Hiking

MASSACHUSETTS

Contact

Dear Readers:

Every effort was made to make this the most accurate, informative, and easy-to-use guidebook on the planet. Any comments, suggestions, and corrections regarding this guide are welcome and should be sent to:

The Globe Pequot Press
c/o Editorial Dept.
246 Goose Lane
Guilford, CT 06437
editorial@globe-pequot.com

We'd love to hear from you so we can make future editions and future guides even better.

Thanks and happy trails!

Hiking

MASSACHUSETTS

An Atlas of Massachusetts'
Greatest Hiking Adventures
by Benjamin B. Ames

FALCON®

GUILFORD, CONNECTICUT
HELENA, MONTANA

AN IMPRINT OF THE GLOBE PEQUOT PRESS

Library of Congress Cataloging-in-Publication Data is available.

ISBN 0-7627-0761-5

Manufactured in the United States of America
First Edition/Third Printing

Ackno

Acknowledgments

Thanks to: Shannon for being proofreader, hiking companion, and patient book widow; Susan Johnson for giving me a GPS receiver, so her son-in-law would someday re-emerge from the woods; Paul Teague and Karen Field for giving me the flexibility from our magazine work to research and write this book; Ned and Jane for sharing their wonder and respect for the natural world, for helping preserve that world, and for being strong parents; and Sue for her schoolteacher's love of the written word. I wish she could have read this.

wledgments

Table of

Contents

Western Massachusetts

Midstate Trail

The Art of Hiking

Meet the Author

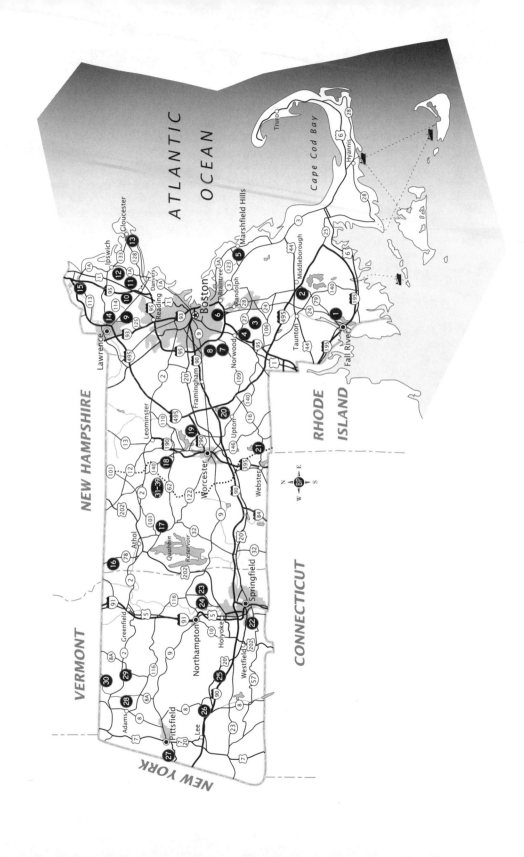

HOW TO USE THIS BOOK

Take a close enough look and you'll find that this little guide contains just about everything you'll ever need to choose, plan for, enjoy, and survive a hike in Massachusetts. We've done everything but load your pack and tie up your bootlaces. Stuffed with more than 200 pages of useful Massachusetts-specific information, *Hiking Massachusetts* features 40 mapped and cued hikes and everything from advice on getting into shape to tips on getting the most out of hiking with your children or your dog. With so much information, the only question you may have is: How do I sift through it all? Well, we answer that, too.

We've designed this FalconGuide® to be highly visual, for quick reference and ease-of-use. What this means is that the most pertinent information rises quickly to the top, so you don't have to waste time poring through bulky hike descriptions to get mileage cues or elevation stats. They're set aside for you. And yet, this guide doesn't read like a laundry list. Take the time to dive into a hike description and you'll realize that this guide is not just a good source of information; it's a good read. And so, in the end, you get the best of both worlds: a quick-reference guide and an engaging look at a region. Here's an outline of *Hiking Massachusetts'* major components.

WHAT YOU'LL FIND IN THIS GUIDE. Each region begins with a **Section Intro**, where you're given a sweeping look at the lay of the land. To aid in quick decision-making, we follow the Section Intro with a **Section Overview**. These short summaries give you a taste of the hiking adventures that will be featured in the section. You'll learn about the trail terrain and what surprises each route has to offer. If your interest is piqued, flip to the hike and you can read more. If not, skip to the next summary.

Now to the individual chapter. The **Hike Specs** are fairly self-explanatory. Here you'll find the quick, nitty-gritty details of the hike: where the trailhead is located, the nearest town, hike length, approximate hiking time, difficulty rating, best hiking season, type of trail terrain, and what other trail users you may encounter. Our **Getting There** section gives you dependable directions from a nearby city right down to where you'll want to park. The **Hike Description** is the meat of the chapter. Detailed and honest, it's the author's carefully researched impression of the trail. While it's impossible to cover everything, you can rest assured that we won't miss what's important. In our **Miles/Directions** section we provide mileage cues to identify all turns and trail name changes, as well as points of interest. Between this and our Route Map, you simply can't get lost. The **Hike Information** box is a hodgepodge of information. In it you'll find trail hotlines (for updates on trail conditions), trail schedules and use fees, local outdoor retailers (for emergency trail supplies), and a list of maps available to the area. We'll also tell you where to stay, what to eat, and what else to see while you're hiking in the area.

We don't want anyone to feel restricted to just the routes and trails that are mapped here. We hope you'll have an adventurous spirit and use this guide as a platform to dive into Massachusetts' backcountry and discover new routes for yourself. One of the simplest ways to begin this is to just turn the map upside down and hike the course in reverse. The change in perspective is often fantastic and the hike should feel quite different. With this in mind, it'll be like getting two distinctly different hikes on each map.

For your own purposes, you may wish to copy the directions for the course onto a small sheet to help you while hiking, or photocopy the map and cue sheet to take with you. Otherwise, just slip the whole book in your backpack and take it all with you. Enjoy your time in the outdoors and remember to pack out what you pack in.

Interstate Highway	
U.S. Highway	
State Road	
County Road	
Township Road	
Forest Road	
Paved Road	
Paved Bike Lane	
Maintained Dirt Road	
Unmaintained Jeep Trail	
Singletrack Trail	
Highlighted Route	
Ntl Forest/County Boundaries	
State Boundaries	
Railroad Tracks	
Power Lines	
Special Trail	
Rivers or Streams	
Water and Lakes	
Marsh	

Airfield		Golf Course	
Airport		Hiking Trail	
Bike Trail		Mine	
No Bikes		Overlook	
Boat Launch		Picnic	
Bridge		Parking	
Bus Stop		Quarry	
Campground		Radio Tower	
Campsite		Rock Climbing	
Canoe Access		School	
Cattle Guard		Shelter	
Cemetery		Spring	
Church		Swimming	
Covered Bridge		Train Station	
Direction Arrows		Wildlife Refuge	
Downhill Skiing		Vineyard	
Fire Tower		Most Difficult	
Forest HQ		Difficult	
4WD Trail		Moderate	
Gate		Easy	

HOW TO USE THESE MAPS

1 Area Locator Map

This thumbnail relief map at the beginning of each hike shows you where the hike is within the state. The hike area is indicated by the white star.

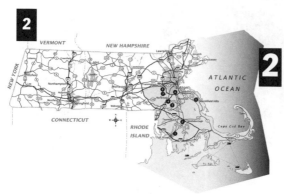

2 Regional Location Map

This map helps you find your way to the start of each hike from the nearest sizeable town or city. Coupled with the detailed directions at the beginning of the cue, this map should visually lead you to where you need to be for each hike.

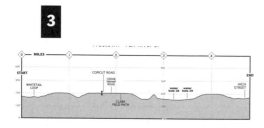

3 Profile Map

This helpful profile gives you a cross-sectional look at the hike's ups and downs. Elevation is labeled on the left, mileage is indicated on the top. Road and trail names are shown along the route with towns and points of interest labeled in bold.

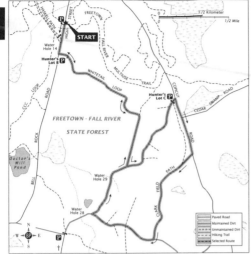

4 Route Map

This is your primary guide to each hike. It shows all of the accessible roads and trails, points of interest, water, towns, landmarks, and geographical features. It also distinguishes trails from roads, and paved roads from unpaved roads. The selected route is highlighted, and directional arrows point the way.

Hike Information *(Included in each hike section)*

🕻 Trail Contacts:

This is the direct number for the local land managers in charge of all the trails within the selected hike. Use this hotline to call ahead for trail access information, or after your visit if you see problems with trail erosion, damage, or misuse.

🕐 Schedule:

This tells you at what times trails open and close. Important winter information is also included.

💲 Fees/Permits:

What money, if any, you may need to carry with you for park entrance fees or tolls.

🄽 Maps:

This is a list of other maps to supplement the maps in this book. They are listed in order from most detailed to most general.

Any other important or useful information will also be listed here such as local attractions, outdoor shops, nearby accommodations, etc.

A note from the folks behind this endeavor...

The producers behind this latest FalconGuide® look at guidebook publishing a little differently. We feel that guidebooks need to be both easy to use and nice to look at, and that takes an innovative approach to design. You see, we want you to spend less time fumbling through your guidebook and more time enjoying the adventure at hand. We hope you like what you see here and enjoy the places we lead you. And most of all, we'd like to thank you for taking an adventure with us.

Happy Trails!

Introduct

Introduction

Massachusetts Weather

I left Cambridge on a sunny March day, congratulating myself as a careful hiker—I'd packed a sweater and long pants, and thrown my winter hat in the pack for good measure. Arriving at a trailhead near the Barre Falls Dam after a short drive, I immediately walked into the woods, and gasped.

With each step, snow flew up my pant legs, packing around my boot cuffs. After 50 yards, I was wading knee-deep. And after 75 yards, I realized my dog was getting nowhere at all—the snow was so deep that it packed under his belly, so his legs couldn't reach the ground!

You'd think I would learn a lesson from that experience, but the next weekend I ventured toward North Andover, an even shorter drive from my sunny, urban block. Sure enough, I traipsed into the woods, and got a little farther—perhaps 200 yards—before returning to the car.

That's Massachusetts weather. And it's one of your most important challenges, even on short day-hikes in the state. Generally speaking, there are three bands of weather in the state: the cape and eastern seashore tend to have moderate weather, with little snow; but when it rains in the east, it snows in the central plains and Connecticut River Valley; and the autumn foliage comes earliest of all in the western, mountainous Berkshires.

Another crucial detail for any hiker is how much daylight he or she has. Massachusetts' sunrise varies from 5 A.M. in June to 7:15 A.M. in December, and sunset varies from 4:15 P.M. in January to 8:30 P.M. in June. These do include Daylight Savings Time, which is defined in the state as setting our clocks forward on the first Sunday of April, and setting them back on the last Sunday of October.

Average monthly temperatures in Boston range from 28 degrees Fahrenheit in January to 72 degrees Fahrenheit in July. But beware that the extremes can reach 40 degrees on either side of those numbers. Seasonally, night time frosts begin in late September and end by early May. Boston's average annual precipitation (including both snow and rain) is 44.23 inches.

Flora and Fauna

Why are birch trees white and laurels green?
Can animals smell fragrant plants like sweet fern and bayberry, as people can?
And wait a minute—look, a polar bear, a tarantula, a python!

OK, there are no polar bears walking wild in Massachusetts, but the state has a little bit of almost everything else. One of the best ways to learn all about it is the EcoTarium, a natural history museum in Worcester (*www.ecotarium.org*).

Choose from three floors of exhibits, an observatory, and a planetarium. Then head outside, riding the Explorer Express Train or walking 60 acres of nature trails, with interpretive signs along the lower pond trail, timescape trail, meadow trail, and other ecosystems. Had enough time with your feet on the ground? Head for the Tree Canopy Walkway, suspended 40 feet up in a grove of oak and hickory, with visitors harnessed to safety cables as they traverse swinging bridges spanning up to 150 feet. There's also a small zoo, with that polar bear and snakes, opossums, and more. And at day's end, EcoTarium features "jazz at sunset."

The nature of modern Massachusetts has been hugely impacted by modern civilization and industry. Today it's the third most densely populated state in the country, but it boasts the nation's sixth largest forest and park system, according to the Massachusetts Association of Professional Foresters (*www.massforesters.org*). Put another way, it's the thirteenth most populous state overall, but ranks just forty-fifth in size.

On the rebound from the age of agriculture, it's changing fast. After farmers cleared most of the land, Massachusetts was about 30% forested in 1900. Today it has grown back to 64% forested, with 3.2 million forested acres, 84% of which (2.5 million acres) is privately owned. The remaining 16% is split between municipal forests (300,000 acres), the state's Department of Environmental Management (264,000 acres), private NPOs (130,000 acres), the Metropolitan District Commission's Division of Watershed Management (100,000 acres), and the Division of Fisheries and Wildlife (50,000 acres).

Massachusetts is a state of small farms, with the number of farms growing from 5,258 to 6,100 from 1992 to 2000. The amount of farm land couldn't keep up, growing merely from 526,440 to 570,000 acres. This lowered the average farm size from 100 to just 93 acres—both miniscule by Midwestern standards. But those Massachusetts farmers are busy! By national rank, the state is second for cranberries, ninth for maple syrup, thirteenth for sweet corn, fifteenth for apples, and eighteenth for tomatoes.

Did I mention cranberries? It's one of the state's claims to fame, with Massachusetts' 14,400 acres delivering fully 37% of the U.S. cranberry crop. Only Wisconsin makes more, with New Jersey in third, then Oregon and Washington.

Along with blueberries and grapes, the cranberry is one of the few fruits native to North America. Its name was originally "crane berry," thanks to early settlers who recognized the shape of its flowers, which last just 10 to 12 days each spring. Full of Vitamin C, it was often brought on long ship voyages to fight scurvy, and Native Americans used it with deer venison and fat to make long-lasting "pemmican." But they're rather stingy with their juice—at a weight of 440 cranberries per pound, it takes about 10 pounds of berries to make a gallon of juice. And despite the beautiful photos of berry harvests, they do not actually grow in water, but in sandy bogs or marshes. Farmers flood these fields for easy harvest, because the berries float.

Also keep an eye out for the black-capped chickadee (state bird), mayflower (state flower—remember the Pilgrims' boat), and American elm (state tree—now very rare because of Dutch elm disease). Of course, the state's beverage is cranberry juice, and the state berry is the cranberry.

Wilderness Restrictions/Regulations

No hunting is allowed on Sundays in Massachusetts. But always use your judgment when heading into the woods in the fall. Think twice about hiking if you see hunters walking the paths at your trailhead. And think three times before bringing an unleashed dog into the autumn woods.

The crucial thing for hikers to know is that shotgun deer season runs November 26 to December 8 statewide, stopping a week earlier on Cape Cod. The rules allow hunting from a half hour before sunrise to a half hour after sunset.

The archery deer season starts earlier but draws fewer hunters into the woods. That runs November 5 to November 24 west of MA 31 (Mount Wachusett), and October 25 to November 24 east of MA 31. Other seasons include pheasant and quail from October 13 to November 24, and turkey seasons from October 29 to November 3 and from April 30 to May 26. Check the Department of Fish and Wildlife site for updates, *www.masswildlife.org.*

The Hikes

Southeast
MASSACHUSETTS

For a small state in a moderate climate, you'd think Massachusetts would have a consistent seashore. But it takes just a few steps for hikers to tell the difference between rocky, exposed Cape Ann to the north, and sandy, marshy Cape Cod to the south.

For classic examples, take a walk at Borderland State Park, Douglas State Forest, Freetown/Fall River State Forest, or Massasoit State Park. In each place, the dry soil is sandy under your boots, with low shrubs spread over a flat, broad landscape. One hike at Ravenswood or Maudslay State Park will show the difference, as you scramble over the steep and stony trails of the north shore.

This soil determines plants and animals, too. Split by Boston in the center, the two capes are like grumpy siblings who look alike, but can't stand each other's sight. The family began 25,000 years ago, when the most recent glacier stalled in this neighborhood. But northern snows kept pushing, and like a conveyor belt, it sent rocky deposits to the state, dropping them as it melted. By 10,000 years ago, it was completely gone, and the state looked entirely different.

The facelift included terminal moraines formed of this glacial till, making the hills and ridges of modern-day Cape Cod and the islands. It also dropped random boulders called glacial erratics, plopped down as if airmailed from hundreds of miles away. And in some places, chunks of the glacier stuck in the earth like terrestrial icebergs, melting until they created ponds with no inlet or outlet, fed only by ground water—kettle ponds.

The region changed very slowly, as the sea's erosion made dunes and barrier beaches. But change accelerated in the mid-17th century, when European settlers arrived, clearcutting southern Massachusetts by 1800, and watching much of the topsoil wash away with the wind and rain. Today you can tell southeastern Massachusetts by its flat, sandy ground filled with plants that love the acidic soil—blueberries, cranberries, pine barrens.

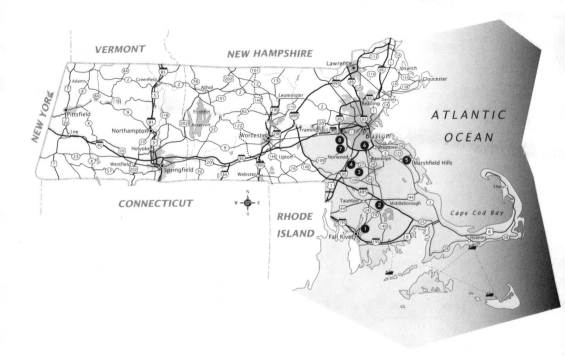

The Hikes

1. Freetown/Fall River State Forest
2. Massasoit State Park
3. Borderland State Park
4. Moose Hill Wildlife Sanctuary
5. Norris Reservation
6. Blue Hills Reservation
7. Rocky Woods Reservation
8. Noanet Woodlands Reservation

Section Overview

Freetown/Fall River State Forest

This sprawling, flat, sandy park is a typical Massachusetts coastal forest, filled with deer, pheasants, and freshwater fish, and surrounded by nearby cranberry farms. Unfortunately, it is also a favorite of dirt bike riders, but this loop sticks to a part of the forest largely avoided by motorized vehicles. *(See page 8)*

Massasoit State Park

Located on the northern edge of Massachusetts' coastal sand plain, this park marks a transition from the more thickly forested hills of northeastern Massachusetts to the flat, sandy lands of Cape Cod and the coast. The trail traces the edge of Lake Rico, with wonderful views of this forested lake and the pitch pines growing on its sandy shores. The walk ends as you reach a cranberry bog near the front gate. *(See page 14)*

Borderland State Park

This wet, sandy land is a typical southeastern Massachusetts ecosystem, with the acidic soil beloved by cranberry bogs and cedar swamps. The park's many ponds were formed by damming its streams, first to spin water wheels for a 19th-century furnace, and later for fishing, boating, and skating. The broad carriage paths that encircle Leach Pond and Upper Leach Pond are filled with baby carriages, mountain bikes, horses, and joggers on a beautiful spring day, while the foot paths that twist around the park's

northern half are more narrow, rocky, and quiet. This loop is a combination of the two, just scratching the surface of the park's four-season variety. *(See page 18)*

Moose Hill Wildlife Sanctuary

This loop begins with a quick climb to the Moose Hill Fire Tower, then settles in for a flat, sweeping stroll through the woods. At the park's southern edge, you get terrific views from Allen Ledge and Bluff Head, where granite cliffs drop off steeply. Look around you—the park is so diverse it has 12 of the 23 habitats listed in *The Nature of Massachusetts*, a wonderful book that's unfortunately out of print. *(See page 22)*

Norris Reservation

This is not a complex or challenging hike, but for its proximity to Boston, it offers amazing views and a unique up-close tour of a salt marsh and the North River. *(See page 26)*

Blue Hills Reservation

Start at a sea level pond and bog, and in just one half mile, climb nearly 500 feet to Tucker Hill, passing through three separate ecosystems. Follow the high ridge along the much-loved Skyline Trail to Buck Hill (496 feet) with its views of the Boston skyline, Boston Harbor and fantastic sunsets. Then complete the loop back to the pond on a wide, cool, wooded trail. *(See page 30)*

Rocky Woods Reservation

This loop begins with a climb up Cedar Hill, for a view of the green waters of Chickering Lake. It then circles behind Whale Rock and Notch Pond for a tour of the park's low swamplands, and their bog-loving trees, frogs, and garter snakes. Thanks to this varied ecology, the park comes alive in the early spring—it seems there is a songbird calling high in each tree and a snake basking on every other sun-warmed rock. *(See page 36)*

Noanet Woodlands Reservation

Like the nearby, affluent town of Dover, this rolling ramble seems built for comfort. Its broad, well-marked trails with their numbered intersections bring you across a brook and over a scenic vista as a proper introduction before leading up to Noanet Peak. At 371 feet, the peak itself offers a peek at the Boston skyline 20 miles to the east. This loop then leads you past an old mill pond and stone mill works, before returning you to your car. *(See page 40)*

Freetown/
Fall River State Forest

Hike Specs

Start: From the dirt parking lot off High Street, just south of its intersection with Copicut Road
Length: 4.8-mile loop
Approximate Hiking Time: 2.5 hours
Difficulty Rating: Easy, with broad trails and little elevation change
Trail Surface: Broad, sandy trails
Lay of the Land: A tour of a coastal sand plain ecosystem, with sandy soil, scrub oak, white pine, and thick laurel undergrowth
Land Status: MA Department of Environmental Management land
Nearest Town: Fall River, MA
Other Trail Users: Mountain bikers, dirt bike and ATV riders, equestrians, hunters (in season), dog sledders, snowmobilers
Canine Compatibility: Dogs permitted

Getting There

From Taunton: Take MA 24 south to exit 10, for North Main St., Assonet, Freetown. Turn left off the exit to head south on North Main Street. Cross over MA 24, and at 0.75 cross through an intersection onto MA 79 south. Ignoring all signs for state park entrances, travel 1 mile before turning left onto High Street. Cross the railroad tracks at 1.4, then cross an intersection in 2.6 miles with Copicut Road. At 3.3 miles, turn right into a gated dirt parking lot. *DeLorme: Massachusetts Atlas & Gazetteer:* Page 57 021

he forest's 5,441 acres yield some fascinating finds, like fuzzy, neon-green caterpillars, and anthills the size of TV sets. The sandy soil holds deer prints, horseshoe prints, tire tracks, and boot prints. And the woods are full of deer and pheasants.

In the 1930s, the Civilian Conservation Corps (CCC) built dozens of stone-lined pits here, to hold water from streams and provide pumping sources for fire engines. Today they are numbered with signs—useful as landmarks—marked on forest maps. This park also includes the 227-acre Watuppa Reservation, which belongs to the Wampanoag Nation and is the site for their annual tribal meeting. The profile of the famous Wampanoag leader, Chief Massasoit, can be seen in Profile Rock, a 50-foot outcropping.

The trailhead parking lot is a favorite place for motorbike and ATV riders to park their trucks. Their noise and fumes can be noxious, but they generally do not ride on the loop you'll be hiking. Also, the park is closed completely to motorized vehicles between the last Sunday of November and May 1st. The forest is also a popular site for mountain bikers, who often race on the trails. However, like the motorbike riders, they seldom ride east of High Street.

The forest's Wildlife Management Area (WMA) is stocked with pheasants to prepare for hunting season, which begins here in mid-October. Together, the Acushnet and Freetown/Fall River State Forest WMAs are 355 acres. The trails are littered with shotgun shells, but there is no hunting allowed on Sundays at any time of year in Massachusetts. Likewise, the state stocks Rattlesnake Brook with brook trout each spring, and anglers flock in season. There are restrooms and free maps at park headquarters.

The land is also part of an exciting new movement to create a 14,000-acre Southeastern Massachusetts Bioreserve stretching from the state forest southward toward Dartmouth and Westport. Although it's located just 10 miles from a major population center, the combined land would encompass a mosaic of ecologies, including three types of water bodies, thirteen kinds of freshwater uplands, and twelve kinds of upland communities. Just the 47th such bioreserve in the country, it would comprise the 3,800-acre former Acushnet Sawmill Property (a former woodlot for furniture and firewood), a combined 10,200 acres of state forest and wildlife management land, some city-owned watershed land, and 2,000 acres of water surface in Fall

MilesDirections

0.0 START at the dirt lot, and turn right onto High St., heading south.

0.1 Pass a sign for Haskell Path, and soon pass Water Hole 14. Then cross the town line from Freetown into Fall River, and immediately turn left, onto the dirt, blue-blazed Whitetail Loop.

0.8 Turn right at an intersection to stay on the Whitetail Loop.

1.1 Turn left at a fork, leaving the Whitetail Loop and heading north on a sandy two-track path.

1.2 Pass by two unmarked paths on the right.

1.6 Pass by an unmarked path on the left.

1.7 Pass through a brown metal gate into a dirt parking lot, called Hunters Lot C. Cross through the lot and turn right onto Copicut Road, heading south.

1.9 Pass by Cedar Swamp Road on your left.

2.1 Come to a pair of footpaths forking to your right, each blocked by three large boulders. Turn right onto the second, more southerly one, called Clark Field Path.

2.2 Carry on as the other path joins from your right.

2.7 Turn right at a T-intersection, heading west.

3.0 Cross another trail at a four-way intersection, continuing on a narrower path. [**FYI.** The wide path that veers to your left here leads in 0.1 mile to a large rock that's a nice stop for lunch. After that, it leaves the forest.]

3.1 Pass by unmarked paths on each side.

3.2 Go right at a fork, then immediately right again, picking up the blue-blazed Whitetail Loop heading north. On maps, this intersection is just north of Water Hole 28.

3.5 Pass Water Hole 29 on your left.

3.6 Go left at a fork. You are now retracing your original steps on the Whitetail Loop.

3.9 Go left at an intersection, to continue following blue blazes.

4.6 Pass by a trail on your left, which leads to Hunters Lot B.

4.7 Turn right onto paved High Street, immediately crossing the town line from Fall River into Freetown. Soon pass Water Hole 14 on your left, and then the Haskell Path.

4.8 Turn left into the dirt parking lot, and find your car.

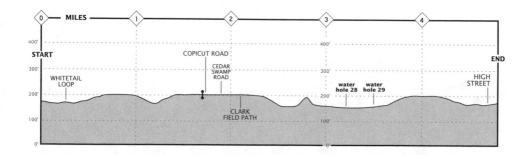

River's two reservoirs. The Trustees of Reservations are planning a 500-acre purchase of part of this land, to build a Gateway Center. This future visitors center would be located south of the state forest, between North Watuppa Pond and Copicut Reservoir.

Among Fall River's many historic sights and sites, one stands out:

Lizzie Borden took an axe
gave her mother forty whacks
when she saw what she had done
she gave her father forty one.

Yes, this is the city where the famous crime occurred. On Fall River's Second Street lived the Borden family: Lizzie, her sister Emma, their father Andrew Jackson Borden, and stepmother, Abby Durfee Gray Borden. On August 4, 1892, the parents were found killed by hatchet blows to their heads. Lizzie was acquitted in the following trial, but was still ostracized by the commu-

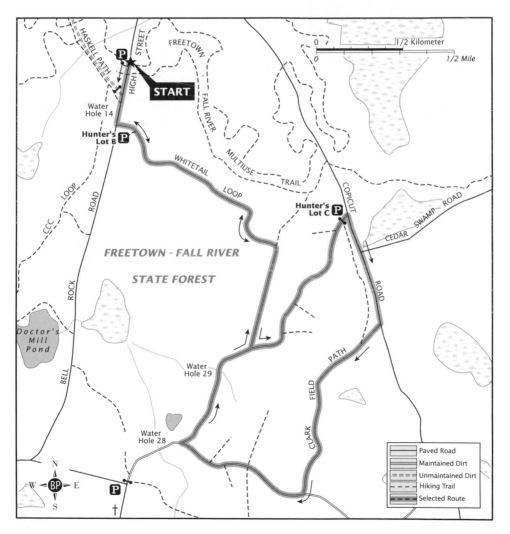

nity. Today there is a bed and breakfast museum, where you can sleep in the same rooms where family members lived (and died), and even eat the same breakfast meal they did on that fateful day—bananas, johnny-cakes, sugar cookies, and coffee.

Hike Information

📞 Trail Contacts:
Freetown/Fall River State Forest, Assonet, MA (508) 644–5522 or www.state.ma.us/dem/parks/free.htm

🕐 Schedule:
The forest is closed from a half hour after sunset to a half hour before sunrise.

💲 Fees/Permits:
No fees or permits required

❓ Local Information:
Fall River city website: www.fallriver.mec.edu/frhomepg.html • Fall River Police Department website: www.frpd.org – has some great info about Fall River and its history

💡 Local Events/Attractions:
The Edaville Railroad, MA (508) 866–8190 or www.edaville.org – This family historical park has a museum and children's train and carousel rides. You can even take a 5.5-mile steam locomotive strip through a 1,800-acre cranberry plantation. The website also lists local hotels and campgrounds. • Battleship Cove, MA (508) 678–1100 or www.battleshipcove.com – A museum of Fall River's rich nautical history. It features ships like the Battleship Massachusetts, Destroyer Joseph P. Kennedy Jr., submarines, PT boats, captured Japanese boats, helicopters, and more. • Fall River Heritage State Park, Fall River, MA (508) 675–5759 or www.state.ma.us/dem/parks/frhp.htm • Fall River Historical Society, Fall River, MA (508) 679–1071 or www.lizzieborden.org

🌐 Accommodations:
Lizzie Borden Bed and Breakfast Museum, Fall River, MA (508) 675–7333 or www.lizzieborden.com

🏛 Organizations:
Friends of the Freetown/Fall River State Forest, Assonet, MA – A conservation group that meets every other month at forest headquarters to protect the forest, and to sponsor trail work, forest cleanup, and other activities.

ℓ Other Resources:
Fun Day in the Forest – An annual outdoors celebration, held in early October, at the forest. It includes guided trail walks, van tours of the forest, a rock climbing wall, pony and hayrides, music and refreshment • Freetown's Big Bang – An annual mountain bike race, held in mid-September, at the forest. Ask for details of both events at the ranger station.

🧗 Local Outdoor Retailers:
Carabiner's Climbing Gym, New Bedford, MA: www.carabiners.com — still under construction—check the website for details.

Ⓝ Maps:
USGS maps. Somerset, MA

Massasoit State Park

Hike Specs

Start: From the parking lot at park headquarters
Length: 4.2-mile loop
Approximate Hiking Time: 2 hours
Difficulty Rating: Easy
Trail Surface: Flat and sandy paths
Lay of the Land: Northern edge of the "sand plain community"; flat, sandy soil dominated by scrub oak and pitch pine, with many cranberry bogs
Land Status: MA Department of Environmental Management land
Nearest Town: Middleborough, MA
Other Trail Users: Mountain bikers, equestrians, and cross-country skiers
Canine Compatibility: Dogs permitted

Getting There

From Middleborough: Take I-495 north to exit 5, for MA 18 South, Lakeville, New Bedford. Follow MA 18 south. Half a mile south of its intersection with I-495, turn right at a blinking yellow light onto Taunton Street (this road's name changes to Middleboro Avenue as you cross the county line). At 2.6 miles, turn left at the sign for the park's main entrance. The parking area is two hundred yards inside, past several gates.
DeLorme: Massachusetts Atlas & Gazetteer: Page 57 H26

The millstone displayed near the main parking lot was pulled from Middle Pond several years ago, when rangers did their annual draining to kill off fast-growing invasive plants. They plan to move this stone back to the park's southern edge and build a full historic display around the 18th-century tool. Along with the cranberry bog near the main parking lot, the park thus holds two of the most enduring symbols of the state's agricultural history. But its name predates them both. Massasoit was a Wampanoag Indian chief—one of the tribes that first welcomed the pilgrims upon their arrival at nearby Plymouth Rock, just 20 miles to the west. Massasoit was born around 1590, near present-day Bristol, RI. He is noted for signing a famed peace treaty with the pilgrims in 1621 that was never once broken throughout the remainder of his life—nearly forty years.

The Peter Adams Trail begins in the parking lot, at the corner closest to the main gate. During the camping season (roughly between Memorial Day and Columbus Day), trail maps are available from the Contact Station on the main road. Otherwise, there is a trail map painted on a wooden kiosk in the parking lot, and extra maps are available inside the headquarters building. The Adams Trail is marked throughout the park with blue triangles.

Adams was a black revolutionary war soldier buried with his family in Talbots Cemetery, a small plot on nearby Sherwood Avenue. His headstone reads simply, "Peter Adams, d. 1841, aged 101 years. A soldier of the revolution." Nearby lies his wife Margaret, who died in 1844 at the age of 92. An adjacent historical marker reads, "Peter Adams, a free Negro man and a soldier of the revolution is buried here."

The sandy soil, seagulls, and clam shells are clues that you're near the ocean. And for proof that this acidic earth is perfect for cranberry crops, you need only look to the nearby corporate headquarters of Ocean Spray, the fruit and juice producer. However, this beach-like ecology does draw crowds of campers in the warmer months; so if you prefer your hikes with privacy, try this one in the off season.

While they were certainly the first to settle the new world, British pilgrims were not the first visitors to arrive in America by boat. There are many signs that Viking explorers reached Cape Cod centuries earlier, and in Middleborough there are signs of an even older visit.

Nearby Lake Assawompsett—the largest natural body of fresh water in Massachusetts— drains into the Nemasket River, which feeds the Taunton River and soon reaches the sea. It's a natural magnet for human settlers; Native Americans relied on the Nemasket for food and water, and Pilgrims built gristmills, saw mills, furnaces, and forges here. They later built cotton mills and shovel works, as the local economy expanded.

One of the oldest signs of habitation here is an archaic village at the mouth of the Nemasket that has been radiocarbon-dated to 2,300 B.C. And when the waters of Lake Assawompsett are very low, there's a rock visible just east of the river mouth that bears an amazing carving—some say it's fake —of a picture of a Phoenician sailing ship, apparently carved by a Native American who witnessed these visitors from the distant Mediterranean.

Hike Information

ⓒ Trail Contacts:
Massasoit State Park, East Taunton, MA (508) 822-7405 or *www.state.ma.us/dem/parks/mass.htm*

ⓢ Fees/Permits:
No fees or permits required

ⓠ Schedule:
During the camping season, the gates remain open since people are staying overnight here. In the winter (between Columbus Day and Memorial Day), they close at 3:30 P.M. to discourage vandalism.

ⓠ Local Information:
Old Colony Historical Society Museum and Library, Taunton, MA (508) 822-1622 or *www.ohwy.com/ma/o/oldcolhs.htm–Fee is $2 for adults.*

ⓝ Maps:
USGS maps: Taunton, MA; Bridgewater, MA

MilesDirections

0.0 START the Peter Adams Trail in the northwest corner of the main parking lot, near the main gate, where the lot narrows to a single road. Walk parallel to the main road, keeping the brown, barn-shaped park headquarters on your left. Immediately climb a steep pitch and see Lake Rico spread out in front of you.

0.2 Bear right at a triangle intersection, then right again, winding your way toward the lake shore. This trail is very windy with many turns, but you can't go wrong by skirting Lake Rico's shore.

0.4 Bear left at a fork, heading straight toward the lake. *[FYI. Unfortunately, the woods here are often littered with beer cans and spray paint. Yet even on a nice day, they are not crowded, and afford pretty lake views.]*

0.5 Left at a fork, bearing away from the lake and up a hillside thick with young pines. Then turn right at a T-intersection. Remember to always keep the lake on your right.

0.6 At the top of a rise, turn left at a four-way intersection, still following blue blazes, then immediately right at a T-intersection, and right again at a fork, dropping down a steep hill, and closer to the lake.

0.7 Turn left at a T-intersection, onto a wide, sandy lane, following blue triangles. Continue to keep the lake on your right as you circle its shore, and soon pass a picnic table with a superb view.

0.8 Turn right at a fork, passing from two-track to single-width trail. Follow the rolling trail that sticks close to the lake's twisting shore. The trail soon emerges onto a sandy ridgeline that traces a steep cliffside above the water.

1.0 Bear right to keep circling the lake.

1.1 Cross a small wooden bridge and immediately turn right over an even-smaller plank bridge. You will soon pass a wooden bench at a breathtaking viewpoint.

1.2 Pass by a trail on your right, then bear right at a fork, and walk along this wide trail onto a broad sandy beach, punctuated with pitch pines that have somehow managed to find nutrients in the ground. Cross the sand to continue along the lake's edge, climbing a small rise and bearing right through thick forest with a marsh full of cattails below you.

1.6 Bear right at a fork, following blue blazes, and soon pass the "Pudding Stone" on your right, a large conglomerate boulder marked with a sign. You then immediately reach the park's campsites, with a paved road (G-Road) encircling dozens of fire pits and picnic benches. Bear right, following the paved road ahead of you for 100 yards and keeping the pond on your right. Just before you reach a bathroom building, turn right, picking up the blue blazes into the woods again at campsite RG-6. Swing right at a T-intersection, leaving the swimming area on your left.

2.1 As you follow the wide sandy path over a dike between Middle Pond and Kings Pond, come through a metal gate, and bear left at a fork. After seeing Little Bear Hole Pond through the trees on your right, stay on the main two-track trail as you pass a left fork.

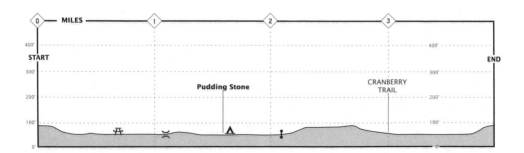

2.4 Turn left at a large X-intersection, following blue blazes and remaining on a two-track trail. The swimming hole is now directly across the lake on your left. Pass by several trails on the right, then a lakeside footpath on the left. Fork left on a path that soon changes to pavement, crosses a stone dam, and passes through a metal gate. Follow this paved road back to your car.

2.6 Pass a gravel road on your right.

2.7 Pass a sign on your right for the Atlantic White Cedar Swamp, hosting acidic soil species like red maple, poison sumac, and holly. Soon pass a junction with the campground's H-Loop on your left.

3.0 Pass a dirt road and paved jughandle on the right. As an alternate route, you can take the Cranberry Trail back to your car. It runs parallel to this paved road, but is confusing, with many unblazed intersections.

3.1 Pass a paved campground road to the left.

3.8 Pass a gated dirt road to the left, then pass the private Perry Cranberry Bogs on the right.

3.9 Reach your car.

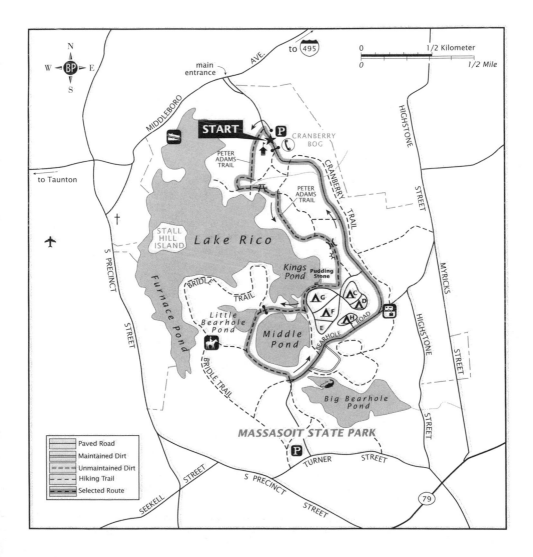

Borderland State Park

Hike Specs

Start: From the visitors center, located off Massapoag Avenue
Length: 4.7-mile loop
Approximate Hiking Time: 2.5–3 hours
Difficulty Rating: Easy, thanks to broad flat trails and minimal elevation change
Trail Surface: Packed dirt trails, with some sections scrambling over bare rock
Lay of the Land: Sandy, marshy ground punctuated with bare rock escarpments in the higher ground
Land Status: MA Department of Environmental Management
Nearest Town: Sharon, MA
Other Trail Users: Mountain bikers, cross-country skiers, equestrians
Canine Compatibility: Dogs permitted (must be kept on leash around visitors center)

Getting There

From Boston: Drive south on I-95 to exit 8, heading toward Foxboro and Sharon. Follow South Main Street toward Sharon, soon passing Ward's Berry Farm, then Audubon's Moose Hill Wildlife Sanctuary. At 3.4 miles, turn right at the light in Sharon Center, onto Billings Street, and immediately go right again, onto Pond Street. At 4.4 miles, reach the rotary at Lake Massapoag, and continue straight on Massapoag Avenue along its shore, following signs for the park. At 7.8 miles, turn left at the park sign, and immediately left again for the visitors center parking lot. *DeLorme: Massachusetts Atlas & Gazetteer:* Page 53 L16

Borderland was tailored for outdoor recreation, earning its name when the Ames family purchased a series of farms that straddled the town lines of Sharon and Easton. The family's four young children dammed several ponds for fishing and boating, and scouted many of its trails. For me, the park has a special significance, because my grandfather was one of those four children, born on the grounds and raised in the great stone mansion. The mansion was built in 1910 by his parents, the Harvard University botany professor Oakes Ames and the artist and suffragette Blanche Ames, and was designed by architect H.H. Richardson.

This hike begins at the visitors center, with its restrooms, free maps, historical photographs, and natural history displays. Walk south along a broad carriage road toward the mansion, encircling Leach Pond (named for General Shepherd Leach, who built it in 1825 to power his furnace). This carriage road winds through swampland, where the sound of mating frogs can be deafening even at noon on a spring day. You circle the pond, home to mallards and ringed by bluebird boxes, continuing on this easy pathway until it reaches Mountain Street, just north of the Upper Leach Pond.

Here, you'll pick up the Granite Hills Trail and the Ridge Trail, leaving the crowds and the ponds behind as you climb to the park's highest points, a series of exposed rock ledges and quarries. The stunted white pine and pitch pine in the sparse soil provide some excellent spots to sit on the sun-warmed, glacier-scarred granite and eat your lunch while hawks circle above.

These narrow trails rejoin the broad carriage loop on Leach Pond's northern shore, soon passing the stone lodge where the Ames family used to build fires for warmth after a day of

ice skating. The pond is fed by Poquanticut Brook and kept by Ollie's Dam, named for my grandfather's elder brother Oliver, who loved to work on it. The broad carriage trail soon returns to the visitors center.

The excellent park staff organizes year-round events that concentrate on natural history. The grounds are also used for everything from dog shows and Civil War reenactments to art exhibits and fishing derbies. Additional events include outdoor concerts, a weekly morning walk, Halloween ghost stories, mushroom hunts, insect walks, and free hay rides. Phone the park for more details.

After your walk, be sure to explore the mansion, which is open for tours every month (except in winter) on the third Friday (from 10 A.M. to noon) and third Sunday (from 1 P.M.

Hike Information

Trail Contacts:
Borderland State Park, North Easton, MA (508) 238-6566 or www.state.ma.us/dem/parks/bord.htm

Schedule:
Open year round – park closes at 6:30 P.M.; summer hours are 8 A.M. to 7:30 P.M.

Fees/Permits:
No fees or permits required

Local Information:
Get Outdoors New England: www.gonewengland.org

Local Events/Attractions:
The park organizes seasonal events, such as bird watching in the woodcock-mating season; star gazing on clear nights, story telling for adults, and tours of the Ames Mansion. Check at the visitors center for details.

Restaurants:
Pizzigando, Sharon, MA (781) 784-8161 – pizza and sandwich shop

Hike Tours:
Check at the visitors center

Local Outdoor Retailers:
Bob Smith's Wilderness House, Boston, MA (617) 277-5858 • City Sports, Boston, MA (617) 782-5121 • Eastern Mountain Sports (EMS), Boston, MA (617) 254-4250 or www.emsonline.com • Hilton's Tent City, Boston, MA (617) 227-9242 or www.hiltonstentcity.com • MVP Sports, Brockton, MA (508) 583-1100 • Patagonia, Boston, MA (617) 424-1776 or www.patagonia.com

Maps:
USGS maps: Brockton, MA

to 3 P.M.). The decorations and furnishings in its 20 rooms have been preserved from the family's residence here, so you can see Oakes' library, and Blanche's paintings, political cartoons, and inventions such as the color wheel, a standardized gradation of painting tones. This extraordinary woman also co-founded the Birth Control League of Massachusetts in 1916. The rooms are stocked with historic mementos of the family's political history, such as a 1910-era Star Spangled Banner, which had 13

stripes and 46 stars. (In 1908, Oklahoma was the 46th state admitted to the union, and New Mexico and Arizona were added in 1912.)

MilesDirections

0.0 START at the visitor center and walk south along the broad carriage road that skims the field and approaches the Ames Mansion.

0.2 Branch left at a fork in the road, just before reaching the mansion's looped driveway. Stay on this main path as you pass signs for the smaller Swamp Trail and Quiet Woods Trail.

0.8 Reach the shore of Leach Pond, skirting its edge as you continue on the broad path, soon passing the wooden boxes of a bluebird nesting area.

1.2 After passing a white farmhouse (a private residence), turn left through a gate, following signs for Pond Trail Walk, Upper Leach Pond, and Puds Pond. Continue straight along this two-track path, ignoring a footpath that forks left in the middle of a clearing.

1.6 At the end of this clearing, cross a cement dam, where Puds Pond (on your right) drains into Upper Leach Pond (visible through trees to your left). Cross a wooden footbridge and continue straight, keeping the shore of Puds Pond close on your right.

1.8 Come through a metal gate and turn left onto a paved road, Mountain Street.

1.9 Turn left through another gate, leaving the pavement and bearing right onto a small path through a clearing. This is the start of the Upper Loop of the Granite Hills Trail, a more narrow and rocky path than the broad carriage roads you've followed so far.

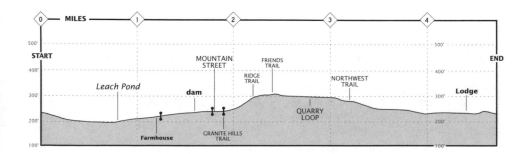

2.2 Go right at a sign for Ridge Trail, then left at an enormous boulder.

2.4 Pass by a sign for the Friends Trail, continuing along Ridge Trail past a rusting automobile.

2.8 Reach an intersection with the Quarry Loop, and go left, following signs for the Ridge Trail. You'll soon cross a wooden boardwalk through a swampy section, then rise again over a series of rocky outcroppings.

3.1 Cross through a stone wall and over a small stream.

3.2 Reach the end of the Ridge Trail, and turn left

onto the Northwest Trail. Soon pass by a sign for the Split Rock Trail.

3.7 Bear left past an intersection with the French Trail.

3.9 Cross a wooden boardwalk as the Northwest Trail ends, and turn right onto the familiar, broad and sandy carriage path.

4.4 Pass by Leach Pond and the Lodge on your left, following the carriage path uphill away from the pond. Quickly bear right at a fork, and you'll see the Visitor Center through the trees.

4.7 Reach your car.

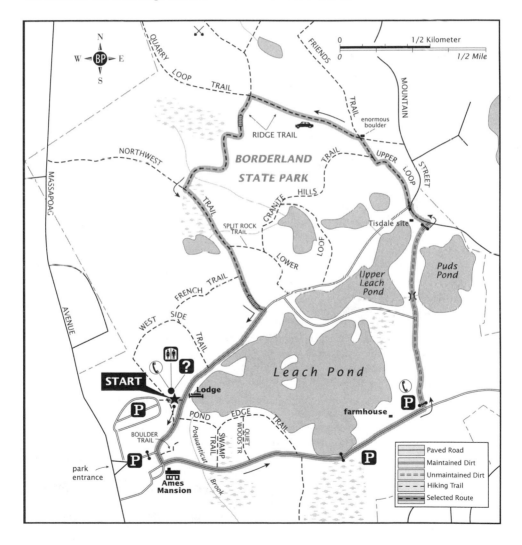

Moose Hill
Wildlife Sanctuary

Hike Specs

Start: From the visitors center off Moose Hill Street

Length: 3.3-mile loop

Approximate Hiking Time: 2 hours

Difficulty Rating: Moderate, due to length and one steep section

Trail Surface: Primarily broad, flat dirt trails, with one steep section and one rocky section

Lay of the Land: A collection of forest, field, and wetland habitats, set in a 2,200-acre wildlife preserve

Land Status: Massachusetts Audubon Society

Nearest Town: Sharon, MA

Other Trail Users: None (Massachusetts Audubon does not allow dogs, bicycles, or horses)

Canine Compatibility: Dogs not permitted

Getting There

From Norwood: Take I-95 south to exit 10 (Coney Street, Walpole, Sharon). Turn left off the exit onto MA 27 north, turning right in 0.3 miles to stay on this road. At 0.9 miles, turn left onto Moose Hill Street. At 2.2 miles, turn left onto Moose Hill Parkway, and immediately enter the sanctuary parking lot. *DeLorme: Massachusetts Atlas & Gazetteer:* Page 52 H13

The red oak forest of the moist flatlands changes quickly to white pine stands as you begin climbing 534–foot Moose Hill, then switches back to oaks and birches as soon as you descend. Since these are mixed wetlands and forests, the trails can be quite wet in spring, so be sure to wear good boots.

You move on from the Summit Trail to the Forest Loop, then the Bluff Head Loop. After looping through a hardwood forest, the trail emerges at Allens Ledge. After your comfortable, flat stroll, it feels like cheating to get such a great view without climbing, but your guilt won't last long as you gaze westward off these bare granite cliffs. A stone chimney stands alone at cliff's edge, the last remnant of a cabin once perched here.

Continuing the loop, you'll soon reach the old stone cistern. It once held water collected from the wetlands to the west; used at one point to feed an orchard that is now lost to the woods you see to the east, and used later for the town of Sharon's drinking water. The modern wooden ramp is a safety measure so clumsy animals (and people) can escape the steep walls.

Like all Audubon lands, trails leading away from the visitors center are blazed blue, and those leading back are blazed yellow. The long-distance Warner Trail passes through the sanctuary, on its way from Canton, Massachusetts, to Rhode Island. The nature center is stocked with helpful books and guides to these woods, as well as maps and restrooms. In the fields around Billings Barn (just west of the nature center), many of the trees are labeled by species. This 2,200-acre sanctuary was founded by Massachusetts Audubon in 1916, the first of its kind in the state.

Moose Hill has an active schedule of speakers, classes, and workshops. You can learn how to attract birds to your backyard, identify wildflowers, study owl behavior, delve into forest or wetland ecology, and plant the best kinds of flowers in your yard to attract butterflies and hummingbirds. You can also learn maple sugaring in February and March and do a summer solstice hayride in June. Keep an eye open year-round for new exhibits in the art gallery at the visitors center.

There are two lingering mysteries about this hike. First, nobody's ever seen a moose in the area, so the sanctuary's name is curious. And second, in its northeast corner, the sanctuary surrounds a fascinating historical collection called the Kendall Whaling Museum. Needless to say, landlocked Sharon has never been a hotspot for whale sightings.

Nevertheless, the museum is engrossing, including such galleries as African Americans in the Whale Trade, British paintings (1740–1900), Dutch paintings (1610–1776), Eskimo whaling, Japanese whaling (1590–present), a full-sized whaling boat, and of course, an enormous collection of harpoons and scrimshaw. And in the grounds outside the museum, there's a hint of Sharon's connection to this maritime industry: larch, white oak, white pine and cedar trees surround the building, each with a plaque describing that timber's value in shipbuilding.

Directions: Leaving the sanctuary parking lot, turn left onto Moose Hill Parkway. In half a mile, turn left onto Upland Road, and at 0.9 miles, turn left onto Everett Street. The museum is at the end of Everett Street. Hours are Tuesday–Saturday, 10 A.M.–5 P.M., and Sunday, 1–5 P.M. The entrance fee is $4 for adults. For more information, call (781) 784–5642 or check the web site at *www.kwm.org*.

MilesDirections

0.0 START at nature center and head west across Moose Hill Street to pick up the Billings Loop, a broad, gravel carriage path that begins at the intersection of Moose Hill Street and Moose Hill Parkway.

0.1 Turn right onto the Summit Trail, blazed with the Warner Trail's white triangles. *[FYI. The Warner Trail is a long-distance hiking path that runs through the sanctuary on its way from Canton, MA to Rhode Island.]* You soon cross over a boardwalk and through a stone wall.

0.2 Cross an intersection with the Moose Hill Loop, following the Summit Trail as it scrambles up a rocky hillside. The trail splits and rejoins itself just before the top.

0.3 Reach the Sharon Fire Tower on Moose Hill (do not climb it). Walk around the tower's fence line, picking up the Summit Trail at the opposite corner, following it downhill.

0.5 At the bottom, cross the Moose Hill Loop, bearing left onto the Old Pasture Trail (which is also part of the Warner Trail).

0.7 Take your first right, beginning the Forest Loop, a smaller trail blazed with the letter "F" on wooden disks. Shortly thereafter, turn right again, at an intersection with a sign for the Forest Loop.

1.1 Follow the trail as it takes a hairpin left.

1.2 Merge left at a fork, following signs to continue the Forest Loop *[Note. A right here would take you off the property]*.

1.5 Bear right at a fork, leaving the Forest Loop. *[Note. This trail can be quite wet in spring.]*

1.7 Swing right at a T-intersection, to begin the west leg of the Bluff Head Loop.

1.8 Bear left at a fork, still following signs for the Bluff Head Loop.

1.9 Reach Allens Ledge, with its lonely chimney and soaring views, and continue along your path, soon reaching another set of cliffs. Bear right after these cliffs, following a yellow blaze downhill.

2.1 Reach another cliffside overlook. Cross these open rocks and bear right, heading downhill to continue, skirting the cliff edge and passing yet more overlooks and the occasional Warner Trail blaze.

2.3 Bear left at a T-intersection (the alternative is a closed trail).

2.4 Swing right at another T-intersection, following signs for the Cistern Trail.

2.5 Pass a junction with the Old Pasture Trail on your left, and soon reach the cistern itself.

2.6 Continue on the Cistern Trail, as you pass another junction with the Old Pasture Trail on your left.

2.7 Follow the trail as it takes a hairpin left.

2.9 Come into an open field and turn left at a sign for the Billings Loop. Walk toward the two barns, then bear right onto a dirt road.

3.0 Turn right at a fork, following the Billings Loop. This is the trail you began on, and you'll soon pass the first turn you took.

3.2 Cross Moose Hill Street.

3.3 Reach your car.

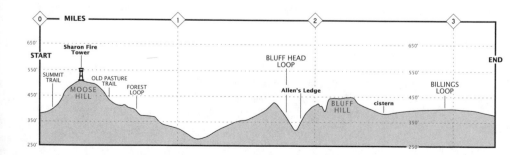

On warm, drizzly days in early spring, watch for Moose Hill's migrating amphibians. They're a little subtler than thundering herds of buffalo, but just as predictable. Each spring, frogs and salamanders awake from their hibernation in the leaf litter of the forest floor, and crawl, hop, or slither to the nearest vernal pool, a fish-free puddle that's safe for breeding. Some of them, like the spotted salamander, even return to the puddle of their birth, like anadromous fish heading up-river from the sea. On average, they make a trip of about 100 meters, but some go nearly half a mile. Moose Hill holds an annual "Frog and Sally Rally" to protect the commuting critters from cars and other traffic.

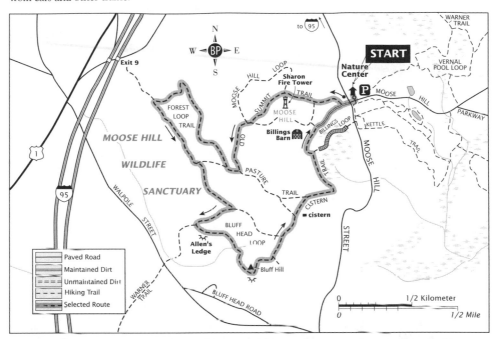

Hike Information

Trail Contacts:
Moose Hill Wildlife Sanctuary, Sharon, MA (781) 784–5691 or *www.massaudubon.org/ Nature_Connection/Sanctuaries/Moose_Hill/ index.html*

Schedule:
Year round, sunrise to sunset, closed Monday – *Nature center open 9 A.M. to 5 P.M., closed Monday*

Fees/Permits:
$3 per adult, or free with Audubon membership

Local Events/Attractions:
Year-round wilderness photography exhibits and **nocturnal wildlife viewing** at Halloween Prowl • **Maple sugaring** in February and March • **Bird-A-Thon Fundraiser** and **Mother's Day nature walk** in May • **Summer solstice** hayride in June

Local Outdoor Retailers:
Eastern Mountain Sports (EMS) Dedham, MA (781) 461–0160 or *www.emsonline.com*

Maps:
USGS maps: Norwood, MA; Brockton, MA

5

Norris Reservation

Hike Specs

Start: From the parking lot at the intersection of West and Dover Streets

Length: 1.6-mile loop

Approximate Hiking Time: 1 hour

Difficulty Rating: Easy, with broad, flat trails

Trail Surface: Wide, woodchipped trails

Lay of the Land: Wooded marshes in North River watershed

Land Status: Trustees of Reservations land

Nearest Town: Norwell, MA

Other Trail Users: Cross-country skiers

Canine Compatibility: Leashed dogs permitted

Getting There

From Braintree: Follow MA 3 south to exit 13, for MA 53 and 123, Scituate, Brockton, Norwell and Hanover. Turn left at the light off the exit ramp onto MA 53 north. At 0.9 miles, turn right at a light, onto MA 123 east (a.k.a Main Street), following signs for Norwell and Scituate. Pass the Norwell Town Offices on your left at 2.6 miles. At 3.9 miles, turn right onto West Street, as you reach the Norwell State Police Station. Immediately cross another road as you follow West Street downhill, past a cemetery on your left. Follow West Street to its end, and turn left on Dover Street. Then immediately turn right, pulling into a gravel parking lot opposite a post office. *DeLorme: Massachusetts Atlas & Gazetteer:* Page 54 F8

T he reservation encompasses 117 acres of wooded upland and salt marsh in the watershed bracketed by Second Herring Brook and the North River. The landscape reveals its recent history, as Eleanor's Trail is named for Eleanor Norris, who donated her family's farmland to form the original 101-acre grant. The balance of the plot includes an adjacent 16 acres from the McMullan family.

Historically, the Wampanoag caught fish and shellfish from the North River here. When the Europeans arrived, settlers built first a sawmill, then in 1690 a mill pond and grist mill. Only rusted farm tools and crumbling stone foundations and mill stones provide reminders of this early industry.

The first European settlers had little room to graze their cattle, so they turned to marsh grass, or "salt hay." Using flat-bottomed boats called gundalows, they hauled up to eight tons of hay per trip, traveling far upriver. This boat-building skill served them well when Britain was running short of lumber and realized that it cost half as much to build a ship in the nascent U.S. Norwell settlers looked around at the 200-foot trees that blanketed the northeast, and met the demand by felling trees that had grown unhindered for 150 centuries.

Today's trees include black tupelo, American holly, and red cedar, but the most significant trees for shipbuilding were white oak, walnut, spruce, and pine. Eventually, more than a thousand ocean-going vessels were launched into the narrow North River, where they were ferried to the sea. Ships built here were as big as the Columbia, a 220-ton schooner that sailed around the globe. Exploring the new west, the ship also served as the namesake for Oregon's Columbia River and Canada's British Columbia.

But poor Norwell has had a series of industrial setbacks. Its shipbuilding era lasted until the newest boats had deeper drafts than the river. The resourceful settlers bought chickens, and

poultry farming was soon the town's biggest business. But a terrible virus wiped out all the local flocks, so the farmers were forced to sell their land to developers. The town changed yet again when returning WWII soldiers used their G.I. Bill loans to spark a residential building boom, and by 1955 they had diversified the Yankee population almost overnight.

Modern hikers can see long wooden boardwalks that stretch to docks and floats from private homes across the North River. Benches along the west bank of the river allow you to breathe in the boggy smell of the muddy salt marsh, and to catch glimpses of water birds' nests in the overhung banks on the far side. But be sure to wear boots; there can still be snow here on Saint Patrick's Day.

After your hike, check out Norwell's James Library & Center for the Arts, which offers concerts and art exhibits. And stop by the Norwell Town Fair, held at the local high school in mid-June, for sights such as the ox-pulling contest. Or if you prefer to get wet, sign up for the Great River Race, a regatta for human-powered craft held on the North River in early August.

MilesDirections

0.0 START in the parking lot, and enter the woods at a trailhead kiosk with map display, following Eleanor's Path.

0.1 Pass a pond on your left as you cross an earthen dike and dam. Turn sharp right on the other side of the dam.

0.2 Pass through a clearing with a millstone.

0.3 Cross a stone wall, and immediately bear right at a fork, onto the River Loop Trail. *[**Option.** This spur trail provides a shortcut.]* Pass through several more stone walls as the trail runs parallel to Second Herring Brook, close by on your right.

0.4 Pass by a narrow trail on your right that leads off the reservation onto private property.

0.7 Cross through two more stone walls and reach a bench with beautiful views of the North River and the private homes on its opposite shore. Bear left, and begin heading north with the river on your right.

0.9 Reach another bench with great views of the river, then continue north, either on a smaller path that runs very close to the river or on the main path, a few yards inland; both paths soon reach a third bench.

1.0 Turn right at a fork onto the McMullan Trail (the spur trail is on your left). Soon enter the McMullan Woods section of the reservation, cross a concrete culvert in the trail, and come to a wooden boathouse with an overhanging porch that's a great place to stop for lunch.

1.3 Turn left just before reaching a green metal gate.

1.4 Cross a wooden boardwalk then another stone wall, as you leave the McMullan Woods.

1.5 Cross over the earthen dike again.

1.6 Reach your car.

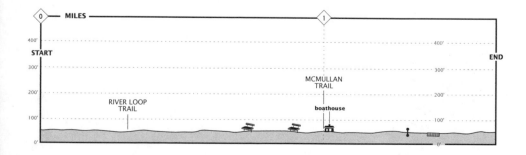

28

Hike Information

☎ Trail Contacts:
The Trustees of Reservations, Beverly, MA
(978) 921–1944 or *www.thetrustees.org*

🕐 Schedule:
Year round, sunrise to sunset

💲 Fees/Permits:
No fees or permits required

❓ Local Information:
Norwell website: *www.norwellma.com*

💡 Local Events/Attractions:
James Library & Center for the Arts, Norwell,
MA (781) 659–7100 or *www.gis.net/~fpnma/
james.html*

🍴 Restaurants:
Papa Ginos, Norwell, MA (781) 878–8417 •
Brueggers, Norwell, MA (781) 829–6552 •
Joe's American Bar and Grill, Braintree, MA
(781) 848–0200

🚶 Organizations:
North and South Rivers Watershed Association, Norwell, MA (781) 659–8168 or
*www.nsrwa.org – sponsors an annual River
Cleanup Day, wetlands education, bird watching, dragonfly watching, river tours, and even
riverside yoga classes*

Ⓝ Maps:
USGS maps: Weymouth, MA

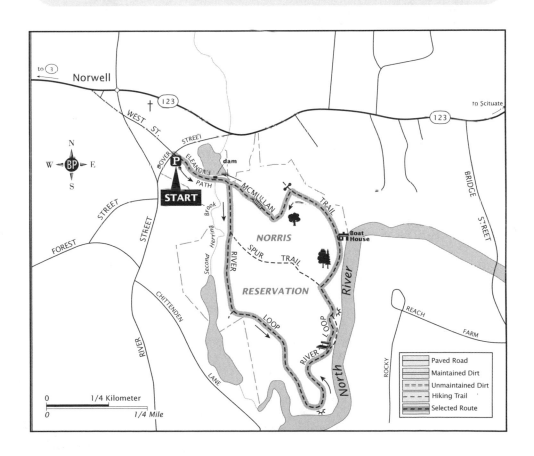

6

Blue Hills Reservation

Hike Specs

Start: From Blue Hills Reservation headquarters
Length: 4.75-mile loop
Approximate Hiking Time: 2.5–3 hours
Difficulty Rating: Moderate due to steepness and rockiness of the trail
Trail Surface: The Skyline Trail is well marked but narrow, steep and rocky. To return, the Massachuseuck Trail is broad and flat.
Lay of the Land: Climb from lily pads, maples and sandy bogs to the pine, hemlock and scrub oak of a rocky ridgeline
Land Status: Metropolitan District Commission
Nearest Town: Randolph, MA
Other Trail Users: Mountain bikers, equestrians, cross-country skiers
Canine Compatibility: Dogs permitted

Getting There

From Boston: Drive south on I-93, and take exit 3, marked Houghtons Pond/Ponkapoag Trail. Turn right off the exit ramp, following signs to Houghtons Pond. In 0.1 miles, turn right again at a stop sign. Turn right again at 0.2 miles, into the large parking lot at Houghtons Pond. *DeLorme: Massachusetts Atlas & Gazetteer:* Page 53 C20

The ten-mile Skyline Trail connects nine peaks through the Blue Hills Reservation and boasts one of the best views of the city's skyline. At 635 feet, Great Blue Hill, the region's flagship peak, is the highest point on the Atlantic coast south of Maine, but this walk features a loop over two less crowded hills with equally broad panoramic views.

This route is a study in contrasts. It begins at a popular swimming beach then passes quickly into quiet paths that lead you from a sandy bog into a hardwood oak and maple forest. You then hike up through hemlock and pine stands and finally onto a windblown ridgeline, populated only by hardy low-bush blueberry and scrub oak.

Begin the hike from the large Houghtons Pond parking lot, with its restrooms, water and snack bar. On summer weekends, the lot is filled with Bostonians wanting a cool swim in this spring-fed "kettle pond." It was formed when mile-high retreating glaciers left a frozen chunk of ice embedded in the landscape. Walk about 300 feet north on the sandy shoulder of Hillside Street and stop at the park's Reservation Headquarters to pick up a trail map for $1.

Directly across the street from the park headquarters are the blue blazes of the Skyline Trail. As soon as you enter the woods, you'll leave 99% of the crowds behind, and progress from the frogs and lily pads of the marshland into stands of red and white oak, Norway maple, and American elm. As you start to climb, the crowd noise fades fast, and the new trail is too narrow and steep for the mountain bikes and horses to follow. You soon climb sharply up a rocky slope, stepping over stone walls and crossing several sandy paths.

Suddenly, the extra altitude tips the forest's balance from oak and maple to low sassafras trees, white pine, balsam, and Eastern hemlock. As you ascend to the ridgeline, you reach Tucker Hill and receive your first reward: a clear view to the west of the weather observatory on Great Blue Hill and the rolling hills behind it. Around you are an exposed rock cap, scrub

oak, and loblolly pine. Follow the Skyline Trail due east, down into a saddle, taking care not to twist your ankles on the loose rock. This small elevation change plunges you back into an open forest again, as you follow the blue blazes across a wider trail. You'll start to climb quickly again, and soon after another intersection, pass several car-sized boulders called glacial erratics, another reminder of things left behind by the huge sheets of ice that shaped these hills.

The Blue Hills trail maps feature four-digit numbers at the major intersections, and you soon come to #2141. Follow the blue blazes up a set of steep stone steps, crest the ridgeline to Buck Hill, and bask in the second superb view of this short hike. This is a great place to stop

for a drink of water, watch the hawks soar close overhead, and, in July, to nibble on low-bush blueberries. To the north, see the Boston skyline and the landmark candy-striped Boston gas tank, with the Braintree/Randolph reservoir to the south. Follow the blue blazes painted on the rocks at your feet, and drop off the hilltop on another set of stone steps.

Near the base, turn right onto the orange-blazed Massachuseuck Trail for your return trip. The state of Massachusetts draws its name from this tribe of native Americans, who fished the kettle ponds and hunted deer on the hills here until they were displaced by colonial settlers. The remainder of the hike is a return to civilization, as you can already hear cars on MA 28. Watch also for mountain bike and horse traffic on this wider, flatter trail. With enough snowfall, it is a wonderful cross-country skiing route.

MilesDirections

0.0 START at Houghtons Pond parking lot, and walk toward Blue Hills Reservation headquarters. Cross the street, and pick up the blue-blazed Bugbee Path.

0.1 Turn left onto the Skyline Trail, following blue blazes uphill on a smaller path. Follow this through an intersection with the green-blazed Tucker Hill Path, and through a second intersection.

0.5 Reach Tucker Hill, and keep following the blue blazes eastward along the ridgeline, and down into a saddle.

0.8 Follow the blue blazes through an intersection with the green-blazed Dark Hollow Path, then through intersection 2117, and through intersection 2141, the Doe Hollow Path.

1.3 Reach Buck Hill. Follow the blue blazes painted on the rocks at your feet off the peak, down a set of stone steps, crossing an intersection with the Buck Hill Path as you descend.

1.5 Turn right at intersection 2210, onto the orange-blazed Massachuseuck Trail.

1.7 Bear left at intersection 2183, following the orange blazes.

2.0 Bear left at a triangle-intersection, 2162.

2.5 Follow the orange blazes past a trail that merges from the left (intersection 2152). Then bear left onto the orange-blazed Doe Hollow Path.

3.0 Turn right at intersection 2137, and follow the orange blazes past several other trails.

3.8 Reach a large intersection, 2094. Cross the trail marked with green dots, following the orange blazes on a smaller trail uphill for one last hilltop.

4.2 As you drop off this small hill, go straight through an intersection with the green-blazed trail. Cross over an abandoned paved road, and bear left to pick up the orange blazes again.

4.4 Bear left through a small clearing, emerge from the woods, and bear right onto the sandy road that circles Houghtons Pond. Follow the shore past the swimmers and picnic tables back to the parking lot.

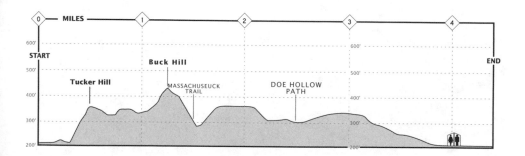

32

The Blue Hills Trailside Museum, run by the Massachusetts Audubon Society, features cultural, historic and natural history displays of this 7,000-acre reserve and its 150 miles of trails.

Events at the museum include public service hearings, such as an information session on the West Nile Virus. There's the annual honey harvest in October, guided owl-watching walks, wilderness photography workshops, and—for kids—seasonal sessions on migration, hibernation, autumn leaves, and the solstices.

It's located at 1904 Canton Avenue in Milton, MA. Hours are 10 A.M. to 5 P.M., Tuesday through Sunday, and holiday Mondays. Admission is $3 for adults; (617) 333-0690 or www.massaudubon.org/Nature_ Connection/Sanctuaries/Blue_Hills for more information.

To get there, take I-93 to exit 2B (Milton, Route 138 North). Follow the exit ramp to the first set of traffic lights. Go straight through the lights. The parking lot is 0.5 miles ahead on the right. The museum is at the end of the parking lot.

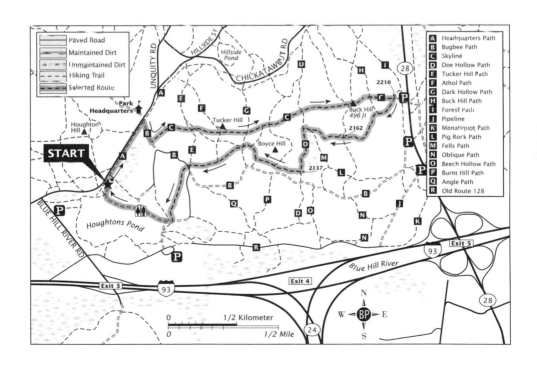

Hike Information

📞 Trail Contacts:
Massachusetts District Commission (MDC): (617) 698–1802 or *www.state.ma.us/mdc*

🕐 Schedule:
Open year round, sunrise to sunset

💲 Fees/Permits:
No fees or permits required

❓ Local Information:
Blue Hills Reservation website: *www. magnet.state.ma.us/mdc/blue.htm* • **The New England Mountain Biking Association:** *http://nemba.org/ma/p_Blue_Hills_ Reservation.html* - *sometimes has useful information on the region (such as weather reports and trail conditions)*

💡 Local Events/Attractions:
Appalachian Mountain Club, Boston Chapter: *www.amcboston.org* • **Appalachian Mountain Club,** Southeastern Massachusetts Chapter: *www.amcsem.org* • **Boston Hiking Guide:** *www.geocities.com/ Yosemite/Trails/1171*

🛏 Accommodations:
MA website: *http://visitnewengland.com/ mass/south*

🚶 Hike Tours:
See Reservation Headquarters.

👥 Organizations:
Friends of the Blue Hills, Milton, MA (781) 828–1805 or *www.motjuste.com/bluehill* - *run year-round outdoor activities and workshops* • **Get Outdoors New England:** *www.gonewengland.org* • **Blue Hills Trail watch:** (617) 698–1802 - *volunteer trail crew*

📖 Other Resources:
The Blue Hills Trailside Museum (see below)

🏪 Local Outdoor Retailers:
Bob Smith's Wilderness House, Boston, MA (617) 277–5858 • **City Sports,** Boston, MA (617) 782–5121 or *www.citysports.com* • **Eastern Mountain Sports (EMS),** Boston, MA (617) 254–4250 or *www.emsonline.com* • **Face Off Sports,** Randolph, MA (781) 963–7825 • **Hilton's Tent City,** Boston, MA (617) 227–9242 or *http://go.boston. com/hiltonstentcity* • **MVP Sports,** Braintree, MA (781) 356–7600 or *www.mvpsports.com* • **Patagonia,** Boston, MA (617) 424–1776 or *www.patagonia.com* • **Sports Authority,** Braintree, MA (781) 380–3380 or *www.sportsauthority.com*

🅝 Maps:
USGS maps: Norwood, MA

Rocky Woods Reservation

Hike Specs

Start: Chickering Lake parking lot, off Hartford Street

Length: 3.7-mile loop

Approximate Hiking Time: 2 hours

Difficulty Rating: Medium; a short section is steep and rocky; the rest is wide and flat

Trail Surface: Mostly flat, packed dirt, with a short section of steep, rocky trail

Lay of the Land: Beginning is on a dry, rocky trail, but the bulk of the loop twists through swampland, with flooded frog ponds, with hemlocks and shagbark hickory

Land Status: The Trustees of Reservations

Nearest Town: Medfield, MA

Other Trail Users: Runners, cross-country skiers, mountain bikers

Canine Compatibility: Dogs not permitted. (A dog moratorium was established in April 2001, during site restoration of Chickering Lake. Check with the Trustees of Reservations to learn when this will be lifted.)

Getting There

From Boston: Take I-95/MA 128 south to exit 16B (for MA 109 and Westwood). Drive west on MA 109 for 1.6 miles, then turn right onto Hartford Street. Continue straight through a stop sign. At 3.1 miles, turn right at a sign for the Trustees of Reservations. *DeLorme: Massachusetts Atlas & Gazetteer:* Page 52 C9

These hills were valuable timberland for New England's early colonists, who cleared them for crops as early as 1640 with a horse and plow. They quarried granite from the ridges, and forged farm tools in the 1800s—the adjacent Fork Factory Brook Reservation is named for the pitchfork factory built along Mill Brook in 1839. The work was easier than it could have been, since much of the land was already prepared for farming thanks to the Native American practice of burning the fields every fall. Fresh grasses would grow back first, drawing wild animals in search of grazing food. So the Indians restocked their hunting grounds.

The town of Medfield was sacked in February of 1676, during King Philip's War, when desperate Native Americans staged a last-gasp assault to push back the European settlers. Eight townsmen were killed and dozens of houses burned, as a force of 1,000 Indians stormed the town. But Philip himself (Metacom was his true name) was killed that August, and the uprising fizzled.

From 1800 until World War II, the town's principal industry was the manufacture of straw hats, which funded factory owners' mansions. But the senior building in Medfield is undoubtedly the Dwight Derby House, built in 1651, and spared in the Indian wars. After careful restoration, the 1651 Shoppe is now open in the old building, stocked with memorabilia commemorating the town's 2001 celebration of its 350th anniversary.

The reservation is located at the corner of Medfield, Dover, and Walpole, three woodsy towns that make the park seem larger than its 625 acres. In fact, this hike is all about keeping

an eye out for the details: the yellow stripe along the ribs of a garter snake, the stone walls left over from the farming era, and the springtime sound of croaking frogs along the Wilson Swamp Trail, echoing so loudly through the trees they often sound like Canada geese.

A great way to study the nature of Rocky Woods is to pick up a copy of the free, self-guided nature trail guide, which describes geology and plants. An interpretive trail map is also available at the ranger station. Featured botany includes the ecology of wood swamps, including forests of white pine, red oak, birch, beech, hemlock, and scattered dogwoods. In the understory, look for pepperbush, swamp honeysuckle, and highbush blueberry. Wildlife loves this diversity of growth, so you find evidence of weasels, red fox, squirrels, raccoons, chipmunks, and skunks, as well as birds like owls, hawks, and kestrels.

Overall, it's a beautiful area despite the existence of an EPA Superfund cleanup site in nearby Walpole. The 30-acre Blackburn and Union Privileges site along the Neponset River was formerly used in manufacturing nails, textiles, asbestos brake linings, and other products. If you

have energy after a hike, stop in Medfield's Zullo Gallery, which has painting and sculpture displays, summer classes, and musical performances of jazz, acoustic rock, and folk. In May, stop by the Dover Days Fair, a collection of dancers, dog shows, hay rides, children's games and amusement park rides, and food.

MilesDirections

0.0 START at the map kiosk near the swings and see-saws at the highest end of the Chickering Lake parking lot. Walk away from the lake, through picnic tables and barbecue pits, on the narrow, dirt Noanet Trail.

0.3 Continue along this path, parallel to a stone wall, as you pass a fork branching off to the right through the wall. The trail soon cuts left, heading sharply uphill toward the granite cliffs above you.

0.4 Reach the top of the rocky trail and turn right, continuing uphill on a broader, crushed-stone trail that twists left as you circle toward the top of Cedar Hill.

0.5 Reach the hilltop and bear left, passing four concrete foundation blocks that once supported a fire tower. Drop downhill on a smaller trail that offers spectacular views to the south and west as you descend.

0.6 Turn right, continuing downhill through a series of switchbacks on a broad, tar and gravel carriage path, the Tower Trail.

0.8 Reach the lakefront and make two right turns, following the stone-chip Ridge Trail at intersection No. 2. Pass by several signs for the Hemlock Knoll Nature Trail (self-guided tour maps are available from rangers).

1.2 Reach the top of a rise and proceed left on a spur trail for 50 yards. After taking in a viewpoint from a rock outcropping, retrace your steps and continue along the Ridge Trail.

1.4 Turn right at intersection No. 5, passing by a sign for the Harwood Notch Trail.

1.5 Bear right at intersection No. 6, picking up the Wilson Swamp Trail.

1.9 Merge left at a fork at intersection No. 9, at the bottom of a pitch below a frog pond. This trail traces the borderline between the bare granite ledges of Mine Hill to your left, and swampland to your right.

2.4 Turn left at intersection No. 10, picking up the Cheney Pond Trail.

2.8 Bear left at intersection No. 11, onto the Ridge Trail.

2.9 Reach June Pond and merge left at intersection No. 8. At the end of the pond, turn right at intersection No. 7, onto the Quarry Trail.

3.1 Cross an intersection with Hardwood Notch Trail at intersection No. 4, and continue on the Quarry Trail.

3.5 Chickering Lake comes into view as you pass a junction with the Bridle Trail. Take a left fork as you reach intersection No. 3.

3.6 Turn right at intersection No. 2, onto the Chickering Pond Trail. This is the same path you started on, as you came off Cedar Hill.

3.7 Reach your car.

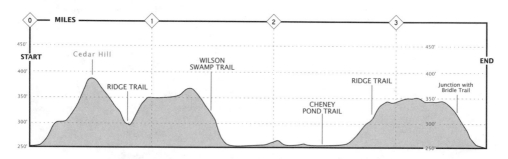

Hike Information

📞 Trail Contacts:
The Trustees of Reservations: Southeast Regional Office, Canton, MA (781) 821–2977 or (508) 785–0339 or *www.thetrustees.org/ttor/ttorspaces.nsf/ReservationLookup/Rocky+Woods — you can phone (978) 921–1944 to order an interpretive trail map*

🕐 Schedule:
The Reservation closes at 6 P.M. daily. Mountain bikers prohibited March 1 to April 30.

💲 Fees/Permits:
$2.50 per person on weekends and holidays

❓ Local Information:
Medfield website: *www.town.medfield.net* • **Suburban World:** *www.suburbanworld.com/medfield.htm* — *local paper* • **Dover website:** *www.doverma.org* or *www.doverrec.com* • **Walpole website:** *www.walpole.ma.us*

💡 Local Events/Attractions:
Dover Days Fair is held in early May • **Zullo Gallery,** Medfield, MA (508) 359–3711 or *www.zullogallery.org*

🍴 Restaurants:
There is a cluster of shops at the intersection of Hartford Street and MA 109.

🐾 Other Resources:
Chamber of Commerce: *www.metrowest.org* • **Further Medfield info:** *www.magnet.state.ma.us/cc/medfield.html*

🚴 Local Outdoor Retailers:
Eastern Mountain Sports (EMS) Dedham, MA (781) 461–0160 or *www.emsonline.com*

Ⓝ Maps:
USGS maps: Medfield, MA

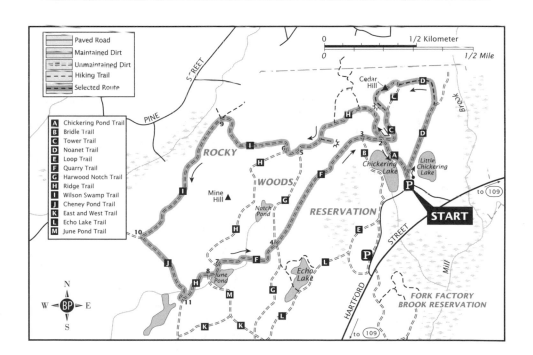

Noanet Woodlands Reservation

Hike Specs

Start: From the ranger station in the parking lot, Caryl Park, Dover
Length: 4.75-mile loop
Approximate Hiking Time: 2 hours
Difficulty Rating: Moderate, due to combination of steep, scrabbly trails, and broad, well-marked ones
Trail Surface: Dirt path
Lay of the Land: Mature white pine and red oak forest, mixed with beech and birch
Land Status: Trustees of Reservations
Nearest Town: Dover
Other Trail Users: Equestrians, mountain bikers, Nordic skiers, runners
Canine Compatibility: Dogs permitted in Noanet Woodlands, but not in Dover-owned Caryl Park—the starting point. See Getting There directions for alternate, dog-friendly trailheads for this hike.

Getting There

From Boston: From I-95, take exit 16 onto MA 109 West. In 1.0 mile, turn right onto Summer Street. At 2.3 miles, turn left onto Westfield Street, following signs to Dover. At 3.1 miles turn left onto Dedham Street, still following Dover signs. The parking lot for Noanet Woodlands is on the left at 5.0 miles. *[Note. There's also a parking lot for Caryl Park in another 0.1 miles.]*

For hikers with dogs: If you have a dog, you should pick up a trail map at the ranger station in Caryl Park, then continue on to a different trailhead. From Caryl Park, continue 0.4-miles further on Dedham Street, then turn left at a stop sign, onto Centre Street. Take an immediate left onto Walpole Street at the light, passing a Mobil Station. Your first alternate trailhead is a fire lane in one mile on the left. There is another fire lane at 1.6 miles, and a third at 2.1 miles (these small turnoffs fill up quickly with cars on a nice weekend). *DeLorme: Massachusetts Atlas & Gazetteer: Page 52 A9*

The drive through Dover's farms, horse stables, and tennis courts is a perfect entry to this ramble along well-marked, color-coded, bark-chip trails. The town-owned Caryl Park offers a soda machine and small ranger station, where you can buy a detailed trail map for $1. If you have time after the hike, local history is on display at the Benjamin Caryl House, located 100 yards further along Dedham Road, and open from spring to fall on Saturdays, 1 to 4 P.M.

Close to the ranger station, the sounds of tennis games, high school playing fields, and a children's playground will follow you into the woods, but the noise fades fast as you press on deeper into the reservation. Its 591 acres of land is bordered by the 1,200-acre Hale reservation, which gives a feeling of being much farther from Boston than you really are.

This hike stays on wide, well-tended trails, following color-coded plastic disks on the trees. In just half a mile, you leave little Caryl Park and cross into Noanet. With permit fees for mountain bikers and horseback riders, and a no-riding rule during the muddy spring months, the trails stay flat and unrutted. This hike follows the red-blazed Larrabee Trail southward to its end, then follows the blue-blazed Peabody Trail back home, with a small detour to Noanet Peak.

Sunday church bells echo through the mature white pine forest as you leave the parking lot far behind. Near the one-mile mark, you'll pass a huge boulder, dropped there by retreating glaciers, and suddenly realize you have left the sounds of civilization far behind. Come up a rise, and the forest fades from pine to eastern black oak and beech. As you continue to climb, you'll also see scarlet oak and northern red oak. It's a beautiful demonstration of the

New England rule that for every 400 feet you gain in elevation, the ecology will change as if you'd gone 100 miles to the north. All these acorns leech tannic acid into the streams. When Native Americans here made acorn cakes, they had to boil the flour in water to remove the bitter taste.

As you climb, be sure also to look down—the loose sandy soil is perfect for amateur tracking. Whether you're with a child or not, it's a fun game to look for prints from dogs, horses, hiking boots, running shoes, and mountain bike tires. Then look up, and on a clear day, the sky may be striped with contrails from jets on their way into Logan. There were five wispy, parallel trails at once when I was there. And look around—these stone walls kept cattle and sheep from eating colonial farmers' crops of corn and hay.

You'll lose a little elevation as you follow the red blazes to their intersection with the northbound, blue-blazed Peabody Trail. Follow the blue for a short ways to intersection #35, where you can choose a straight, flat trek back to your car, or a short detour that adds 0.5 miles to your route as it climbs to Noanet Peak. As you climb, you'll quickly find yourself walking through eastern red cedar, where they cling to the rocky slope. Enjoy the view then continue north along the ridgeline, and you'll soon reach intersection #36 and the familiar, homebound blue trail. You'll come across the stoneworks and waterfall for the old mill site here, where the Dover Union Iron Company built its ironworks in 1815. The brook was too small, and the company went out of business in 1830, but landowner Amelia Peabody rebuilt the dam in 1954.

You'll soon hit the intersection where you first started along the red trail. Retrace your steps into Caryl Park, and back to your car.

Hike Information

Trail Contacts:
The Trustees of Reservations (508) 785–0339 or Southeast Office (781) 821–2977 or *www.thetrustees.org/ttor/ttor spaces.nsf/ReservationLookup/Noanet+ Woodlands*

Schedule:
Open year round, sunrise to sunset

Fees/Permits:
No fees or permits required for hikers; equestrian and mountain biking permits required

Local Information:
Ranger station on site, staffed year-round, weekends and holidays, 9 A.M. to 5 P.M.

Local Events/Attractions:
The New England Mountain Biking Association: *http://nemba.org/ma/p_ Noanet_Woods.htm - sometimes has useful information on the region such as weather reports and trail conditions*

Other Resources:
Wellesley website: *www.wellesleyweb.com - gives information on Wellesley, Weston, and Dover*

Local Outdoor Retailers:
Eastern Mountain Sports (EMS), Dedham, MA (781) 461–0160 or *www.emsonline.com*

Maps:
USGS maps: Medfield, MA

MilesDirections

0.0 START immediately behind the ranger station in Caryl Park. Follow the Caryl Trail, blazed with plastic yellow disks nailed to trees.

0.3 Take a left fork, following the yellow blazes and a sign for Noanet Woodlands.

0.4 Turn left at intersection No. 3, following a sign that announces you are leaving Caryl Park and entering Noanet Woodlands Reservation, featuring an arrow directing you to the red and blue trails.

0.5 Immediately bear left again at intersection No. 4, picking up the red-blazed Larrabee Trail.

0.6 Continue to follow red blazes at intersection No. 33.

1.0 Follow the trail through intersection No. 28, passing a huge boulder.

1.1 Turn left at intersection No. 27, following the red blazes as you skirt a small pond.

1.2 Bear left again at intersection No. 26, following red blazes.

1.3 Bear right at intersection No. 25, following red blazes as you step through a break in a ramshackle stone wall.

1.5 Continue straight uphill through intersection No. 23, soon turning left at intersection No. 22.

1.9 Take a right at a T-intersection marked No. 21, following red blazes as you crest a hill there.

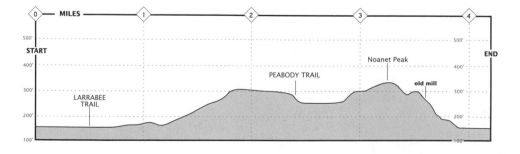

2.1 Turn right at a T-intersection marked No. 20, immediately bearing left at a fork (No. 19).

2.4 Cross a buried natural gas pipeline, and turn right at intersection No. 18, picking up the northbound, blue-blazed Peabody Trail.

2.6 Bear right at a fork at intersection No. 34, following the blue blazes.

2.7 Begin your detour to Noanet Peak, leaving the blue-blazed Peabody Trail behind, turning left up a slope at intersection No. 35.

2.8 Bear right at intersection No. 9, then immediately right again, at a large stone cairn and a "no mountain biking" sign.

3.2 Reach Noanet Peak. Continue northward along the ridgeline.

3.4 Bear right at a fork with a broader trail, and quickly bear right again, at another fork (you are still heading north).

3.6 Turn left at intersection No. 36, picking up the blue blazes again as you pass the old mill and mill pond on your right.

4.2 Fork left at intersection No. 4, where you had first picked up the red blazed trail at the start of this hike. And immediately turn right at intersection No. 3, to pick up the yellow blazes and follow signs for Caryl Park and the parking lot.

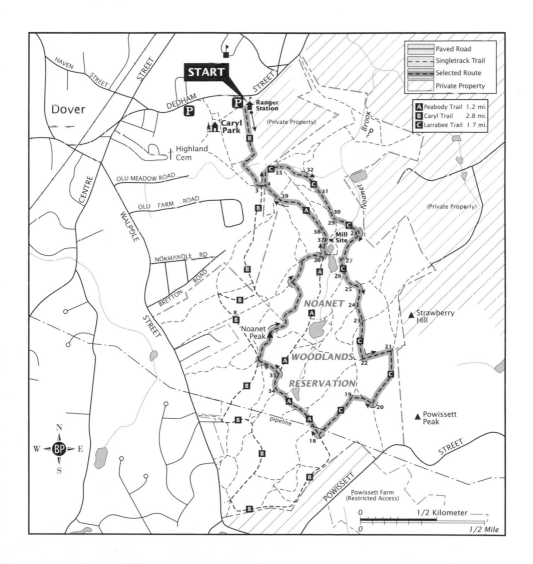

Northeast
MASSACHUSETTS

G eologists call the land inside the I-495 loop "the Boston Basin," a flat, low transition between original bedrock to the west, and newer glacial deposits on the cape and islands. Further seaward, inside the MA 128 loop, there is more evidence of the glaciers' footprints—eskers (long, snaking hills) and drumlins (tear or pear-shaped hills), created when the melting glaciers dropped their earthen loads.

Hikers in the northeast will see more exposed rocky shelves than along the south shore, with taller trees and steeper pitches. Check out Noanet Woodlands, Maudslay State Park, Ravenswood, Rocky Woods, Ward Reservation, and Weir Hill Reservation. At each of these destinations, the very shape of the hiking path under your feet has been shaped by awesome glacial forces.

The Ward Reservation itself contains two such drumlins, known as Boston and Holt Hills, and large enough that they're favored by backcountry skiers. Likewise, Weir Hill itself is a 200-foot high, two-peaked drumlin. And Ravenswood is a 300-acre moraine, right on the cusp of Gloucester Harbor. With rocky ledges throughout, the soil is marshy, culminating in the Great Magnolia Swamp. Likewise at Rocky Woods, the terrain alternates between granite ridges and frogponds—the land is wet and flooded between Cedar Hill and Chickering Lake, and between Whale Rock and Notch Pond.

This region has also spawned great diversity of flora and fauna in its wetlands, such as the Ipswich River Wildlife Sanctuary and Norris Reservation. At Ipswich you will find the Great Wenham Swamp, a huge freshwater wetland bursting with birds (and their predators and prey).

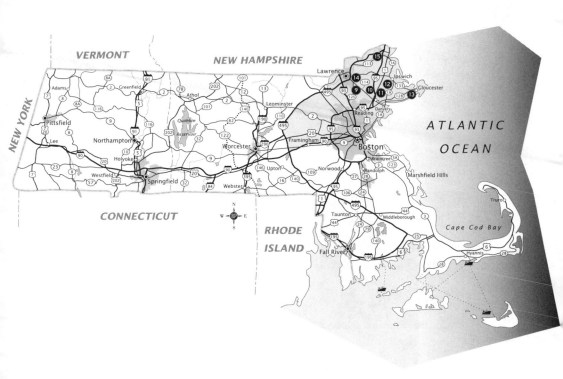

The Hikes

9. Ward Reservation
10. Boxford State Forest
11. Ipswich River Wildlife Sanctuary
12. Bradley Palmer State Park
13. Ravenswood Park
14. Weir Hill Reservation
15. Maudslay State Park

Section Overview

Ward Reservation

The reservation is split evenly by the Andover and North Andover town line, with drumlins on either side: Holt Hill in Andover and Boston and Shrub Hills in North Andover. The Cat Swamp lies between them, ensuring that your loop will feature a contrast of low and high ground. *(See page 48)*

Boxford State Forest

This walk through the woods doesn't offer steep climbs or views, but for its proximity to civilization, Boxford State Forest offers quiet trails and glassy ponds, with signs of beaver, deer, and birds all around. The path traces the shore of Crooked Pond, then climbs the gentle Bald Hill before descending to the stone foundation of the Russel-Hooper Farmhouse. It closes the loop with a short stroll on a paved road. *(See page 52)*

Ipswich River Wildlife Sanctuary

At 2,800 acres, this is Massachusetts Audubon's largest sanctuary, covering woods, meadows and wetlands, including the Great Wenham Swamp, the largest freshwater wetland on the north shore. This loop tours the sanctuary's open fields, marshes and beaver ponds, as well as the thickly-wooded Averill's Island, before returning for one more pass through the bustling wildlife neighborhood of the marshland. *(See page 56)*

Bradley Palmer State Park

This loop begins on an educational, self-guided nature trail, then veers off to follow the Ipswich River as it cuts between Bradley Palmer State Park and the adjacent Willowdale/Cleaveland Farm State Forest. Together, they offer 721 acres and over 20 miles of trails. Our hike leaves the river at the park's edge, and circles through rolling fields, up to Blueberry Hill, before returning to the start. *(See page 62)*

Ravenswood Park

Start at the harbor edge of this 600-acre glacial moraine, and head north through fields of boulders dropped by the glaciers as they retreated at the end of the last ice age. You'll pass by ocean views before heading west and dropping through wooded flatlands. Reach the Great Magnolia Swamp, and cross a series of boardwalks to return on a broad carriage path to your car. (*See page 66*)

Weir Hill Reservation

Weir Hill is a two-peaked drumlin rising between Stevens Pond and the two-mile-long Lake Cochichewick. This hike crosses the meadow on its top, then drops 200 feet to trace the peninsula's perimeter. Looking around, the town of North Andover has more than 3,000 acres of preserved open space, so it's easy to feel you're in a wilder place than you really are. (*See page 70*)

Maudslay State Park

This flat loop around a 480-acre park begins with a visit to the ruins of an historic mansion, with commanding views of the Merrimack River and stunning summer flower blooms. The path then traces the edge of a cliff side just above the river edge—a favorite winter roosting area for bald eagles. After a quick trip to the park's highest point (a modest 150-foot hill), it loops back to the start. (*See page 76*)

9

Ward Reservation

Hike Specs

Start: From dirt parking lot off Prospect Road

Length: 3.3-mile loop

Approximate Hiking Time: 2 hours

Difficulty Rating: Medium, with modest elevation change and some narrow footpaths

Trail Surface: Mostly two-track dirt paths, with some narrower dirt paths through woods

Lay of the Land: Two drumlins rise above boggy marshland

Land Status: Trustees of Reservations

Nearest Town: Andover, MA

Other Trail Users: Cross-country skiers, equestrians

Canine Compatibility: Dogs permitted

Getting There

From Reading: Head north on I-93 to exit 41, for MA 125, Andover and North Andover. Turn right off the exit onto MA 125 north. At 3.0 miles, pass the entrance to Harold Parker State Forest, and at 5.0 miles pass a Getty gas station. At 5.4 miles turn right onto Prospect Road, and at 5.8 miles turn right into the reservation's dirt parking lot. ***DeLorme: Massachusetts Atlas & Gazetteer:*** Page 29 G19

At 420 feet, Holt Hill is the highest point in Essex County, with views of the Boston skyline and Blue Hills Reservation on a clear day. Knowing this, local citizens gathered here on June 17, 1775 to watch as Charlestown burned in the Revolutionary War.

Today, Holt Hill is better known for the compass-pointing Solstice Stones at its peak. Arranged by Mabel Ward, who donated her family's property for the reservation, the stones point to the compass' cardinal points, and to both pairs of solstices and equinoxes.

Here's when to look. Around March 21 and September 23, the sun rises due east and sets due west—these are the vernal and autumnal equinoxes. Around June 21, the sun will rise in the northeast quadrant of the circle and set to the northwest during the longest day of the year—the summer solstice. And about December 22, the sun will rise in the southeast and set in the southwest quadrant, marking it the shortest day of the year—the winter solstice. A particular stone in the circle marks each of these points.

Another point of interest is at Holt Hill's feet—Pine Hole Bog, a rare "quaking bog." This phenomenon occurs when a wetland forms across the surface of a shallow pond. Based on a floating mat of entangled mosses, rushes, and shrubs, it typically shimmies and shakes when walked on, and can support botany found nowhere else. Other signs of nature are here for the looking. During one winter visit, I stumbled across a pile of turkey feathers in the wooded lowlands, encircled by fox prints in the snow.

Marked by these two drumlins and two wetlands, the reservation is a study in contrast. The Trustees of Reservations maintains a self-guided nature trail along the 700-foot boardwalk that stretches from Holt Hill to the center of the Pine Hole Bog. Numbers that correspond to a pamphlet titled "Bog Nature Trail" mark the walk. The trails here are poorly blazed, but there are maps at major intersections.

Part of the reason its trails seem to meander at their pleasure is likely due to the haphazard formation of the reservation, which was glued together with pieces from 43 separate parcels of farm and pasture land. Since they were used for so long as independent businesses, they are uniformly walled-in. According to the Trustees of Reservations, 15 of the parcels are bordered on all sides by stone walls, 27 are partially bordered, and just one has no walls. That brings the total stone wall distance inside the reservation to 17 miles!

Massachusetts' High Points

Although it's sovereign of a modest domain, Holt Hill is nonetheless listed on a fascinating website called County Highpointers (http://cohp.org), a guide to climbing the highest point in all 3,141 counties in the U.S. They range from Alaska's Mt. McKinley (20,320 ft.) to a 10-foot high swamp in Terrebonne Parish, Louisiana. Our own 420-foot Holt Hill occupies a modest, middle rung. Feel free to e-mail the site's creator if you have additions or corrections!

Massachusetts' other highpoints include:

- *306-foot Pine Hill in Barnstable Co.*
- *Three unnamed 390-footers in Bristol Co.*
- *An unnamed 311-foot point near Peaked Hill in Dukes Co.*
- *2,841-foot Crum Hill in Franklin Co.*
- *1,794-foot Round Top Hill in Hampden Co.*
- *2,125-foot West Mountain in Hampshire Co.*

- *800-foot Nutting Hill in Middlesex Co.*
- *630-foot Great Blue Hill in Norfolk Co.*
- *Two 111-foot regions near Sankaty Head in Nantucket Co.*
- *395-foot Manomet Hill in Plymouth Co.*
- *330-foot Bellevue Hill in Suffolk Co.*
- *2,006-foot Mt. Wachusett in Worcester Co.*

The reservation is also crossed by the white-blazed Bay Circuit Trail. This staccato loop passes through 21 towns as it rings Boston on a hiking path that arcs between the MA 128 and I-495 beltways. First proposed in 1929, the ring is still taking shape—when completed, the

MilesDirections

0.0 START Leave the parking lot and turn right to continue uphill on Prospect Road. Immediately turn left, passing through a green metal gate on a paved road.

0.1 Turn left into the woods onto Margaret's Trail, marked with yellow or orange disks.

0.3 Cross a stream on a wooden plank footbridge.

0.4 Turn right at an intersection, to follow the Ward Trail, which winds between a small hill on your right and swamp to your left.

0.8 Pass by a narrow trail forking off to your right, then turn right at a T-intersection where the Ward Trail dead-ends at the Mass Electric power station, with its field full of humming transformers. You are now on Old Chestnut Street, which runs between Shrub and Boston Hills.

0.9 Pass by a footpath on your right and Jeff and Eric's Trail on your left. Shortly thereafter, cross a stream.

1.1 Turn left onto the Graham Trail, following it uphill.

1.2 Pass by a right turn onto Lynn's Trail.

1.4 Turn right, following a chain link fenceline on your left. Shortly thereafter, bear right through an open field to reach a great scenic overlook from atop Boston Hill.

1.5 Pass by fenced-in radio towers, satellite dishes,

and cell phone antennas on your left. Shortly thereafter, reach Elephant Rock, a glacial erratic boulder in the middle of a field. *[**FYI**. From here, there are great views of the Boston skyline.]*

1.6 Continue in the same direction, heading downhill and sweeping gently right to pick up your trail into the woods.

1.8 Drop steeply downhill as you cross a stream and then a stone wall.

1.9 Turn left onto Old Chestnut Street.

2.0 Bear right to follow yellow and blue blazes.

2.1 Cross a stream and pass close by the Hoehn Farm, with its barking dogs and crowing roosters. Pass by a blue-blazed trail that branches off to your right.

2.3 Pass by the Five Crossings Trail on your left.

2.4 Bear right at a fork (a left here would take you onto the Field Loop).

2.5 Continue following blue blazes as you cross an intersection with another trail, then bear right when you reach a private house. Your trail passes between two parallel rows of trees, with a paved road below on your left.

2.7 Emerge from the woods at the green gate you passed through at the start of this hike, and retrace your steps on Prospect Road to your car.

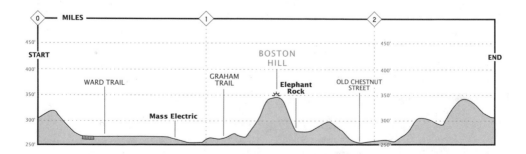

200-mile path will cross through 50 towns and cities, touching 79 areas of preserved land. Today, 150 miles of the trail are blazed and open for hiking.

Be careful when you dress to come here. There is significant snow remaining in the woods in mid-March, requiring snowshoes or cross-country skis. In fact, Boston and Holt Hills are favorite spots for telemarkers and backcountry skiers.

Hike Information

Trail Contacts:
The Trustees of Reservations, Beverly, MA (978) 921–1944 or *www.thetrustees.org* • **Friends of the Ward Reservation,** Andover, MA – *This group publishes a free, quarterly newsletter*

Schedule:
Open year round, gates close at sunset

Fees/Permits:
No fees or permits required

Local Information:
Andover Trails Committee: *www.town. andover.ma.us/commun/trails/maps.htm*

Organizations:
Bay Circuit Alliance, Andover, MA (978) 470–1982 or *www.baycircuit.org* • **Bay Circuit Trail Information:** *www.serve.com/ baycircuit/towninfo.htm*

Other Resources:
Geology of the Ward Reservation by George E. Zink

Maps:
USGS maps: Lawrence, MA

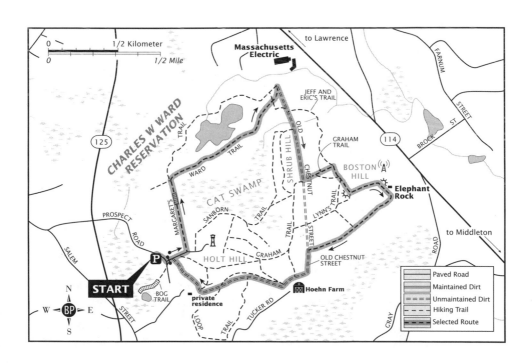

Boxford State Forest

Hike Specs

Start: From the intersection of Lockwood and Middleton Streets

Length: 4.6-mile loop

Approximate Hiking Time: 2 hours

Difficulty Rating: Easy, with flat, broad trails

Trail Surface: Rough dirt

Lay of the Land: Boggy lowlands surrounding a flat-topped hill

Land Status: MA Department of Environmental Management

Nearest Town: Danvers, MA

Other Trail Users: Cross-country skiers, snowmobilers, equestrians

Canine Compatibility: Dogs permitted

Getting There

From Danvers: Head north on I-95 to exit 52, for Topsfield Road, Topsfield and Boxford. Turn left off the exit onto Topsfield Road, and cross over I-95, following signs for Boxford. At 1.6 miles, bear left onto Main Street at a three-way intersection, keeping a cluster of small monuments on your right. Reach a stop sign at 2.0 miles, and turn left again, onto Middleton Street. At 3.4 miles, reach an intersection with Lockwood Lane and park on the shoulder. *DeLorme: Massachusetts Atlas & Gazetteer:* Page 29 G26

H ikers will be rewarded here for keeping their eyes open for signs of wildlife—it's easy to find squirrel nests in trees above piles of broken, shelled beech nuts; and deer have left their tracks and scat everywhere, some quite near hunters' deer stands. And the historic Russel-Hooper Farmhouse at the base of Bald Hill—today just a crumbling stone foundation—is a sign of early inhabitants, who cleared the land and built the stone walls.

The state forest is adjacent to the J.C. Philips Wildlife Sanctuary, and part of its land is protected by the Essex County Greenbelt Association. Hunting is permitted in some areas here, according to season. There are no blazes or trail names, but numbered intersections aid in navigation. There are no motorized vehicles allowed in this wildlife sanctuary, so the trails are in great shape, although they can be deeply flooded during the spring melt.

Bald Hill itself is part of the Bald Hill Reservation, a 1,624-acre plot split between Boxford State Forest, the Philips Wildlife Sanctuary, and the Essex County Greenbelt (and thus between the towns of Boxford, North Andover, and Middleton). Protected here are ponds, wildflowers, and historic landmarks. For more details and trail descriptions, check the *Boxford Bay Circuit Guidebook.*

After your hike, don't miss Boxford's annual Apple Festival each autumn. Held on the third Saturday of September on Elm Street, East Boxford, it features more than a hundred crafters selling their homemade goods. Also, the local historical society sells homemade apple pies. For a complete listing of orchards where you can pick your own apples after a strenuous hike, check out *www.apples-ne.com/masspickyourown.html.* For a listing of what to do with all those apples, browse the recipes at *www.apples-ne.com/newrecipes.html.* You'll find ideas from apple chicken stir-fry and apple halibut kebobs to apple pizza and silky sweet potato and apple bisque.

In the holiday season, you can cut your own Christmas tree at Herrick Tree Farm. Stop in to choose your favorite tree from a wide range of spruce and fir. (Call ahead for hours.) In the spring, check out the Harlan P. Kelsey Arboretum, located on the grounds of the Kelsey-Highland Nursery (address below). This 4.2-acre plot protects the remnants of a former 500-acre collection of plants imported from North Carolina, and today managed by the Horticultural Society of Boxford, which is planning a visitors center and parking lot. You can walk along footpaths through this show garden.

Hike Information

Trail Contacts:
Department of Environmental Management **(DEM),** Boston, MA (617) 626-1250 or *www.state.ma.us/dem/parks/trails/BOXF. pdf* – for an online trail map

Schedule:
Open year round

Fees/Permits:
No fees or permits required

Local Information:
Boxford website: *www.haverhillchamber. com/communities/boxford/index.html* • The Haverhill Gazette: *www.hgazette.com* • **Tri-Town Transcript,** Danvers, MA (978) 887-4146 – *Boxford's newspaper*

Local Events/Attractions:
Harlan P. Kelsey Arboretum, Boxford, MA (978) 462-7310 • **Boxford Historical Society,** Boxford, MA (978) 887-5078 • Herrick Tree Farm, Boxford, MA (978) 887-5477 or (978) 372-2509

Restaurants:
Benson's Ice Cream, West Boxford, MA (978) 352-2911

Hike Tours:
The Essex County Greenbelt Association, Essex, MA (978) 768-7241 or *www.ecga.org* – *A land trust focused on preserving open space and ecosystems in Essex County, MA. The group seeks to create continuous open land (greenbelts) of unbroken trails, rivers, and other intact corridors • See **www.ecga. org/events/walksche.htm** for a schedule of the group's monthly guided-walks.*

Organizations:
Essex National Heritage Area (978) 740-0444 or *www.essexheritage.org* • **Merrimack Valley Planning Commission:** *http://mvpc.org*

Local Outdoor Retailers:
MVP Sports, Danvers, MA (978) 774-7512 • **Ski Market Underground,** Danvers, MA (978) 777-3344 • **Sports Authority,** Danvers, MA (978) 774-9400

Maps:
USGS maps: Lawrence, MA

MilesDirections

0.0 START Enter the woods on a westbound hiking trail opposite Lockwood Lane, 15 yards further south on Middleton Street.

0.1 Bear left at a fork and continue to follow this rutted, muddy, two-track trail.

0.3 Turn left at intersection No. 25, and soon cross a wooden boardwalk.

0.5 At the bottom of a hill, turn right at a T-intersection where the trail meets Fish Brook. Following this broad, sandy path, you soon walk along the banks of Crooked Pond (a marsh) on your left.

0.6 Continue straight through intersection No. 15, passing by a trail on the right.

0.8 Bear left at intersection No. 14, curling closely around the pond and over a wooden boardwalk.

0.9 Bear left at intersection No. 13, crossing another trail and soon passing a left turn at intersection No. 13A.

1.2 Turn right at intersection No. 12 and begin a gentle climb up Bald Hill, still following the broad, two-track trail.

1.3 Emerge into a clearing atop Bald Hill, then follow the trail as it turns left and drops downhill halfway across the meadow.

1.4 Halfway down the slope, bear right at a fork (although both choices end up in the same place); at the base of the hill pass by the stone foundation of the Russel-Hooper Farmhouse. Immediately bear right, then right again at intersection No. 10, and follow the trail northwest in a gentle downhill, with the hill rising above you on the right.

1.6 Continue straight through intersection No. 9, passing by a trail branching left.

1.7 Bear left at a fork at intersection No. 8A.

1.9 Cross two boardwalks over streams, the legacy of a 1997 Boy Scout project.

2.3 Turn right at intersection No. 8, and head northeast.

2.8 Turn right at a fork at intersection No. 31, soon passing an unmarked trail on your left.

3.8 Bear right at intersection No. 19, then left at intersection No. 20.

4.0 Bear left at intersection No. 20A.

4.1 Turn right on Middleton Street, heading south.

4.6 Reach your car.

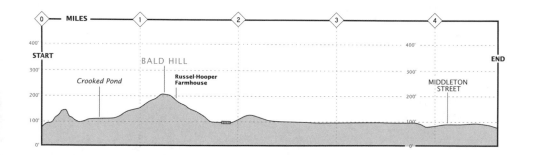

Together with Middleton and Topsfield, Boxfield is in a "Tri-Town Area" within Essex County. The town has maintained its rural, agricultural appearance partially through a minimum lot size of two acres, unchanged since 1949. Settled in 1645, Boxford hews close to traditional New England small town form with its two town centers. East Boxford Center boasts the town hall, post office, bank, church, and a country store, while West Boxford is the site of another church and country store, as well as Benson's, a locally famous ice cream shop with homemade flavors like red raspberry.

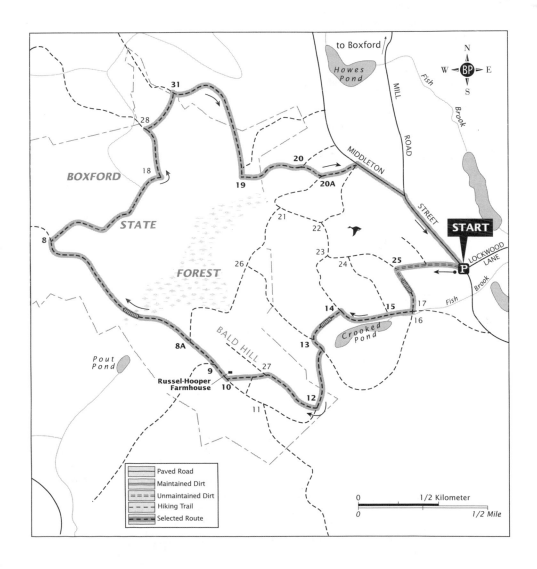

Ipswich River Wildlife Sanctuary

Hike Specs

Start: From visitors center at main parking lot, off Perkins Row

Length: 3-mile loop

Approximate Hiking Time: 2 hours

Difficulty Rating: Easy, with flat, rolling trails

Trail Surface: Dirt single-track paths that can get very wet in the spring, even on the boardwalks

Lay of the Land: Mixed upland forests surround acres of wetlands and eight miles of the Ipswich River

Land Status: Massachusetts Audubon Society

Nearest Town: Topsfield, MA

Other Trail Users: Cross-country skiers. Massachusetts Audubon does not permit dogs, bicycles, horses without permits, or joggers

Canine Compatibility: Dogs not permitted

Getting There

From Danvers: Take I-95 north to exit 50 (Topsfield) and follow U.S. 1 north for 2.8 miles. Turn right onto MA 97 south (following signs for Beverly and Danvers) and at 3.2 miles turn left onto Perkins Row. At 4.2 miles, turn right at the sanctuary entrance, and park at the main lot, at 4.5 miles. *DeLorme: Massachusetts Atlas & Gazetteer:* Page 29 H30

Originally home to the Agawam tribe, this land was part of the original Massachusetts colony in 1643, and the office and visitors center has stood since 1763. Of course, this human history is dwarfed by geologic features such as eskers, kames, and a drumlin, created by a glacier 15,000 years ago. Look for these features as you walk: an esker is the sediment left behind as a glacier melts, often in the shape of a winding ridge like a raised railroad bed. A kame is similar, since it derives from the sediment dropped by melting glaciers into depressions, which slowly grow into small hills. Today they are often mined for sand and gravel. A drumlin is a long, rounded hill that was formed of existing till molded by glaciers as they moved, so they point in a parallel direction to the glacier's path.

The variety of ecosystems here is stunning, from freshwater meadows and marshes, to the silver maple floodplain forest along the riverside, and the tall pine-hemlock stands on Averill's Island. This mixture of wetlands and uplands is the perfect mix for birders, and the sanctuary keeps some meadows mowed for bluebird and woodcock habitat (the mailbox-size birdhouses on posts are for the bluebirds). There is an observation tower for watching waterfowl at Bunker Meadows, and a bench on the boardwalk near Waterfowl Pond that extends deep into the marshes. And although it's not on this loop, the Rockery Trail was designed as an arboretum in the early 1900s, with exotic trees and shrubs planted around enormous glacial boulders.

One point of this sanctuary serves as an epicenter for diversity—the Stone Bridge. An active beaver lodge and dam keep Waterfowl Pond full, while garter snakes slither at your feet, hawks circle over the marsh, and Canada geese feed and fight in the rushes. At some point on your hike, take a minute to stop on the trail, shut your eyes and just listen. (For one game, you can try to count the number of different bird species by their songs.)

Birds aren't the only flying creatures so closely tracked—naturalists have identified more than 44 species of butterflies here. Check at the visitors center for trail conditions, bird and butterfly sightings, wildlife guidebooks, maps, and restrooms. And the excellent nature center has exhibits of different nests, skeletons, tracks, and photos. As with all Massachusetts Audubon properties, trails that lead away from the visitors center are blazed blue, and those leading back to it are blazed yellow. Remember to check for ticks after warm weather hikes here.

MilesDirections

0.0 START on Bradstreet Lane, the double-track dirt road behind the visitor center.

0.3 Turn left at a T-intersection, onto the Drumlin Trail. And in 50 yards, bear right at a fork in a beech grove, onto Stone Bridge Trail. This trail passes between the long, low mound of an esker (a glacial hill) on your right and marshland on your left.

0.7 Cross a wooden bridge and continue along the Stone Bridge Trail, through birch and white pine.

0.8 Turn right at a fork, crossing the stone bridge at Waterfowl Pond. Just over the bridge, take a sharp right onto the Averill's Island Trail, looking to your right at a beaver lodge. [**Note.** This path is sometimes very wet.]

1.1 Bear right at a fork, for the eastern leg of the Averill's Island Loop, and soon pass through a grove of impossibly straight, tall white pines and hemlocks.

1.5 Merge right at a fork at the end of the island, picking up the White Pine Loop. Cross a short berm

between two marshes, and immediately bear left for the southern leg of this loop.

1.9 Bear left at an intersection with the northern leg of the loop.

2.0 Turn sharply left at a sign for the Hassocky Meadow Trail.

2.4 Come up a rise to a T-intersection with the North Esker Trail and swing left, continuing southward along the edge of the marsh.

2.5 Drop off a low ridge line onto a 20-yard boardwalk and turn left, crossing the Stone Bridge again. Immediately over the bridge, turn right, onto the Waterfowl Pond Trail.

2.7 Turn left onto the boardwalk, picking up the Innermost Pond Trail. [**Side-trip.** And take a short detour to stop at the observation bench, thrust far out into the marsh.]

2.8 Continuing along the Innermost Pond Trail, cross an intersection with the Drumlin Trail, and walk uphill toward the Visitor Center.

3.0 Reach your car.

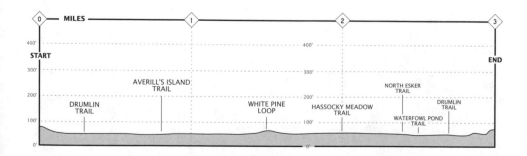

If you're here in the fall, make sure to stop at the Topsfield Fair, held in the first week of October. Founded in 1818, the event bills itself as "America's Oldest Agricultural Fair." It features giant pumpkins, sand sculptures, a cattle show, and amusement park rides for children. In fact, there's plenty going on at the fairgrounds in the rest of the year, too: oriental rug auctions, bridge tournaments, dog and horse shows, car shows, a Native American festival, and antique and crafts fairs. Check the web site for dates.

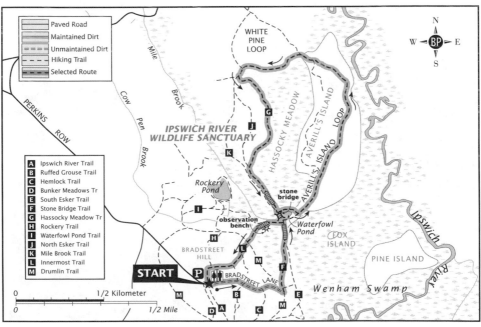

Birding at Ipswich

Birders have studied this area for so many years that they have a good idea what to expect in a given season and region. The following information is from the sanctuary's trail map; for the curious, there are far more details available at the Nature Center.

- *The open fields around Bradstreet Hill are nesting and feeding grounds for the tree swallow, Eastern bluebird, American kestrel, and bobolinks. In the spring and summer, chimney swifts may nest in the chimney of the large house here.*
- *From the Observation Tower, look over the buttonbush shrub swamp for seasonal visitors: in the spring and fall, blue- and green-winged teals, ring-necked ducks, and hooded mergansers will rest and feed here during their migrations. And in the spring and summer, look for tree and barn swallows, great blue herons, glossy ibises, and great egrets.*
- *The Great Wenham Swamp may hold rare finds such as the American bittern and pied-billed grebe, as well as more common waterfowl and migrating songbirds.*
- *The silver maple floodplain forest alongside the Ipswich River is often home to warblers, vireos, and rose-breasted grosbeaks.*
- *At Waterfowl Pond, there are wood ducks nesting in tree holes close to the waters' edge. In spring and fall, this is a feeding ground for warblers.*
- *On the upland wooded trails, there are wood thrush, pileated woodpecker, ovenbird, scarlet tanager, rose-breasted grosbeak, and an occasional great horned owl.*

Hike Information

☎ Trail Contacts:
Massachusetts Audubon, Topsfield, MA (978) 887–9264 or *www.massaudubon.org/ Nature_Connection/Sanctuaries/Ipswich_ River/index.html – There are also maps available online at this site.*

◔ Schedule:
Trails open sunrise to sunset, closed Monday – Visitors Center open 9 A.M. to 4 P.M. Tuesday–Friday, 9 A.M. to 5 P.M. weekends and Monday holidays May–October, and 10 A.M. to 4 P.M. weekends and Monday holidays November–April.

ⓢ Fees/Permits:
$3 per adult

❓ Local Information:
Topsfield website: *www.state.ma.us/cc/ topsfield.html* • **Ipswich website:** *www. ipswichma.com*

ⓠ Local Events/Attractions:
Rent canoes from Audubon to paddle on the eight miles of the Ipswich River that flow through this sanctuary (available May to November) • **The Topsfield Fair,** Topsfield, MA (978) 887–5000 or *www.topsfieldfair.org*

– Fair grounds are located on MA 1, just south of its intersection with MA 97 (High Street).

🛏 Accommodations:
Camping is allowed on Perkins Island, located 0.5 miles upriver from the sanctuary HQ, or rent a four-person cabin on sanctuary grounds.

👫 Organizations:
The Ipswich River Watershed Association, Topsfield, MA (978) 887–8404 or *www. tiac.net/users/irwa – The association studies and monitors the river's 45-mile path. They offer maps, current events, a natural history, and more.*

🔄 Other Resources:
The United States Geological Survey (USGS): *http://ma.water.usgs.gov/ipswich – studies the river carefully since conditions were so dry in the summer of 1999 that the river dried up.*

Ⓝ Maps:
USGS maps: Ipswich, MA

12   Bradley Palmer State Park

Hike Specs

Start: Park headquarters, at main entrance off Asbury Street

Length: 3.15-mile loop

Approximate Hiking Time: 1.5 to 2 hours

Difficulty Rating: Easy, with smooth trails and small hills

Trail Surface: Grassy fields and dirt trails

Lay of the Land: Ranges from mountain laurel and rhododendron groves to freshwater wetland along Ipswich River, and evergreen forest on higher land

Land Status: State and Essex County Greenbelt Association

Nearest Town: Topsfield, MA

Other Trail Users: Mountain bikers, equestrians, cross-country skiers, snowshoers, snowmobilers

Canine Compatibility: Dogs permitted

Getting There

From Boston: Take I-95 north to exit 50. Drive north on U.S. 1 for 4.25 miles, then turn right at the light onto Ipswich Road. At 5.5 miles, turn right onto Asbury Street. At 5.9 miles, turn left at a stone gate following signs for the park. Turn right at an intersection, and then turn left into the parking lot. *DeLorme: Massachusetts Atlas & Gazetteer:* Page 30 F1

T ogether with Willowdale/Cleaveland Farm State Forest, this land was the private estate of Bradley Webster Palmer (1866–1946), a Boston lawyer who represented Sinclair Oil in the Teapot Dome Scandal and President Woodrow Wilson at the Versailles Peace Conference at the end of World War I.

He called the estate Willowdale, and at its peak it contained 32 buildings, employed 40 people, and spanned five square miles, including a full steeplechase course for horse racing. He used the Tudor mansion for enormous parties, but also loved philanthropy; by the time of his death, he had donated all of the land to the state. Today, it is a busy park for everyone from horseback riders to inline skaters, with free trail maps and restrooms at the park headquarters building.

The hike starts on the nature trail, a mile-long loop with marked stations that illustrate the full variety of the land's plants and history. It's a perfect way to get acquainted with the land before you walk into the woods. We learn that wild turkeys were reintroduced here in 1990 after the native birds were nearly hunted to extinction in Massachusetts at the beginning of the last century. You'll also find trees including black cherry, rhododendron, mountain laurel, Scotch pine, Norway spruce, eastern cottonwood, white and red pines, and Canada hemlock. Also keep your eyes open for the three shiny leaves of poison ivy, and for purple loosestrife, an imported plant that is edging out many indigenous species. Our hike leaves the nature loop halfway through, but if you have time after this hike, it's worth completing the loop.

Once you leave the tour-trail, your path shadows the lazy river for nearly a mile, before doubling back through open meadows. You'll step around several equestrian jumps—part of the traditional steeplechase course—before heading uphill to cross a plateau in the center of the land. Dropping back downhill, you follow the bridle paths in a looping trail back to your car.

Long used for hunting and transportation by Native Americans, the Ipswich River has archeological sites along its banks with Indian artifacts more than 10,000 years old. In its next stage, the river was frequently dammed for textile mills, many in the town of Ipswich. Several of these dams still exist, though the river spills over them easily as it makes its way from its headwaters in the town of Wilmington toward the ocean, meeting saltwater between Ipswich's Crane Beach and Plum Island. Today it still pro-

> *If you're here at holiday time, stop by Nutter's Tree Farm to pick up a hand saw and cut your own Christmas tree. Choose between white spruce and Fraser fir, and pay by the foot for a tree that will fit perfectly in your house. The farm is located at 170 Ipswich Road, on your left as you drive to the park. Call (978) 887–9835 for details.*

Hike Information

Trail Contacts:
Bradley Palmer State Park Headquarters: (978) 887–5931 or *www.magnet.state.ma.us /dem/parks/brad.htm*

Schedule:
Open year round, sunrise to sunset

Fees/Permits:
No fees or permits required

Local Information:
The Essex County Greenbelt Association, Essex, MA (978) 768–7241 or *www.ecga.org* — *scheduled hikes and nature walks, local information, education and more* • **Willowdale State Forest,** Ipswich, MA: (978) 887–5931 or *www.state.ma.us/ dem/parks/ wild.htm* • **Ipswich River Watershed Association,** Ipswich, MA (978) 356–0418 or *www.ipswichriver.org*

Local Events/Attractions:
Appalachian Mountain Club, Boston Chapter: *www.amcboston.org* • **Appalachian Mountain Club,** Southeastern Massachusetts Chapter: *www.amcsem.org* • **Boston**

Hiking Guide On-line: *www.geocities.com/ Yosemite/Trails/1171/*

Accommodations:
Visit New England: *http://visitnewengland. com/mass/south* • **Massachusetts vacation website:** *www.mass-vacation.com/ index.shtml*

Organizations:
Massachusetts' birds website: *www.mass bird.org* – *If you're a birder, check it out.*

Other Resources:
Essex, MA website: *www.cape-ann.com/ essex.html* – *local maps, lodging, restaurants, shopping directories, and more*

Local Outdoor Retailers:
Essex River Basin Adventures, Essex, MA (978) 768–3722 or *www.erba.com* • **Moor & Mountain,** Andover, MA (978) 475–3665 • **Eastern Mountain Sports (EMS),** Peabody, MA (978) 977–0601 or *www.emsonline.com*

Maps:
USGS maps: Ipswich, MA
Trail maps located at the headquarters building.

vides drinking water and recreation to thousands of people, and is a great place for hikers to spot wildlife, from fish to birds to aquatic mammals.

Like any river, it occasionally overflows its banks, usually during the spring melt. Seasonal flooding flushes silt off the river bottom and guides anadromous fish back to their freshwater breeding grounds from the ocean. And in this watershed, floods fill another purpose, providing water to the silver maple floodplain forest located in Middleton and Topsfield. Several rare plants here depend entirely on the flooding Ipswich for their survival.

The park's neighbor, Willowdale State Forest, has no developed recreational facilities, but does boast the 100-acre Hood Pond as well as 40 miles of trails. It is split by MA 1, with its eastern block abutting Bradley Palmer State Park.

MilesDirections

0.0 START at the beginning of the "self-guided walking tour." There are maps at the trailhead under a tall white pine behind the headquarters building, fifty yards downhill from the bathrooms.

0.1 Turn gently right, along the river, at walking tour stop No. 7. (Ignore the sharper right turn that leads into a pine forest.) Your trail is marked with blue triangle blazes with bear paw logos inside.

0.2 Bear left onto a wider path, still following the River Trail's blue triangle blazes. The river continues to flow parallel to the trail, just fifty feet to your left.

0.3 Turn left at a sign for the River Trail, still marked with blue triangles.

0.4 Reach a wood and stone bridge crossing the river to your left, and continue straight past it.

0.7 Still following the river, see a sign in the trail that you are crossing from state land into land protected by the Essex County Greenbelt Association.

0.9 Reach a dam across the river, and turn right onto a smaller, uphill trail. Then immediately turn right again, as the trail emerges into a wide, open path. You'll soon cross back onto state land as you step over a stone wall.

1.1 Bear right onto a dirt road as you emerge into an open field.

1.6 Cross over a small, rickety wooden bridge, and turn left onto a smaller trail uphill, just before you reach a paved road.

1.8 At the top of the hill, bear left at a fork. Then quickly take your first right.

2.1 Merge left at another fork, and continue straight, dropping downhill and ignoring two trails that merge from the left.

2.4 Turn gently right in a clearing at the bottom of the hill, ignoring a hairpin right turn that leads to a steeplechase jump.

2.7 Reach a clearing at the intersection of many trails, and follow your broad, flat path as it curves gently to the right.

3.0 Cross straight through an intersection. Then bear left at a fork, along the edge of a small pond.

3.1 Reach a paved road, and cross it to reach the main parking lot, and your car.

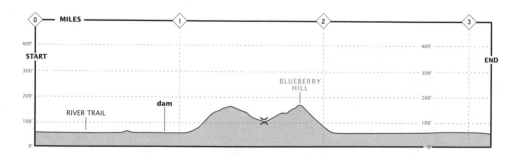

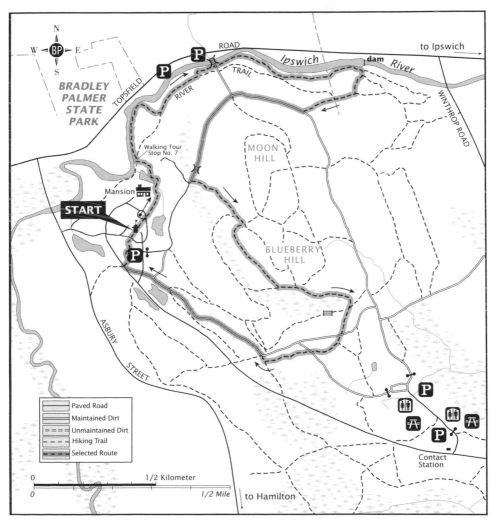

N
W — BP — E
S

ROAD

P P

to Ipswich

BRADLEY
PALMER
STATE
PARK

Ipswich   dam River

TOPSFIELD

RIVER   TRAIL

WINTHROP ROAD

Walking Tour
Stop No. 7

MOON
HILL

Mansion

START

BLUEBERRY
HILL

P

ASBURY

STREET

P

P

Paved Road
Maintained Dirt
Unmaintained Dirt
Hiking Trail
Selected Route

0   1/2 Kilometer
0   1/2 Mile

to Hamilton

Contact
Station

13

Ravenswood Park

Hike Specs

Start: From the small parking lot at the trailhead off of Route 127, just south of Gloucester

Length: 4.8-mile loop

Approximate Hiking Time: 2.5–3 hours

Difficulty Rating: Easy, due to broad, flat trails and modest elevation gain

Trail Surface: First 1.5 miles alternate between marshy flatlands and glacial boulder fields. The rest is broad trails through marshy flatlands, with occasional boardwalks.

Lay of the Land: The glaciers left their fingerprints on this 600-acre marshy moraine in the form of the rocks and boulders they dropped as they melted. Vistas from the highest points provide views of Gloucester Harbor.

Land Status: The Trustees of Reservations and City of Gloucester Watershed

Nearest Town: Gloucester, MA

Other Trail Users: Mountain bikers, cross-country skiers

Canine Compatibility: Dogs permitted

Getting There

From Beverly: Drive north on MA 128 to exit 14, the first Gloucester exit. Follow MA 133 east for three miles to the edge of Gloucester Harbor, then turn right onto MA 127 South, a.k.a Western Avenue. At five miles, turn right, into a small parking lot marked with a Trustees of Reservations sign hanging from a tree. *De-Lorme: Massachusetts Atlas & Gazetteer:* Page 30 J14

As you drive along the arm of Cape Ann toward Gloucester, the trip down Route 133 is like touring a museum of the region's modern history. You pass by marinas filled with shrink-wrapped sailboats in dry dock, and cat tailed marshes draining into the Atlantic. Tugs, barges, and lobster boats are moored at their piers near the city's State Fort Park. And the curious Hammond Castle stands on the harbor's rocky beach like a monument to the sea.

Ravenswood Park is a more ancient kind of museum. The park itself is a moraine—a long mound of dirt and rock left behind by melting glaciers. Its ponds and swamps were formed when the glaciers left huge chunks of ice stuck in the earth, intersecting the water table and leaving holes full of water and sediment when they melted. Fernwood Lake is an example of these "kettle ponds," and the Great Magnolia Swamp is a glacial bog.

Your hike begins and ends on the Old Salem Road, a broad carriage path that bisects the park. Within a quarter mile, you leave it, following the yellow-blazed Ledge Hill Trail as it winds through forest land scattered with boulders and ocean views. There is so much stone in these birch and pine woods that when farmers finished building stone walls, there was enough left over to line the trails, like natural guard rails.

In about two miles, you cross Old Salem Road at the Hermit's Plaque, a marker to Mason Walton, who arrived here in 1884 and lived alone in a cabin in these woods for the next 33 years. His book about the experience is in the town library.

Be sure you have good boots, as you follow the muddy, blue-blazed Fernwood Lake Loop to the park's northwest corner. Tall white pines here are mixed with the moisture-loving hemlocks that make the streams run red with tannin. Pick up the red-blazed Magnolia Swamp Trail that shadows the swampland through rhododendron groves, then crosses through the swamp itself on a chain of wooden boardwalks. When you reach the familiar Old Salem Road, it's less than a quarter mile to your car.

Used since 1623, Gloucester calls itself "America's Oldest Seaport," and it has plenty of action to back up the claim. Activities include sea chantey concerts on a retired schooner anchored in the harbor, the Gloucester Fishermen's Museum on Seven Seas Wharf, and the

Hike Information

Trail Contacts:
The Trustees of Reservations: Northeast Regional Office, Ipswich, MA (978) 356–4351 or www.thetrustees.org/ttor/ttorspaces.nsf/ReservationLookup/Ravenswood+Park

Schedule:
Open year round

Fees/Permits:
Mountain bikers prohibited from March 1 to April 30 in the park, and barred year round from the Magnolia Swamp Trail.

Local Information:
Gloucester on-line: www.cape-ann.com/gloucester.html • City of Gloucester website: www.ci.gloucester.ma.us

Local Events/Attractions:
Hammond Castle, Gloucester, MA (978) 283-7673 or www.hammondcastle.org – the museum and home of inventor John Hays Hammond Jr. (see sidebar) • Schooner Adventure, Gloucester, MA (978) 281-8079 or www.schooner-adventure.org – Business organization that's restoring the 122-foot fishing vessel Schooner Adventure • Schooner Sails: Thomas E. Lannon, Seven Seas Wharf,

Gloucester, MA (978) 281-6634 or www.schooner.org • Gloucester Fishermen's Museum, Seven Seas Wharf, Gloucester, MA (978) 281-1820

Restaurants:
Tony's Magnolia House of Pizza and Italian Cuisine, Magnolia, MA (978) 525-3030 – From the trailhead, drive north on MA 127 (Western Avenue). In 0.5 mile, turn right onto Hesperus Ave. In another 0.7 mile, pass Hammond Castle, and at 1.9 miles, reach the village of Magnolia, MA. Tony's is in Cole Square, at the intersection of Fuller and Norman Streets. Nearby Lexington Ave. is also full of shops, restaurants, and hotels.

Other Resources:
Gloucester Daily Times: www.gloucestertimes.com

Local Outdoor Retailers:
Moor & Mountain, Andover, MA (978) 475-3665 • Eastern Mountain Sports (EMS), Peabody, MA (978) 977-0601 or www.emsonline.com

Maps:
USGS maps: Gloucester, MA

Essex Shipbuilding Museum. And if you're here in the fall, be sure to check out the Gloucester Schooner Festival, held each Labor Day. Old ships and replicas participate in sailing races, and you can enjoy deck tours, fish fry dinners, and fireworks. Check out *www.gloucesterma.com/calendar.htm* to learn what's happening on the day that you'll be there.

Also, don't miss Gloucester's most famous landmark, the one and a half-times life-size *Fisherman at the Wheel*, sculpted in 1923 by Leonard Craske. Standing on Stacy Boulevard, it honors the more than 10,000 Gloucester fishermen lost at sea in nearly four centuries. An additional "Wall of Remembrance" was added in 2000, naming 5,400 of those lost sailors.

MilesDirections

0.0 START at the Trustees of Reservations trailhead. Walk north on Old Salem Road, a broad, flat path.

0.2 Turn right at a sign for the Ledge Hill Trail, marked with yellow disks nailed to trees.

0.3 Pass through a stone wall, then turn left at a T-intersection (a green-blazed trail goes right).

0.4 Bear right at a T-intersection (a green-blazed trail goes left here).

0.7 Follow the yellow blazes through the curves as you take a left fork, then a right fork.

0.9 Reach a hilltop with a view of Gloucester Harbor visible to the east.

1.2 Passing a small granite quarry on the right, follow the yellow blazes through an intersection as you cross a wider path, then drop into a shaded hemlock grove.

1.6 The yellow blazes end here as you merge left at a T-intersection on the Old Salem Road.

1.9 Bear right into the woods onto the blue-blazed Fernwood Lake Trail, at the spot where the carriage path forks. *[FYI. The Hermit's Plaque is about 50 yards further along the right fork, a simple brass plate bolted into a boulder.]*

2.1 Continue to follow the blue blazes as you cross an intersection with a broader path, then cut through a stone wall and bear left.

2.3 Take a hairpin left turn.

2.8 Cross a stream and bear sharply right, following the blue blazes as you catch glimpses of Fernwood Lake through the trees.

3.1 As you reach the lake, bear sharply left, then bear right, uphill.

3.3 Swing left at a T-intersection, following the blue blazes.

3.8 The blue blazes end here as you turn right onto the red-blazed Magnolia Swamp Trail. *[FYI. For a possible side trip, a boardwalk branches to the left through the swamp here.]*

4.3 Continue along a boardwalk as the trail cuts directly across the swamp.

4.4 Cross an intersection as you follow the red blazes uphill through thick rhododendrons.

4.6 The red blazes end here as you turn right onto the familiar Old Salem Road.

4.8 Reach your car.

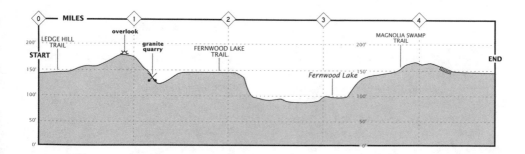

Hammond Castle

John Hays Hammond Jr., an inventor who worked on guided missiles and radio communications, built Hammond Castle in 1929. After making a fortune in African diamond mines as a mining engineer, he built the structure for the Hammond Research Corp., where he allegedly invented over 800 items, claiming more than 400 patents. One of the most important was remote control, which he tested by sailing empty ships around Gloucester harbor. Today the building houses his collections of medieval art, tiles, and paintings. Check the schedule for chamber music concerts, dinner-theater, historical fairs, and Shakespeare productions.

From the trailhead, drive north on MA 127 (a.k.a. Western Avenue). In half a mile, turn right onto Hesperus Avenue. In 0.7 miles turn right into the castle's parking lot, 80 Hesperus Ave. Open 10 A.M. to 4 P.M., on weekends only from November to May, and daily in June, July, and August. Tickets are $6 for adults, $4 for children.

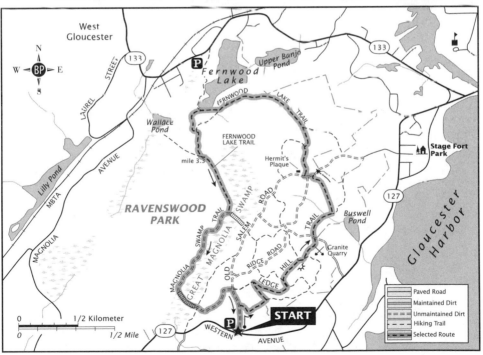

Weir Hill Reservation

Hike Specs

Start: From reservation entrance on Stevens Street

Length: 1.9-mile loop

Approximate Hiking Time: 1.5 hours

Difficulty Rating: Easy, with gentle elevation changes and broad trails

Trail Surface: Two-track dirt trails and lakeside footpaths

Lay of the Land: A 200-foot double drumlin surrounded by a mile of lakeshore trails

Land Status: Trustees of Reservations

Nearest Town: North Andover, MA

Other Trail Users: Cross-country skiers

Canine Compatibility: Dogs permitted

Getting There

From Reading: Take I-93 north to exit 41. Turn right off the exit onto MA 125 north. At 7.1 miles, turn left at a light to continue on MA 125 north, and shortly thereafter pass the Merrimack College campus on your left. At 7.7 miles, turn right at a light to continue on MA 125 north. At 8.0 miles, turn right at a light onto Andover Street. Then at 8.6 miles, fork right, curving around the large town common. Cross onto Great Pond Road, passing the large white church on your left (the North Parish Unitarian Universalist). Proceed one block, then turn left onto Stevens Street. At 9.4 miles, turn right to continue on Stevens Street, dropping downhill between two parts of Stevens Pond. At 9.8 miles, see the entrance to the reservation and park on the shoulder. *DeLorme: Massachusetts Atlas & Gazetteer:* Page 29 D19

Settlers first built their homes in nearby North Andover in 1646—originally naming the town after Cochichewick Brook. Likewise, they named this hill after Native Americans' fish weirs in the same waters.

The weirs were underwater fence-like structures made of a woven latticework, supported on wooden stakes. Placed in streams and flowing lakes, water would flow through them while fish would be trapped, speared, or netted. Used by Native Americans across the continent, the woven structures were removed for the winter in colder climes, leaving the stakes or dikes behind. European settlers quickly realized this was a far more efficient way to fish than their own methods, and began to build large-scale, commercial weirs on local rivers.

Those settlers also grazed sheep and cattle on the shoulders of Weir Hill. Then a funny thing happened. Given several centuries to rebound, the forest grew back slightly differently on its two exposures. The Trustees of Reservations describes the woodland now as pitch pine and oak on the west side of Weir Hill, and white birch, shagbark hickory, aspen, beech, maple, and white pine on the east side.

This land is in the Merrimack River drainage basin, which covers 279 square miles of eastern Massachusetts. Among the 76 lakes and ponds in this region, only Lake Cochichewick—at 592 acres—is larger than 500 acres. The river flows toward Newburyport, where it becomes a tidal estuary for its final nine miles before emptying into the sea.

To relax after a hike, try a magic or puppet show, or catch some local ventriloquists and musicians. Throughout the summer, the town sponsors free events on its common, located on

Massachusetts Avenue. For more information, phone the town's Recreation Department at (978) 688–9579. The town's bathing beach is right here at Stevens Pond, though the beach is open to residents only.

Another option is to stop by the Stevens-Coolidge Place in North Andover, listed on the National Register of Historic Places. The 92-acre, meticulously landscaped estate is owned by the Trustees of Reservations, and is open to the public (see hours in the Hike Information section). The Stevens Estate is another historic attraction. Also in North Andover, the 33-

room mansion was built in 1886 by textile magnate Moses T. Stevens in a prime location on Osgood Hill overlooking the lake. Now owned by the town of North Andover, it is rented out as a conference and meeting center. The building also hosts murder mysteries and comedy theater performances.

Although this is a modest hike, be sure to dress with care, since the shore path can be very muddy in early spring. Fortunately, all motorized vehicles are prohibited from the reservation, so the trails are in good condition. And like the land's first inhabitants, ice fishermen today can be seen dragging their heavy sleds on the ice of Lake Cochichewick, as late in the spring as mid-March. This water body is the sole source of drinking water for North Andover and the largest body of fresh water in Essex County.

MilesDirections

0.0 START from the reservation sign, walk uphill through the clearing and pick up the trail into the woods in the far left corner.

0.1 Turn right at a fork, going steeply uphill on the Stevens Trail.

0.2 Reach a stone bench in the midst of a hillside clearing, with beautiful views of the surrounding hills; this is the shorter shoulder of Weir Hill. Continue straight over the top and down the other side, passing under a power line at mile 0.3.

0.5 At the edge of a clearing, curve gently left into the woods, crossing a seasonal stream and dropping downhill.

0.6 Reach the edge of Stevens Pond at an intersection marked with a trail map, and proceed straight ahead onto the Alewife Trail, keeping the pond on your immediate right.

0.8 Stick to the shore path as the Weir Hill Trail leads uphill to your left. Soon, fork right onto Millers Path, which wanders right by the water's edge.

1.0 Continue to trace the shore of Lake Cochichewick as the Alewife Trail rejoins from the left. Soon cross a wooden boardwalk.

1.2 Cross several stone walls, then over another boardwalk, and pass by another trail leading uphill to your left.

1.3 Turn right as you reach an intersection with a posted trail map, continuing along the shore.

1.4 Follow the trail as it forks left uphill away from the water, onto the Edgewood Farm Trail.

1.5 Cross a dirt road.

1.6 Turn right on a wide trail, then immediately left again onto your hiking path, as you reach the boundary of the reservation. Soon cross another boardwalk.

1.8 Pass by your original turning point where you climbed Weir Hill, and retrace your steps to your car.

1.9 Reach your car.

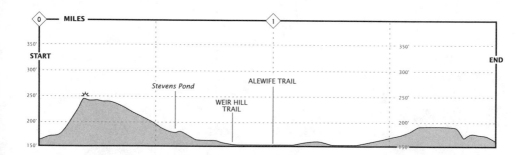

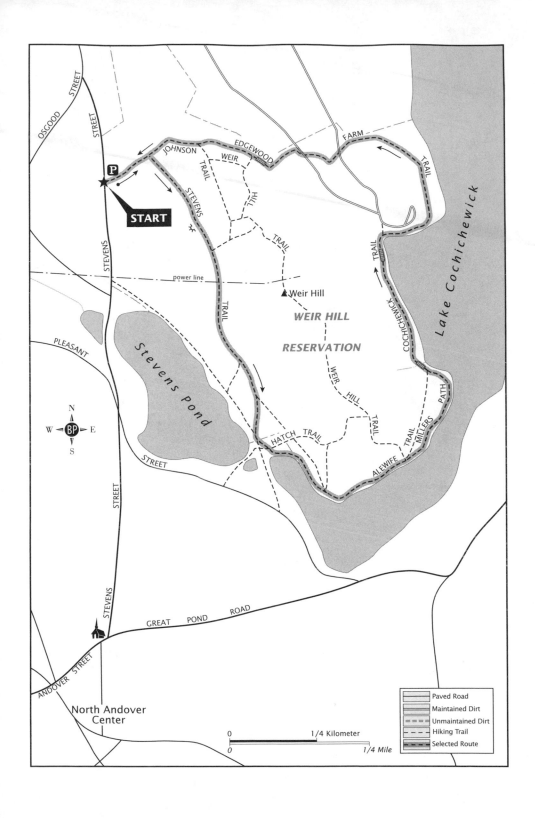

OSGOOD STREET

STREET

P
★
START

JOHNSON

EDGEWOOD

FARM

WEIR

TRAIL

HILL

STEVENS

TRAIL

power line

TRAIL

▲ Weir Hill

WEIR HILL

RESERVATION

COCHICHEWICK

TRAIL

Lake Cochichewick

PLEASANT

Stevens Pond

N
W ◄●BP●► E
S

WEIR

HILL

PATH

TRAIL

MILLERS

HATCH   TRAIL

ALEWIFE   TRAIL

STREET

STEVENS

STREET

GREAT   POND   ROAD

STEVENS

ANDOVER   STREET

North Andover Center

	Paved Road
	Maintained Dirt
	Unmaintained Dirt
	Hiking Trail
	Selected Route

0
1/4 Kilometer
0
1/4 Mile

Hike Information

Trail Contacts:
The Trustees of Reservations (978) 682–3580 or (978) 356–4351 or *www.thetrustees.org*

Schedule:
Open year round, open sunrise to sunset

Fees/Permits:
No fees or permits required

Local Information:
North Andover web site: *www.townofnorthandover.com* • **Lawrence Eagle Tribune:** *www.eagletribune.com – local paper* • **Stevens Memorial Library,** *North Andover, MA: (978) 688–9505* • **The Appalachian Mountain Club's Andover Chapter:** *www.thecompass.org/amcandover/index.html* • **The Andover Village Improvement Society:** *http://avisandover.org — local conservation group*

Local Events/Attractions:
Stevens-Coolidge Place, North Andover, MA (978) 682–3580 — *Gardens open year round, sunrise to sunset; house open Sundays 1–5 P.M., and during the summer Thursdays 2 to 4 P.M.* • **Stevens Estate,** North Andover, MA (978) 682–7072 or *www.stevensestate.com*

Restaurants:
There are several restaurants in the town center, near the North Parish Church • **General Store,** North Andover, MA (978) 688–4116 — *sandwiches and drinks* • **Top of the Scales,** North Andover, MA (978) 681–8848

Organizations:
Essex National Heritage Site: *www.essexheritage.org — part of a 500 square mile area of eastern Massachusetts intended to preserve the historic, cultural, and natural resources of the region*

Maps:
USGS maps: Lawrence, MA

15

Maudslay State Park

Hike Specs

Start: From the ranger station

Length: 3.6-mile loop

Approximate Hiking Time: 1.5 to 2 hours

Difficulty Rating: Easy

Trail Surface: Dirt paths

Lay of the Land: Rhododendron groves and pine forests overlooking the Merrimack River

Land Status: State of MA

Nearest Town: Newburyport

Other Trail Users: Mountain bikers, equestrians, runners, and cross-country skiers

Canine Compatibility: Leashed dogs permitted

Getting There

From Boston: Take I-95 north to exit 57 (for West Newbury/Newburyport). Follow MA 113 east for 0.3 miles, then turn left through a cemetery onto Noble Street. At a stop sign, turn left onto Ferry Road and follow it as it bears left at a fork, following signs for the park. The street's name changes to Pine Hill Road, and then to Curzon Mill Road—just keep following it, and in a mile you'll see the park entrance on the left (3.3 miles total from I-95). *DeLorme: Massachusetts Atlas & Gazetteer:* Page 19 K20

A cquired by the state in 1985, and famed for its groves of mountain laurels, this land has a long history. Framed by the Artichoke and Merrimack Rivers, it was a riverfront site for early Native American settlements, then in 1668 it was a crossing point for the Amesbury-Newbury ferry. It was purchased in 1805 by the wealthy Moseley family when they settled in Newburyport. By 1900, they had bought up surrounding land and named the estate Maudsleigh, after their original home in England. Its mansions included the 22-room gothic wooden "Moulton's Castle" (razed in 1900), Frederick Moseley's 40-room summer home (razed after his death in 1955), and his daughter Helen's large colonial (burned down in 1978).

The family also had a gift for building gardens, and thankfully for us, these have survived. From the formal gardens and stone bridges to the 16 miles of carriage roads, spring and summer are the time to see blooms on the flowering shrubs, ornamental trees, azaleas, rhododendrons, and, of course, the laurels. And in the southeast corner, the Theater in the Open features summertime performances for the public.

Pick up a free trail map in the plywood kiosk in the parking lot, then begin your hike by walking west along Curzon Mill Road, past the rangers office. When you turn right, passing through an entranceway in the stone wall, the dirt road leads you through a chute of tall, shady oaks and 20 foot tall rhododendrons to a flat, open field with a breathtaking view of the Merrimack River. It's easy to see why this was the site for Frederick Moseley's main house. Pass the green-doored garage, walking through a gate in the wall, and past a row of seven small headstones (in honor of the family's dogs) on your way to the Merrimack River Trail, marked irregularly with small square blazes of the trail's wagon-wheel logo. This trail was conceived as a long-distance path to stretch from Newburyport's Plum Island to Canada, but it currently covers just a fraction of that distance.

This narrow trail scrambles along the steep cliff, with the river on your left supplying views of Newburyport's houses, boats, and marinas. If you're hiking in the winter, you'll soon reach a fence around the eagles' roosting area, and will detour around this area, returning back to the river edge on the other side. A quick trail takes you up to Castle Hill, the park's highest point.

Then our hike continues along the river edge, to the park's northeastern corner, before doubling back around Castle Hill. The trip home is a good place to stretch your legs, as you stroll a smooth, broad trail along the park's edges and back to the parking lot.

If you have time after your hike, check out Newburyport, with museums such as the historic Cushing House Museum & Garden, the Custom House Maritime Museum, Massachusetts Audubon's Joppa Flats Education Center and Wildlife Sanctuary, and many more. Or leave the land behind and take a whale-watching cruise out to Stellwagen Bank, a shallow offshore sand bank where the plentiful fish attract humpback, fin, and minke whales.

MilesDirections

0.0 START your hike by walking west along Curzon Mill Road, past the rangers office, the state park sign, and a small break in the stone wall.

0.2 Turn right, through a once-grand entranceway in the stone wall, onto a wide dirt road lined with soaring oaks and elms.

0.4 Reach a river overlook, at the site where the main mansion once stood (point #1 on trail map available at park headquarters). In the trees behind you there's a shingled, green-doored carriage house, near seven small headstones for the Moseley's dogs. Walk to the river edge of the clearing, then bear right along the cliff, and soon enter a grove of tall white pines.

0.5 As you emerge from the pine grove, bear left onto a small, dirt trail, which runs even closer to the river – the Merrimack River Trail. [**FYI.** *This long-distance hiking trail runs through Andover, Tewksbury and Lowell, and one day may follow the river all the way to Canada.*] Keeping the river on your left, follow this rocky trail as it clings to the cliff's edge.

0.6 Cross a small wooden bridge over a stream, and emerge into a windy clearing, near Point #7 (Rhododendron Dell) on your trail map. Continue on the path, hugging the shore and following the green and blue wagon wheel blazes for the Merrimack River Trail.

0.7 Cross a small cement bridge, and rejoin the sandy, double-track main path (called Mile Circle on your trail map), soon passing a memorial granite bench, located just ten feet from where the cliff drops sharply to the water's edge.

0.9 A fence will soon block your trail, protecting the bald eagle winter roosting grounds. Follow the fence-line, turning right, then immediately left, and see a pond through the trees on your right. Cross the dam, reaching Point #17 on your trail map, and turn right.

1.1 Turn left onto the Main Road, following this wide path through a pine forest, past several junctions with smaller paths.

1.4 Bear left onto Castle Hill Trail when you step out of the trees, catching sight of the rolling meadows of map point #15 (Open Fields) to your right. Immediately reach another intersection, and take the middle path, walking uphill just to the right of a small bog. This bark chip path – called the Line Road – traverses a small ridge-line. When the land opens up in a clearing on your left, follow the road as it curves left, skirting the edge of the field.

1.5 Go through an intersection, then immediately turn right at a T-intersection at the cliff edge, coming onto the Merrimack River Trail. You'll pass a few more irregular blazes for the Merrimack River Trail.

1.6 Reach a marker for map point #21 (Bootlegger's Field), and bear left, walking through tall pines and staying close to the river on a windy trek along the rocky river edge.

1.8 Follow the trail in a hairpin right turn when you reach orange posted signs where state property ends and a tree plantation begins.

2.1 Reach the marker for map point #21 again, retracing your steps along the river cliffs. Soon turn left, and walk across the open field, circling Castle Hill to your right. Retrace your original steps along this path, Line Road.

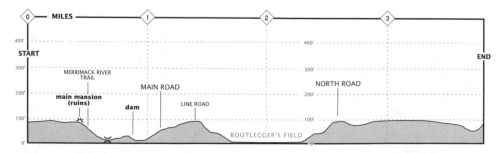

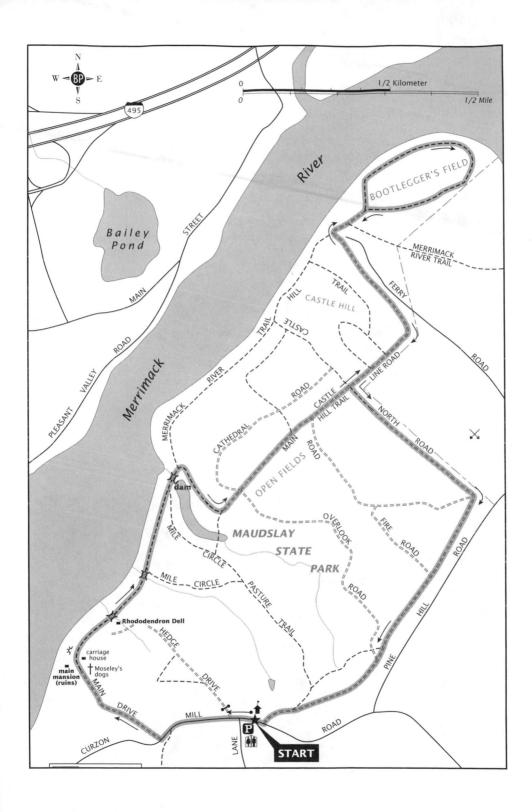

N
W · E
S
BP

495

Bailey
Pond

STREET

MAIN

ROAD

PLEASANT VALLEY

Merrimack

River

BOOTLEGGER'S FIELD

MERRIMACK
RIVER TRAIL

CASTLE HILL

TRAIL

HILL

CASTLE

TRAIL

FERRY

ROAD

MERRIMACK

RIVER

ROAD

CATHEDRAL

MAIN

CASTLE

LINE ROAD

HILL TRAIL

NORTH

ROAD

ROAD

OPEN FIELDS

ROAD

dam

MILE

CIRCLE

MAUDSLAY

STATE

PARK

OVERLOOK

FIRE

ROAD

ROAD

MILE

CIRCLE

ROAD

PASTURE

TRAIL

ROAD

Rhododendron Dell

HEDGE

PINE

HILL

carriage
house

† Moseley's
dogs

DRIVE

main
mansion
(ruins)

MAIN

DRIVE

MILL

ROAD

CURZON

LANE

P

START

1/2 Kilometer
0
0
1/2 Mile

2.6 Reach the small bog again and turn sharply left, onto North Road, a broad, flat, tree-lined trail.

3.0 Reach a thick clump of rhododendrons, and bear right through the intersection, walking parallel to paved Pine Hill Road on your left, the road you drove in on. Carry on straight along this path as you pass intersections with other trails, then emerge into an open field, and soon catch sight of the parking lot.

3.8 Reach your car.

Maudslay's botanical offerings are one of the sole remaining vestiges of the once-mighty mansions on the grounds. Visit the park in these times to catch the peak blooming seasons:

April   purple trillium, large flowered trillium, crocus, daffodil

May   1st week – dogwoods begin, hawthorns, crab apple
2nd week – roses begin, trout lily, wild geranium, jack-in-the-pulpit, royal azalea, lilac
3rd week – hybrid rhododendrons begin, kaempferi azalea, lady slipper, apple trees, carolina rhododendron
4th week – lily of the valley, bunchberry

June   1st week – ghent/exbury azaleas
2nd week – roses peak, mountain laurel begins, phlox, coreopsis, foxglove
3rd week – mountain laurel peak, rock columbine, ox-eye daisy
4th week – maximum rhododendron begin

July   1st week – harebells, wood lily
2nd week – indian pipe, black-eyed susan, pipissewa, blueberries
3rd week – spotted wintergreen

August   goldenrod, pasture thistle, asters

Source: Massachusetts Dept. of Environmental Management

Hike Information

☏ Trail Contacts:
Maudslay State Park Ranger Station: (978) 465-7223 or *www.magnet.state.ma.us/dem /parks/maud.htm*

⏱ Schedule:
Open year round, 8 A.M. – sunset daily

$ Fees/Permits:
No fees or permits required

❓ Local Information:
The New England Mountain Biking Association: *http://nemba.org/ma/p_ Maudslay_State_Park.html – sometimes has useful information on the region—such as weather reports and trail conditions* • **Newburyport website:** *http://newburyport. net*

💡 Local Events/Attractions:
Theater in the Open (978) 465-2572 (for schedule and information) – *a local acting troupe located at the state park. Past productions include plays by Moliere and Thornton Wilder, haunted skits at Halloween, and Vermont's famous Circus Smirkus* • **Newburyport Whale Watch Newburyport,** MA (978) 499-0832 or *www.Newburyport WhaleWatch.com* • **Cushing House Museum & Garden,** Newburyport, MA (978) 462-2681

or *http://newburyport.net/WebLink/Cushing HouseMuseum* • **Newburyport Maritime Society's Custom House Maritime Museum,** Newburyport, MA (978) 462–8681 or *http://newburyport.net/WebLink/Custom HouseMaritimeMuseum* • **Joppa Flats Education Center and Wildlife Sanctuary,** Massachusetts Audubon Society, Newburyport, MA (978) 462–9998 or *http:// newburyport.net/WebLink/JoppaFlats EducationCenter*

🏃 Organizations:
Maudslay State Park Association, Newburyport, MA – *a non-profit, tax-exempt organization dedicated to the protection of the park*

ⓛ Other Resources:
Greater Newbury Friends of our Trails (FOOT): *www.thecompass.org/foot* • Information on the New Hampshire coast: *www.seacoastnh.com*

🛒 Local Outdoor Retailers:
Moor & Mountain, Andover, MA (978) 475–3665 • **Eastern Mountain Sports (EMS),** Peabody, MA (978) 977–0601 or *www.emsonline.com*

Ⓝ Maps:
USGS maps: Newburyport, MA

Central
MASSACHUSETTS

I magine if the Rockies were located in Worcester.

West of the I-495 belt is the "erosion region," the base of what once were granite mountains 20,000 feet high. Geologists say they were an extension of New Hampshire's White Mountains. But millennia of erosion have carved these peaks down to a series of plateaus 1,000 feet high, laced with river-carved valleys.

Today, all that remains of those original giants are Mounts Wachusett and Watatic. This context makes it fun to visit Mt. Wachusett, Mt. Grace State Forest, or the Midstate Trail, to see these rocky, ancient uplands. Mt. Grace is steep enough to have a deserted alpine ski resort on one shoulder. This isolated peak stuck out so clearly from the landscape that the Wampanoag tribe of Native Americans used it as an important landmark. Likewise, the Midstate Trail completes its trip from Rhode Island to New Hampshire by crossing over a succession of peaks, including Mt. Wachusett, Brown Hill, Mt. Hunger, and finally Mt. Watatic.

Change here has come more quickly since the arrival of European settlers. The state has over 1,100 lakes and ponds, but the largest two of these are both manmade, and both reside in this region—the Quabbin Reservoir (24,704 acres) and Wachusett Reservoir (4,160 acres) were both created to serve the drinking needs of greater Boston. The land, too, is changing—once nearly clear-cut, today abandoned farms are quickly giving way to suburbs and young forests.

While hawks migrate over the Berkshires each fall, migratory songbirds prefer the farmland and wooded hills of the central plains and river valley. And the Quabbin Reservoir has hosted several pairs of breeding bald eagles each year since the late 1980s. Visit the Brooks Woodland Preserve and Moose Hill Wildlife Sanctuary to catch more glimpses of this rich tableau.

We can still see erosion in progress—even today, the Connecticut River uncovers dinosaur fossils and 300-million year old lava flows as it cuts through the state. The mighty river runs quickly through its narrow valley in the north, but spreads out, twisting and lazy, in the south, dropping tons of fertile topsoil there every year. Robinson State Park is a great example, as a hike here shows the Westfield River, a tributary of the Connecticut River, as it carves through steep, dry bluffs.

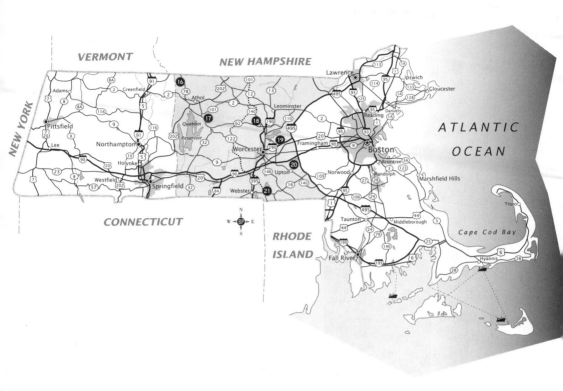

The Hikes

Section Overview

Mount Grace State Forest

With a tall, eight-platform fire tower at its peak, and the long-distance Metacomet-Monadnock (M-M) Trail running up its flank, Mt. Grace deserves more attention than it gets. But located on the New Hampshire border, far from large towns, the forest is quiet and the trails are usually empty. The recent logging activity on its south face is a reminder that not everyone has forgotten about these thick woods. (*See page 86*)

Brooks Woodland Preserve

This loop begins and ends along the water in the Swift River valley. Following well-marked numbered intersections throughout the hike, you climb into the Harvard Forest, then drop back down to the riverside. The trail passes stone cellars that remain from early settlers' homes, and then recently chewed tree stumps that show modern beavers are hard at work building their own homes. (*See page 90*)

Wachusett Mountain State Reservation

A ridgeline ascent to the highest point in Massachusetts east of the Berkshires, this hike is located on a state reservation with over 17 miles of trails. The loop passes through a succession of mature hardwood forests and mystical hemlock groves, as well as stone rivers of glacial till. Although its proximity to Boston, paved summit road, and chairlift to the peak can make it quite crowded, it is also famed in the fall as one of the east coast's premier foliage and hawk-watching spots. (*See page 96*)

Mount Pisgah, Northborough Conservation Lands

Mount Pisgah is 715 feet above sea level, but is scarcely elevated at all from the trailhead. This flat hike winds through mature trees and a grid of stone walls, then skirts a steep ridgeline, offering two sweeping views as a reward for very little sweat. A great hike for families and kids. *(See page 100)*

Upton State Forest

Well-marked dirt trails lead you past Lady's Slipper flowers and lichen-crusted boulders to Dean Pond, a great place to stop for lunch. Return to your car on the Mammoth Rock Trail, scrambling between more boulders as you pass through the flat, thickly-wooded forest. Hunting is permitted here in season, so take care if you're hiking here in the fall. *(See page 104)*

Douglas State Forest

This 4,640-acre forest sits at the corner of Massachusetts, Connecticut, and Rhode Island. Far from being just a flat, sandy flood plain, the land includes the cedar swamp and basin marsh ecosystems, as well as the rare Atlantic White Cedar habitat. This loop tours the shore of Whitin Reservoir in the forest's northern end. *(See page 108)*

16

Mount Grace State Forest

Hike Specs

Start: From Ohlson Memorial Field, at park headquarters off MA 78

Length: 4-mile loop

Approximate Hiking Time: 2 hours

Difficulty Rating: Moderate, due to some steep climbs

Trail Surface: Broad dirt paths, with some narrow trails

Lay of the Land: Steep, thickly wooded forest

Land Status: MA Department of Environmental Management

Nearest Town: Warwick, MA

Other Trail Users: Mountain bikers, cross-country skiers, snowmobilers

Canine Compatibility: Dogs permitted

Getting There

From Greenfield: Take MA 2 east to MA 2A (this intersection is in Erving, between exits 13 and 14). Drive east on MA 2A 2.0 miles, turning left onto MA 78 (a.k.a. Winchester Road). Go north on MA 78, and at 9.0 miles, park in the large paved lot at Ohlson Memorial Field, adjacent to the park headquarters. *DeLorme: Massachusetts Atlas & Gazetteer:* Page 24 D5

T
his loop begins with a gentle descent, heading northward along the valley slope above Mountain Brook and MA 78. After passing the rusting remnants of a ski lift shack (more on this later), you meet the Metacomet-Monadnock (M-M) Trail and begin a steep climb, leaving the tall white pines of the valley floor and entering a mixed region of hemlock, birch, and beech. The M-M runs 117 miles from the Metacomet Trail (named for a Wampanoag tribal chief) on the Connecticut state line to Mt. Monadnock in New Hampshire.

At the summit, the unlocked fire tower atop Mt. Grace affords clear views of Mt. Monadnock to the north, the Berkshires to the west, and the heavily wooded 1,689-acre state forest below. But the stiff breeze cools a sweaty t-shirt so fast that you won't stay up there long. Several mountain biking groups are in the midst of cutting and blazing a Round-the-Mountain Trail that circles the peak, and you pick up these blue blazes on your descent. Pass through a soaring stand of white pines as you return to the picnic tables and restrooms at Ohlson Field.

At 1,625 feet, the peak is the state's second highest, east of the Connecticut River (Mt. Wachusett is 2,006 feet). It was doubtless this altitude that attracted early skiers to hike up its northeastern slope for a schuss down the mile-long Pro Trail or 0.8-mile Novice Trail. In later years a rope tow pulled skiers to the top. However, no one has done any organized skiing here since the 1970s. With the slopes grown in, the lift poles toppled, and the lift engine buried under its collapsed hut, it's a safe bet that no one will try it again anytime soon.

Mt. Grace gained its name in grisly fashion when a kidnapped woman buried her infant child here during the Colonial Era. Mary Rowlandson of Lancaster was kidnapped in 1676 by Wampanoag Indians during King Philip's War. During the group's march toward Canada, the infant baby Grace died, and Mary buried her on the spot.

The nearby town of Warwick was settled in the 1740s and founded in 1763 by tough settlers who ground out a living in these hills just six miles east of the Connecticut River, under

continuing attacks from the French and Indians. The first established industry here included mid-19th-century sawmills, blacksmith shops, tanneries, and factories that made pails, staves, and axes.

In fact, the tough fiber of these early colonists may persevere today—modern Warwick residents are famed for their longevity. Though the town claimed just 740 residents in the last

MilesDirections

0.0 START in the northern end of the parking lot, furthest from the headquarters buildings. Skirt the right edge of this large, open field, entering the woods in 100 yards. Follow blue blazes as you traverse Round-the-Mountain Trail through a thick birch grove.

0.2 Cross a wooden foot bridge over a stream.

0.5 Pass by a picnic table and heavy wooden car bridge (this bridge leads to a dirt road which intersects MA 78). Follow the blue blazes as the trail twists uphill and crosses a small stream, then continues its northward traverse parallel to Mountain Brook and MA 78, both visible to your right.

0.8 Pass by an unmarked trail that enters from the left.

1.0 Pass by an abandoned ski lift, complete with a rusted engine and series of pulleys stretching uphill through the undergrowth.

1.2 Turn left as you reach an intersection with the broad, dirt M-M Trail, following its white blazes steeply uphill.

1.4 Fork right at a stream crossing, staying on the broad two-track path and soon reaching a wooden lean-to. Pass by it and continue uphill.

1.7 At a stream crossing, fork left to follow the white-blazed M-M Trail, as the blue-blazed Round-the-Mountain Trail branches off toward Flower Hill Road.

2.2 The trail splits around a streambed, but keep following the white blazes uphill (the two paths soon

rejoin anyway), and soon pass by an unmarked trail, which enters from the left.

2.5 Your trail merges with the dirt Fire Tower Road, which enters from the left. You will immediately reach the eight-platform fire tower at the peak. Continue along the M-M Trail as it passes between the tower and a large boulder, and drops downhill along a pole line, soon passing a crop of satellite dishes.

3.1 Keep following the white blazes for your descent as a logging road enters from the right.

3.2 Reach a large clearing full of timber and stumps. Take a sharp left across a two-track rocky road, and pick up the blue-blazed Round-the-Mountain Trail.

3.4 Bear left, on the larger trail, as the Round-the-Mountain Trail splits.

3.6 Keep descending as a trail marked "Summit" (the Fire Tower Road) enters from the left.

3.7 Go left at an intersection, following the blue blazes, as you can hear traffic on nearby Wendell Road. [**FYI.** The trees have changed back to white pines again here, and the nearly branchless trunks seem perfectly straight.]

3.9 Emerge into Ohlson Field, with its lean-to, picnic tables, and portable toilets.

4.0 Reach your car.

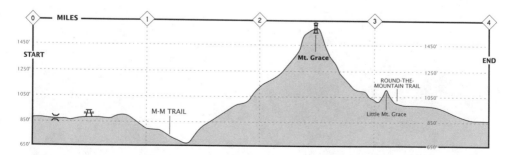

census, rumor dictates that their town's healthy climate will keep them all around for a long time to come.

When you're done with the hike, another local attraction is the "Indian Cave," a natural rock formation located north of Stevens Swamp and south of the Old South Road to Northfield. It is said to include a 30-foot tunnel that opens into a 12-square-foot opening.

Hike Information

☎ Trail Contacts:
Mount Grace State Forest, Warwick, MA (978) 544-3939 or *www.state.ma.us/dem/ parks/mgrc.htm*

🕐 Schedule:
Open year round

💲 Fees/Permits:
No fees or permits required

❓ Local Information:
Warwick, MA website: *www.co.franklin.ma. us/warwick.htm* • **New England Lost Ski Areas Project,** Mount Grace, Warwick, MA:

www.nelsap.org/ma/grace.html - *for more information on the early ski area here* • **Warwick Historical Society,** Warwick Center (978) 544-3461 or (978) 544-3628 for hours - *has photos, furniture, historical diaries, and factory relics*

🛈 Other Resources:
Metacomet-Monadnock Trail: *www-unix.oit. umass.edu/~berkamc/mmtrdisc.html* and *www.amcberkshire.org*

🅝 Maps:
USGS maps: Northfield, MA

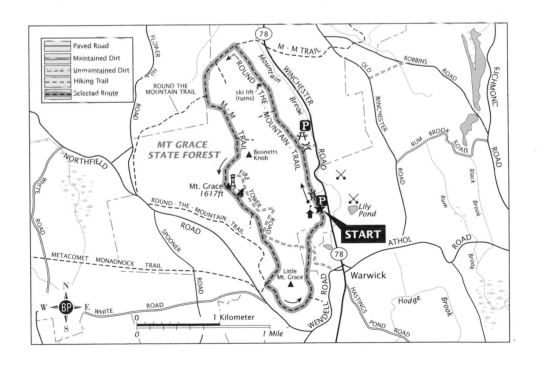

Brooks Woodland Preserve

Hike Specs

Start: From parking lot on Quaker Drive

Length: 4.5-mile loop

Approximate Hiking Time: 2.5 hours

Difficulty Rating: Moderate, with broad, flat trails that roll up and down the valley hills around the Swift River

Trail Surface: Broad, dirt, usually two-track

Lay of the Land: Tall white pine and hemlock forest on both sides of the valley surrounding the Swift River, punctuated with hardwood stands and thick rhododendron undergrowth

Land Status: Trustees of Reservations

Nearest Town: Petersham, MA

Other Trail Users: Cross-country skiers

Canine Compatibility: Dogs permitted

Getting There

From Leominster: Drive west on MA 2 to exit 21, for Templeton and MA 101. Follow MA 101 south for 8.7 miles, then turn left onto MA 32 south. At 10.2 miles, turn left onto MA 32/122 south. At 11.6 miles, turn left onto Quaker Drive, and at 11.8 miles park at a small dirt lot on the left shoulder, just before a bridge. *DeLorme: Massachusetts Atlas & Gazetteer:* Page 37 B16

The Brooks Woodland Preserve is like a history book, and you can practically hike through the pages of its chapters. It began as home to the Nipmuck Indians, who ground corn and acorns into bread flour using the stone hollows they scraped into large boulders here. You can find many of these today in the northeast part of the property (the Swift River Tract). Petersham was founded in 1754, and the settlement of Europeans ultimately forced the Nipmucks out. European settlers converted the woods to open farmland, built miles of stone walls, and left behind only the stone cellars beneath their homes. Keep your eyes open for a half-dozen of these foundations as you hike. Another colonial remnant is a ten-acre marsh, which was once an open pond feeding water to a downstream mill.

Today, the Trustees of Reservations are trying to return the forest to its primeval state. The trees, jumping at the opportunity, are dominating the land with soaring white pines and hemlocks, scattered with birches, red oak and shagbark hickory, and rhododendron growing underneath. In the spring, drowsy garter snakes will wriggle across your trail, while beaver families busily dam the Swift River and Moccasin Brook, creating deep pools and leaving gnawed, pointy stumps along the waters' edge. The reservation also serves as a wildlife sanctuary, supporting a balance of deer, fox, moose, coyote, porcupines, hawks, owls, bald eagles, wild turkeys, and herons.

The trails are not named or blazed, but they feature numbered intersections that serve as helpful landmarks for this hike. The preserve is bordered by the Harvard Forest (a 2,000-acre woodlands research center managed by Harvard University, and founded in 1907), a Massachusetts Audubon Society reservation (the 1,500-acre Rutland Brook Sanctuary), and state-owned lands. It is composed of three sections—the North Common Meadow, Brooks Woodland Preserve, and Swift River Preservation—but this loop stays primarily in the Brooks

The Harvard Forest, located adjacent to Brooks Woodland Preserve, has a wealth of knowledge about the natural history of this region. Its 3,000 acres are highlighted and explained at the Fisher Museum, originally designed to display twenty-three 3-D dioramas on the subject of the management and ecology of New England forests, beginning with the era before the first European settlement in Petersham.

The museum and its outdoor self-guided hiking trails are free (although they appreciate donations). They are open year round from 9 A.M. to 5 P.M. Monday–Friday, and additionally from noon to 4 P.M. on Saturday and Sunday from May to October. Contact the Harvard Forest, at 324 N. Main Street, Petersham, MA (978) 724–3302 or http://lternet.edu/hf/.

GETTING THERE:

From the east or west, take Route 2, turn off at Exit 17 (intersection with Route 32), turn right on 32 south toward Petersham and travel 3 miles south on Route 32. Harvard Forest is on the Left.

From the Worcester area go north on Route 122 to Petersham and take Route 32 north through the town center and Harvard Forest is 3½ miles north on the right.

section, given to the Trustees by the estate of James Willson Brooks, a turn-of-the-century lawyer, diplomat, and co-founder of the United Shoe Machinery Company.

A great way to get to know this land is to pitch in on an annual trail-working day. Each spring, volunteers clear fallen trees and overgrowth from the trails. Check the Trustees' web site for dates. With 1,200 people, modern-day Petersham boasts an anemic population density of just 21 people per square mile (compare this to Worcester's 4,520 per square mile, and Cambridge's 14,899 per square mile). It is listed in the National Register of Historic Places, featuring the town common and about 45 buildings that were built in the early 19th century. In summertime, there are frequent band concerts staged at the renovated bandstand.

MilesDirections

0.0 START at the green metal gate in the small, dirt parking area. Follow this broad, two-track dirt road as it parallels the East Branch of the Swift River, on your right. Pass by several forking trails to your left, but continue to walk upstream beside the river.

0.8 Follow the trail in a hairpin left turn, as you leave the river and start a series of switchbacks working your way uphill.

1.1 As the trail levels off on the hilltop, go right at a fork, soon passing through a stone wall. *[FYI. This left turn goes to MA32.]*

1.4 Cross another trail at intersection No. 30, walking through a wooden gate and another stone wall.

1.6 Go right at a fork at intersection No. 21.

1.8 Come through a stone wall, and at intersection No. 22 go left at a T-intersection, heading downhill.

1.9 Bear right at intersection No. 23, continuing your traverse along the steep hillside.

2.2 Go left, heading downhill at intersection No. 32.

2.3 Go right at a T-intersection (at intersection No. 33), then soon ignore a right fork (at intersection No. 34), continuing your downhill path.

2.4 Reach intersection No. 35, with its basement stone works—the John Cornell Cellar Hole—and go left, heading downhill.

2.5 Cross the East Branch of the Swift River on a wooden bridge, and immediately go right at intersection No. 45.

3.1 Walking downstream, parallel to the river, pass by intersection No. 46 which branches steeply uphill to your left.

3.9 Go right at intersection No. 49, crossing a wooden bridge over Moccasin Brook.

4.0 Come over a rise and bear right at intersection No. 52, crossing an open field and walking through a stone wall at its edge.

4.2 Turn right at intersection No. 53, onto the pavement of Quaker Drive.

4.5 Cross a bridge and reach your car.

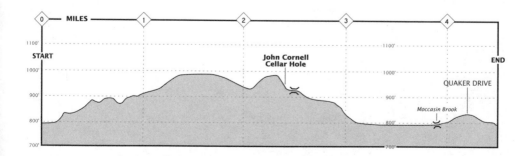

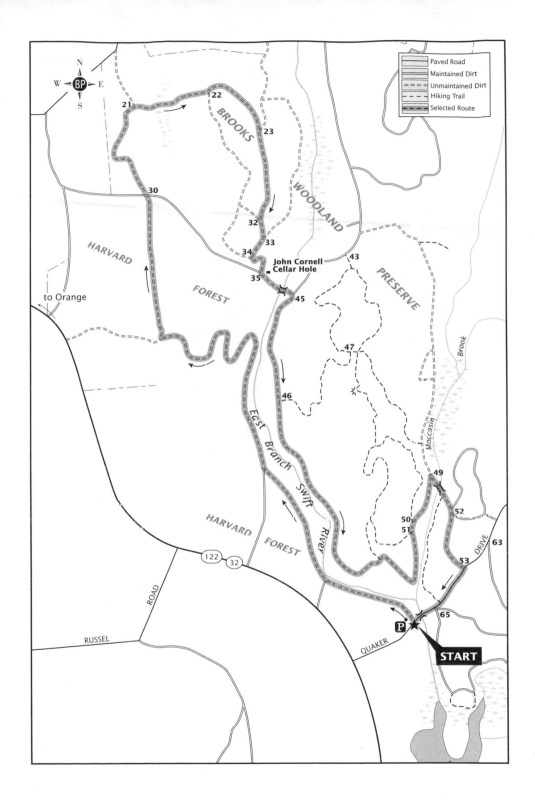

N
W ⊕BP E
S

Paved Road
Maintained Dirt
Unmaintained Dirt
Hiking Trail
Selected Route

21   22
23
BROOKS
WOODLAND
30
32
33
34
35
John Cornell
Cellar Hole
43
45
PRESERVE
HARVARD
FOREST
to Orange
47
46
East Branch Swift River
49
50
51
52
63
53
HARVARD FOREST
122 32
DRIVE
65
RUSSEL
ROAD
P
QUAKER
START

Moccasin Brook

Despite their proud history in early manufacturing, there is one deed of modern history that residents of central Massachusetts have never forgiven—the flooding of the Quabbin Reservoir. The state's eastern cities had outgrown their local water supplies by the 1920s, and began to buy up land around the Swift River, nearly 100 miles inland. One by one, these towns were emptied, buildings bulldozed, graveyards dug up, and millions of acres of trees razed. An enormous dam was built in Belchertown in 1939, and by 1946, the central Massachusetts towns of Dana, Enfield, Greenwich, and Prescott were buried beneath almost 40 square miles of water. The reservoir was named for a Native American chief called Nani-Quaben, or "well-watered place."

Hike Information

📞 Trail Contacts:
The Trustees of Reservations, Central Regional Office, Leominster, MA (978) 840–4446 or *www.thetrustees.org* - *Cheap maps can be ordered through this site or by phoning the Trustees at (978) 921–1944.*

🕐 Schedule:
Open year round, sunrise to sunset

💲 Fees/Permits:
No fees or permits required

❓ Local Information:
Petersham, MA, online: *www.petershamcommon.com* • Greater Gardner Chamber of Commerce, Gardner, MA (978) 632–1780 or *www.gardnerma.com* - *for local weather forecasts, shopping, and restaurant and hotel guides* • Worcester County Convention & Visitors Bureau, Worcester, MA (508) 753–2920 or *www.worcester.org*

💡 Local Events/Attractions:
The Johnny Appleseed Trail Association/Visitor Center, Leominster, MA (978) 534–2302 or *www.appleseed.org* - *Why is it here? The famed Johnny Appleseed of our camp songs was born here in Leominster in 1774, although he was known then as John Chapman.*

👥 Organizations:
Appalachian Mountain Club: Berkshire Office, Lanesboro, MA (413) 443–0011 • Narragansett Historical Society, Templeton, MA (978) 939–2303 • Petersham Memorial Library, Petersham, MA (978) 724–3405

🗘 Other Resources:
New England Orienteering Club, Arlington, MA (781) 648–1155

🚴 Local Outdoor Retailers:
New England Backpackers Inc., Worcester, MA (508) 853–9407

Ⓝ Maps:
USGS maps: Barre, MA

Wachusett Mountain State Reservation

Hike Specs

Start: From the reservation headquarters and visitors center off Mountain Road
Length: 4-mile loop
Approximate Hiking Time: 3 hours
Difficulty Rating: Moderate, due to steepness
Trail Surface: Rocky dirt trails
Lay of the Land: Hardwood forests and hemlock groves
Land Status: MA Department of Environmental Management
Nearest Town: Princeton, MA
Other Trail Users: Alpine skiers on northern face of mountain, but not on trails
Canine Compatibility: Dogs permitted

Getting There

From Worcester: Drive north on I-190. Take exit 5 to MA 140 north. Turn left on MA 62 West, toward Princeton, then left again onto MA 31 south. At Princeton Square, turn right onto Mountain Road, passing the gazebo. In 3.1 miles, turn left at the sign for the visitors center and Summit Road. *DeLorme: Maine Atlas & Gazetteer:* Page 38 A2

Pick up a free trail map at the visitors center, which also has water and restrooms, and a fascinating collection of bird, wildflower, and natural history displays. The Bicentennial Trail begins in the corner of the parking lot, and is clearly marked with blue triangles, the same blazes used for all Wachusett's trails.

Follow Bicentennial for about a mile as it traverses the steep hillside, being careful not to twist your ankles on several hundred meters of glacial till. Continue past the Loop Trail branching uphill to your right (this will be your return path), and enjoy the mature hardwood forest of tall oaks, maples, beech, and hickory. Your traverse ends as you come over a small rise into a gorgeous clearing with views to the southwest. The High Meadow Trail leads steeply uphill for a short, heart-thumping ascent to the ridgeline. This quick elevation gain proves the wisdom of names: Wachusett means "by the great hill" in Algonquin, the same root as the word Massachusett, "people of the great hill."

As you walk the ridge, the trail drops suddenly into a half-mile of thick, shaded hemlock grove. At the abrupt end of this grove, you'll pass over a series of smooth, pillow-shaped bedrock, polished by the glaciers when they retreated 10,000 years ago. At the next intersection, turn left onto the Link Trail, hiking uphill and across the paved summit road to the top.

Even on a cloudy day, the summit can be crowded, but the view from the 2,006-foot peak is thrilling, with the Boston skyline to the east, Lake Quinsigamond and Worcester to the south, Mount Tom and Greylock to the west, and Mount Monadnock to the north. In September and October, this spot is one of the east coast's premier bird-watching points, directly in a migration route for hawks, ospreys, falcons, and eagles.

For a return route, you'll cross the summit and pass the fire observation tower, to begin a corkscrew around the shoulders of Mount Wachusett, re-joining your original path near the end. Pass the ski lift and scramble down a series of switchbacks over rock ledges. You'll soon cross the Summit Road again, and see some familiar sights: more glacier-polished rock, and another thick hemlock grove. Soon you return to the neighborhood of tall, full-canopied oaks.

Hike Information

📞 Trail Contacts:
Wachusett Mountain State Reservation, Princeton, MA (978) 464–2987 or *www. magnet.state.ma.us/dem/parks/wach.htm*

🕐 Schedule:
Open year round - visitors center open 9 A.M. to 6 P.M. and parking lot open 7 A.M. to dusk

💲 Fees/Permits:
No fees or permits required

❓ Local Information:
Wachusett online guide: *www.wachusett. com* • **Greater Gardner Chamber of**

Commerce, Gardner, MA (978) 632–1780 or *http://gardnerma.com - for local weather forecasts, shopping, and restaurant and hotel guides*

💡 Local Events/Attractions:
The Johnny Appleseed Trail Association, Leominster, MA (978) 534–2302 or *www. appleseed.org*

🚴 Local Outdoor Retailers:
Squannacook River Outfitters, Townsend, MA (978) 597–5332

Ⓝ Maps:
USGS maps: Sterling, MA

The corkscrew continues as you hold the mountain on your left throughout the descending traverse, and begin to see signs for the visitors center. Soon you'll pick up the Bicentennial Trail and retrace your steps to the visitors center, and your car.

Wachusett itself is known geologically as a monadnock, the remnant of a lone peak that once rose high above the surrounding plains, independent of any mountain range. How high?

MilesDirections

0.0 START at trailhead for Bicentennial Trail, marked with a sign in the parking lot. Follow this blue-blazed path as it traverses the mountainside, quickly passing junctions leading uphill on your right for the Pine Hill Trail and Loop Trail.

0.8 Cross an old stone wall, and continue past a junction with the Mountain House Trail, leading uphill on your right.

1.0 Come over a small rise and into an open clearing. Turn right onto the High Meadow Trail, climbing steeply uphill.

1.3 At the hilltop, turn right onto the Jack Frost Trail for a flat stroll along the ridgeline and into a thick Hemlock grove.

1.5 Turn left onto the Link Trail, then quickly right onto the Mountain House Trail, following the path uphill and across the paved Summit Road to the top.

1.9 Reach the summit and its gorgeous views. To continue, walk through the summit parking lot, past the fire observation tower, and onto the Old Indian Trail. Immediately pass the ski lift and follow yellow and blue blazes down a series of switchbacks over rock ledges. Your descent will be a corkscrew around the mountain, always keeping the peak on your left.

2.4 Still on the steep mountainside, turn left onto the West Side Trail.

2.6 When you reach a picnic table, turn left again, crossing Summit Road onto Semuhenna Trail. You'll soon walk over a wooden boardwalk, past more glacier-polished rock, and into another thick hemlock grove.

3.0 Turn left onto the Harrington Trail for a short, steep ascent, shortly thereafter turning right onto the Link Trail.

3.2 Walk under a power line, then bear right, following Link Trail past its junction with the Mountain House Trail.

3.3 Turn left onto Loop Trail, following signs for the visitors center.

3.5 Continue downhill on Loop Trail, passing a junction on your right for the Mountain House Trail.

3.7 Bear left onto the Bicentennial Trail, and you're now backtracking your original steps from the very beginning of the hike.

3.8 Continue along Bicentennial past its junction with Pine Hill Trail, following signs for the visitors center.

4.0 Reach your car in the lot.

Alternate hikes: *there are 20 miles of marked and named hiking trails in these 2,050 acres.*

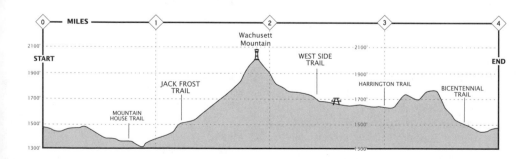

Theory dictates that the peak was once a towering 23,000 feet (Mount Everest in Nepal is 29,035 feet), but was worn down by glaciers and erosion.

If you still have energy left after this hike, there are always events planned by the Reservation and by the Ski Mountain. Check at the visitors center on Mountain Road for natural history events such as a poetry walk featuring the work of Robert Frost, a hike through old-growth forest, lessons on wind power at Wachusett, a tour of the Wachusett watershed, wild animal tracking, and the annual hawk migration watch. This bird migration is a natural wonder, with up to 20,000 birds of prey passing overhead in a single day during the peak of the October-to-November period.

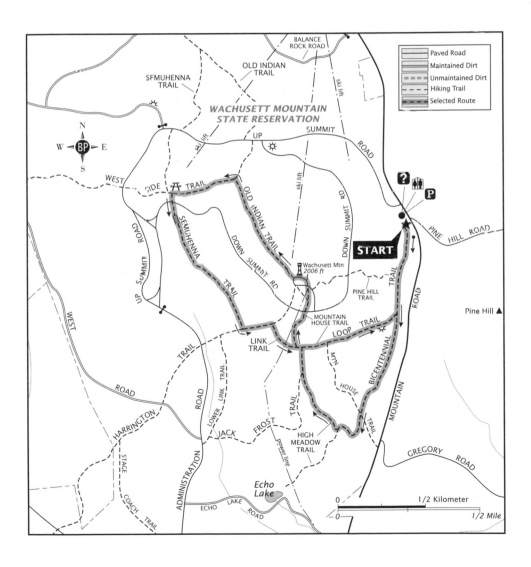

Mount Pisgah, Northborough Conservation Lands

Hike Specs

Start: From the trailhead parking lot is on Smith Road, near its intersection with Green Street, about 4 miles from Northborough town center.

Length: 3-mile loop

Approximate Hiking Time: 1–1.5 hours

Difficulty Rating: Easy—the trail can be rough underfoot, but it is wide and has a flat pitch throughout

Trail Surface: Rocky, forested trail

Lay of the Land: Mature, white pine and red oak forest

Land Status: Conservation lands

Nearest Town: Northborough, MA

Other Trail Users: Mountain bikers, equestrians

Canine Compatibility: Dogs permitted

Getting There

From Worcester: Drive east on I-290 to exit 24, for Church Street, Boylston/Northborough. Take a right off the exit ramp, heading north toward Boylston and Clinton, and immediately take another right onto Ball Street, just before you reach the Davidian Brothers Farm and its big red barn. Drive uphill, and at 1.3 miles, pass the Tougas Family Farm on your right. Keep going, and at the end of the road (1.8 miles) turn left onto Green Street. At 2.3 miles, bear right at a fork just before a stone wall onto Smith Road. At 2.5 miles, come to a small gravel parking area on the right. Park here. *DeLorme: Massachusetts Atlas & Gazetteer:* Page 39 I16

E arly New England farmers pulled the thick trunks and heavy rock out of the earth to clear this land and farm it. They left for the cities in the mid-1800s, so their legacy today is a mature, third-generation forest, with stone walls stretching in straight lines for hundreds of yards. There are breaks in the walls where they meet at neat right angles, and as you step through these breaks, it is easy to imagine a farmer driving his team of horses on the same path two centuries ago. (But watch where you step, as there is often fresh dung on the trail from more recent horses.)

The land is still rich for farming, and if you hike here in the fall, be sure to stop by one of the farms as you drive to the trailhead. The Davidian Brothers Farm is right near the highway exit, and the Tougas Family Farm on Ball Street offers apple picking and pumpkin carving until November.

Mount Pisgah is on a plateau, which means you get a lot of views for a little climbing, simply by walking to the edge and peering over. Begin at the trailhead, and the path quickly enters a forest of tall white pine, pitch pine, and red oak, punctuated by birches, with some sassafras, beech, and hornbeam understory. This congress of mature trees sharing the sunny canopy is a great example of the long-range effects of agriculture, as the old fields gave all kinds of trees a chance to grow. The ruler-straight stone walls represent a lost art, built without mortar, and standing the effects of hundreds of New England winters. When the trail passes close by a stone cellar, you can see that the craft of building in stone was not merely decorative, but formed a strong, enduring foundation for the many labors of these pioneer farmers.

In the leafless autumn, the wind whips through these trees, making trunks creak against each other. Many of the older pines have twisted into gnarled wooden shapes. And when woodpeckers knock the trees as you walk, it is easy to imagine the long tale of a tree's life, sub-

jected to weather and bugs and birds and farmers. Farther on, you pass through a thick grove of young white pine saplings; none taller than a man, and the cycle seems complete.

Soon, the path pulls parallel to a stone wall, and when you reach its junction with another wall, step through the break and onto an exposed rock ledge for a splendid lookout to the southeast. Retrace your steps to the stone wall corner, turn left, and continue along the plateau edge, walking southwest. The trail starts to roll and pitch as you go, and within a mile

The Tougas Family Farm

The back roads of Worcester County are full of family farms and roadside stands, selling fresh food and pick-your-own fruits and squash. The Tougas Family Farm, located along Ball Street on your way to the trailhead, offers this list of the best picking seasons for the region:

strawberries: *mid June to early July*
raspberries: *late June to mid July, and late August to mid October*
blueberries: *early July to early September*
blackberries: *August to late September*
peaches: *August to mid September*
apples: *late August through mid October*
pumpkins: *mid September through October*

See the farm's web site for more information at www.tougasfarm.com, or phone their automated picking line for hours and availability, at (508) 393–6406.

The Massachusetts Roadside Stand and Pick Your Own Association offers the following recipe to complement your fresh-picked food.

Cranberry Pumpkin Muffins

1¼ cups cranberries	1 tsp cinnamon
2 cups flour	½ tsp allspice
1 cup sugar	½ cup butter
½ tsp baking powder	2 eggs
1 tsp baking soda	1⅔ cups cooked pureed
1 tsp salt	pumpkin

Halve cranberries; set aside. Sift together flour, sugar, baking powder, baking soda, salt, cinnamon, and allspice. Add butter, eggs, and pumpkin, and mix together with a pastry blender until just combined. Stir in cranberries. Fill 18 greased muffin cups almost full. Bake in a preheated 350-degree oven for 35 minutes or until a toothpick inserted into the center comes out clean. (Makes 18 medium muffins.)

MilesDirections

0.0 START at trailhead parking lot, and walk east on a wide trail, perpendicular to Smith Road. Blazes are inconsistent, but begin by following a pair of plastic disks, white over red *[FYI. If you look over your shoulder, they're single yellow disks heading the other way.]*

0.2 Bear left at a fork, following a white plastic arrow eastward on a narrow path. You are now following single white disks.

0.5 Pass a stone foundation on the left, and immediately reach an intersection with a wide dirt road, the Pisgah Slope Trail. Continue straight through this, following the white disks eastward.

0.8 Reach the corner of a junction between two stone walls, walk through the break, and bear left. Follow this new wall for 0.1 miles and reach the first lookout. After enjoying the view, retrace your steps to

the junction, and turn left, following white blazes southwest, parallel to the plateau's edge.

1.5 Pass by a trail that branches off to the right.

1.8 Bear left at a fork, and in 0.1 mile reach the second lookout. Retrace your steps, bearing left at the fork, and down a short pitch.

2.1 Turn right at a T-intersection, following a yellow plastic arrow, and follow the single yellow blazes northward.

2.4 Bear left, following the yellow blazes.

2.8 Continue straight as another small path enters on the right. This was the trail you took in the beginning.

3.0 Reach your car, returning along the same trail on which you started.

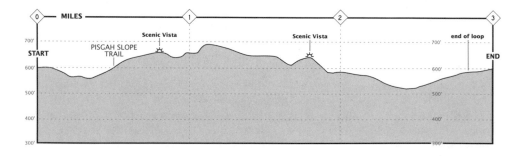

you reach the second lookout. It's another bare bedrock shelf, peering southeast. The trail brings you home after a short downhill drop, as you hike northward through a young oak forest mixed with pine. You cross more stone walls, walk through another thick grove of human-sized white pines, and follow the blazes to your car.

Mount Pisgah is also the site of one of the almost 600 hidden, waterproof boxes scattered around the country for a little-known competition called "letterboxing," which requires hikers to follow clues to find the small boxes, then use a rubber stamp to mark their logbook as a prize. Get more information on this fun treasure hunt at *www.letterboxing.org*.

Hike Information

📞 Trail Contacts:
Northborough Conservation Commission, Northborough, MA (508) 393–5015 - *town parks and recreation commission*

🕐 Schedule:
Open year round, sunrise to sunset

💲 Fees/Permits:
No fees or permits required

❓ Local Information:
Northborough online: *www.northborough.com*

📍 Local Events/Attractions:
Apple and pumpkin picking in autumn

🎒 Local Outdoor Retailers:
New England Backpackers Inc., Worcester, MA (508) 853–9407 or *www.newengland backpacker.com* • **Recreational Equipment Inc. (REI),** Framingham, MA (508) 270–6325 or *www.rei.com*

🗺 Maps:
USGS maps: Marlborough, MA

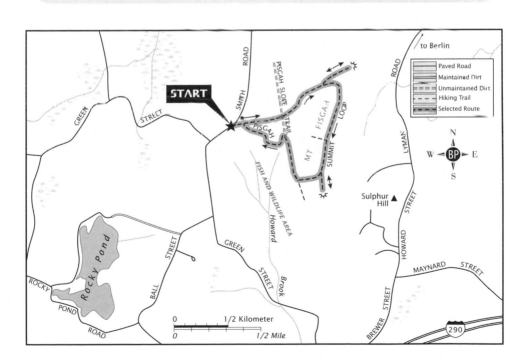

Upton State Forest

Hike Specs

Start: From main parking lot at park headquarters, off Westborough Road

Length: 3.3-mile loop

Approximate Hiking Time: 2 hours

Difficulty Rating: Easy, due to moderate elevation change and well-kept trails

Trail Surface: Broad carriage roads and narrow dirt trails

Lay of the Land: Marshy wetlands filled with tall white pines and scattered with huge boulders

Land Status: MA Department of Environmental Management

Nearest Town: Upton, MA

Other Trail Users: Mountain bikers and equestrians

Canine Compatibility: Dogs permitted

Getting There

From Framingham: Take I-495 south to exit 21B, for West Main Street/Upton. Drive west on West Main Street, which changes names to Hopkinton Road as it crosses the county line from Middlesex into Worcester. In 3.5 miles from the interstate, make a hairpin right turn onto Westborough Road. At 5.5 miles, turn right onto Southboro Street (called Spring Street on maps) at the state park sign. Take the middle fork at a junction, following a dirt road to the parking lot.

DeLorme: Massachusetts Atlas & Gazetteer: Page 51 C19

T his little-known, 2,660-acre forest in the Blackstone River Valley is a favorite for mountain bikers, but most of your loop is along narrow twisting trails that discourage much bicycle traffic. The thick woodland is laced with boulders dropped by the melting glaciers of the last ice age. And the low-lying marshland between the boulders encourages flowers like the pink lady's slipper, a member of the orchid family, which grows a single drooping flower on a tall stalk between May and June. Overhead, the canopy is dominated by tall white pines, with maple and chestnut saplings below.

After you leave the carriage road at the beginning of the hike, the Whistling Cave Trail passes by a stack of boulders that form a small tunnel, or cave. You reach Dean Pond in a little more than a mile, and even on a sunny weekend, you can enjoy it without crowds. There's not much elevation change on this hike, but you climb gently to the Hawk Trail as you leave the pond, and then follow the Mammoth Rock Trail past enormous glacial boulders. At the end of the hike, you follow the paved Spring Street downhill past swampland and to your car.

This land was originally a seasonal hunting ground for the Nipmuc tribe, who joined with other Native Americans in King Philip's War (1675–76) to discourage settlement here through the end of the 17th century. The town of Upton was incorporated in 1735, not as a usual settlement of Massachusetts's wild, western lands, but cobbled together from the borders of four surrounding towns; Hopkinton, Mendon, Sutton, and Uxbridge. Since they had settled so close to other populated areas, Upton's subsistence farmers had an easy means to supplement their agricultural income—bootmaking. After more than a century of this home-based, cottage business, changing times forced them to find a new industry, and they quickly adopted their skills to making straw hats. By 1837, William Knowlton had built a successful hat factory, which remains on the National Register of Historic Places today, although it shut down

around 1970 and the building (134 Main Street) now contains apartments. At the beginning of the 20th century, farmers began to convert their land from agriculture to dairy, poultry, flowers, and woodland.

Hike Information

Trail Contacts:
Upton State Forest Headquarters, Upton, MA: *www.state.ma.us/dem/parks/uptn.htm*

Schedule:
Open year round, sunrise to sunset

Fees/Permits:
No fees or permits required

Local Information:
Upton, MA website: *http://uptonmass.com* - features local yellow pages, restaurant listings, a calendar of local events, and more • Upton, MA/ Worcester County website: *www.state.ma.us/cc/upton.html* - offers further information on Upton and Worcester • Upton, MA watersheds website: *www.mywa-* tershed.com/im/ ma/imupton.htm – lists the various rivers and watersheds in the Upton region • official government website for Upton, MA: *www.upton.ma.us*

Restaurants:
Country Club Sooper, Upton, MA (508) 529-3161 • Upton House of Pizza, Upton, MA (508) 529-6666

Other Resources:
Blackstone River Theater, Cumberland, RI (401) 725-9272 or *www.riverfolk.org* • Waters Farm, Sutton, MA: *www.watersfarm.com*

Maps:
USGS maps: Milford, MA

Upton straddles the Narragansett Bay watershed—where the West and Blackstone Rivers drain into Rhode Island—and the Concord River watershed, where water flows into the Merrimack River and finally into the Gulf of Maine. Upton's local water sources include Warren Brook, Center Brook, and Mill River, all historic sites of mills during the region's agricultural heyday.

Modern Upton shares its loyalties with northern Rhode Island and central Massachusetts, with proximity to I-495, Framingham, and Worcester. A great cultural resource is the Blackstone River Theater, in Cumberland, Rhode Island, with folk music performances showing from June through December, and Irish step dancing classes available for those who need to brush up on their skills. Also, Waters Farm, in nearby Sutton, hosts year-round events such as a horse-drawn Sleigh Rally in February; the hitch, harness, and driving clinic in July; an apple crisp bake-off each September; Waters Farm Days in October; and Christmas in Historic Sutton.

MilesDirections

0.0 START at the map kiosk in the parking lot, and walk through the metal gate along a broad carriage road with marshland on either side. *[**Note.** The mosquitoes can be thick here in summer months.]*

0.1 Turn right onto Park Road at a fork.

0.3 Continue on Park Road, passing by the Middle Road connector path, which joins from the left.

0.6 The road widens into a small clearing, and you turn left onto the narrow, blue-blazed Whistling Cave Trail. Follow it over a rock escarpment, then drop down a steep slope to the flat land below, soon passing the trail's namesake.

1.1 Turn right at the three-way junction of Whistling Cave Trail with Middle and Loop Roads, following a broad two-track path 100 yards to Dean Pond. After enjoying the pond, backtrack to the junction, and take the middle fork, onto Middle Road. This broad path narrows to a dirt trail as you head north.

1.5 Turn right at a fork onto the blue-blazed Hawk Trail.

1.7 Turn left onto the Loop Road, and soon pass by a right turn for the Hawk Trail.

1.9 Turn right, uphill, onto the Grouse Trail. Step over a stone wall here, and turn left onto the Mammoth Rock Trail, which is also blue-blazed.

2.1 *[**Side-trip.** Reach Mammoth Rock, following a 25-yard spur to the right if you wish to climb on top.]* Otherwise, continue northwest along the Mammoth Rock Trail.

2.5 *[**Note.** Your trail passes close to several private homes, so be sure to keep your dog leashed and your voice down.]*

2.7 Reach the paved Spring Street and turn left onto it.

2.9 Continue along the paved road as you pass by the Swamp Trail on the left.

3.2 Reach the front gate of the park, and turn left along the dirt road that leads to the parking lot.

3.3 Reach your car.

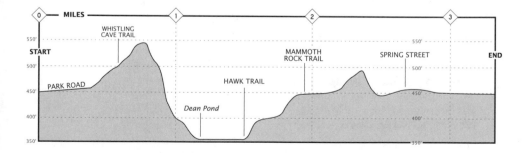

The Upton Country Store and Antique Center is a shop that looks as if it hasn't changed much in 40 or 50 years. From crumbly, old Life magazines to lampshades, tea sets, and furniture, it seems to have a little of everything—including a candy bar and cold soda to revive a tired hiker. Reach it by turning left onto Westborough Road from the state forest, and crossing the intersection with West Main Street/Hopkinton Road at 2.1 miles. After the intersection, the road is called School Street. Then turn right onto MA 140 north (Main Street) at 2.9 miles, reaching the Antique Center on your left at 3.1 miles.

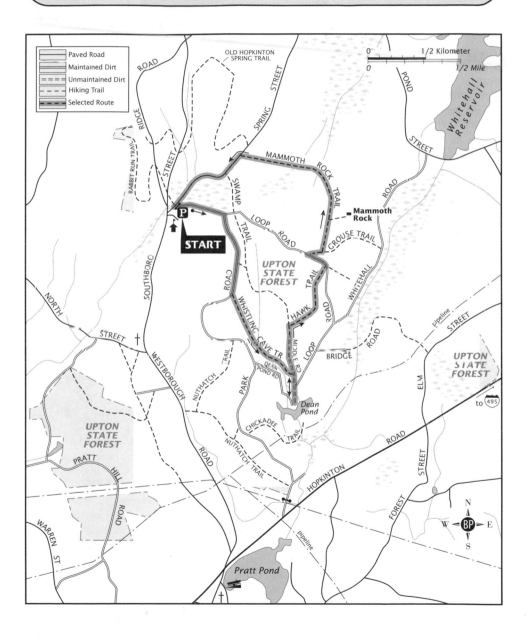

Douglas State Forest

Hike Specs

Start: From the dirt parking lot at the trailhead off MA 16

Length: 4.5-mile loop

Approximate Hiking Time: 2 hours

Difficulty Rating: Easy, with broad trails and little elevation change

Trail Surface: Broad, two-track dirt paths

Lay of the Land: Cedars and hemlocks fill this swampy, sandy land, which drains into ponds and reservoirs

Land Status: MA Department of Environmental Management

Nearest Town: Webster, MA

Other Trail Users: Mountain bikers, cross-country skiers, and equestrians

Canine Compatibility: Dogs permitted

Getting There

From Worcester: Take I-395 south to exit 2. Drive east on MA 16 (a.k.a. Webster Street) for 4.3 miles, and pull into a dirt parking lot on your right, marked with a "trailhead" sign and map kiosk. *DeLorme: Massachusetts Atlas & Gazetteer:* Page 50 L8

The wetlands that cover this sandy forest provide far more diversity than a visitor would guess. But this richness was no secret to the Native Americans who have left signs of their stay here from up to 6,000 years ago. When the pilgrims arrived in America, these people were known as the Nipmuc Tribe. European settlers used the land initially for logging, brickmaking, charcoaling, granite quarrying, and harvesting ice from Wallum Lake. The land was bought by the state in 1934 for the Civilian Conservation Corps, who cleared land for the beach and trails we see today.

Although this hike is in the northern end of the park, perhaps the best way to appreciate Douglas State Forest is to do a tiny, second loop—the Cedar Swamp Trail. The trail is a red-blazed, 0.7-mile, self-guided nature loop that begins at the Nature Center, located on Wallum Lake near the park's main entrance. An attraction of this trail is the frequent sprouts of the American chestnut, once the most common tree in the entire northeast, but tragically killed off in three quick decades by a blight mistakenly imported from Asia in 1904. The species still creates seedlings that grow to maturity, but as soon as they stretch beyond 15 or 20 feet tall, cracks develop in their bark, and the blight quickly kills them. Other attractions are the granite quarry worked from 1893 to 1906, glacial "erratic" boulders, and the Atlantic white-cedar swamp. Retreating glaciers 15,000 years ago left "kettle hole" ponds where enormous chunks of buried ice intersected the water table. Ponds formed when they melted, and as the climate warmed, the cedar quickly established itself here. Seventeenth century European settlers used the cedar tree for house building since it is lightweight and water resistant.

The hike begins at a trailhead off MA 16, away from the crowds of the Nature Center, picnic tables, and boat launching ramp. It heads north, parallel to the long-distance Midstate

Trail, then curves along the shore of Whitin Reservoir. A shaded peninsula at the northwestern tip of the reservoir makes for a beautiful spot to stop for lunch and linger by the shore. With boulders scattered among the hemlocks in these marshy, sandy woods, the forest has a beauty that doesn't demand mountaintop vistas.

Since the British-born Samuel Slater settled it as a mill town in 1812, nearby Webster has been valued most for its abundant fresh water, particularly Lake Manchaug (see the sidebar). Slater founded villages to house entire families who would work on his water-powered textile mills. This was later known as the Rhode Island System. The town of Webster was founded in

MilesDirections

0.0 START at the trailhead parking lot, cross MA 16, step around a brown metal gate, and head north on a broad, sandy path.

0.3 Go left at a T-intersection.

0.4 Cross a wooden bridge over a stream, with a small, round, stone-lined pool on one side.

0.6 Cross another bridge.

0.8 Go right at an intersection.

0.9 Bear left at a fork following this wet trail up a short hill. *[FYI. The alternative leads only to a gravel pit 50 yards away]*.

1.2 Go right at a fork — beginning the loop portion of this hike — and continue past several smaller trails entering from either side.

1.6 Reach Wallis Pond (visible through trees to your right) and the stonework dam where its waters drain into the reservoir. *[FYI. The tannin-rich cedars have stained this water red, which fades to a pale yellow in the turbulence.]* Instead of crossing the dam, bear left, crossing through a stone wall and following the water downstream.

2.0 Trace the shore, keeping the reservoir on your right.

2.5 As the reservoir gets narrow, bear right at a fork, and emerge onto the hemlock-shaded peninsula, with its gorgeous water views. Then return to the shoreline trail and turn right, continuing your path.

2.7 At the end of the reservoir, bear left, climbing a small, steep hill away from the water's edge.

3.1 Emerge onto a sandy trail and go left, beginning your southward trek home.

3.3 Continue straight (go right) at a fork (the other direction is the spur trail).

3.7 Go straight through an intersection, rejoining your original trail, and ending the loop portion of this hike.

3.9 Cross the wooden bridge.

4.1 Cross the other bridge.

4.2 Turn right onto a broad, sandy path.

4.5 Cross MA 16 and reach your car.

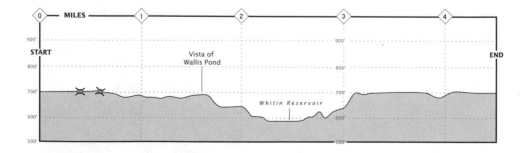

1832, and textile and show industries thrived here when the railroad arrived in 1840. Within the park, Whitin Reservoir and Wallum Lake are also vast water sources and popular destinations for fishing and other recreation. Mountain bikers like this location because of its more than 30 miles of wide trails and dirt roads. Pick up a free trail map at park headquarters. And for further information on this location, see the Midstate Trail section of this book.

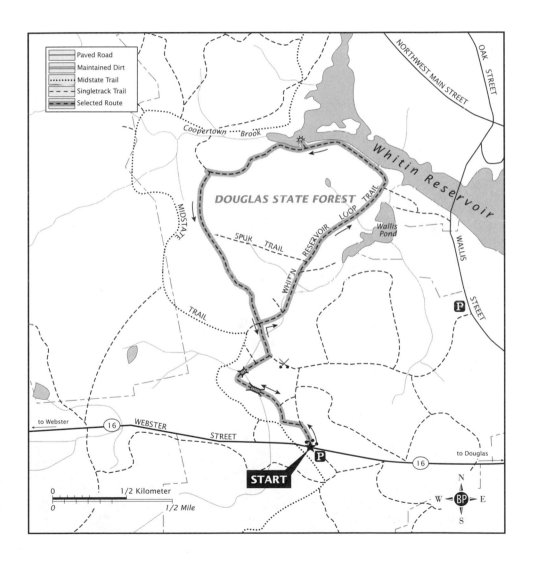

Lake Manchaug

Webster's five-mile-long, 1,442-acre **Lake Chargoggagoggmanchauggagoggchaubunagungamaugg** was named by the local Nipmuc tribe of Native Americans. History ordains that the lake was neutral territory, so local tribes including the Narragansett, Pequot, and Mohegans often met here. Tradition dictates that the name means "you fish on your side, I fish on mine, nobody fishes in the middle," but a more accurate translation is likely "the fishing place at the boundaries and neutral meeting grounds." Modern locals simply call it Lake Manchaug. Today you can even buy a t-shirt bearing the lake's name at www.bestofnewengland.com/lakechar.asp.

The Nipmuc were among the Algonquian tribes who first lived in central New England, and were the Native Americans who first met the European settlers in the 1600s. Nipmuc translates as "fresh water people" since they made their villages near water throughout their Nipnet territory, which ranged "from the present day Vermont and New Hampshire borders, through Worcester County in Massachusetts, into northern Rhode Island, and into northeastern Connecticut as far south as Plainfield," according to the Nipmuc Indian Association of Connecticut, based in Thompson, CT. For more information on this tribe check out www.nativetech.org/Nipmuc.

Hike Information

Trail Contacts:
MA Department of Environmental Management, Douglas MA (508) 476–7872 or www.state.ma.us/dem/parks/doug.htm

Schedule:
Open year round – The picnic area at the main entrance is open 10 A.M. to 8 P.M.

Fees/Permits:
No fees or permits required

Local Information:
Webster, MA websites: www.magnet.state.ma.us/cc/webster.html • Current MA trail conditions: www.lexicomm.com/trail/ma/index.html • The Appalachian Mountain Club: www.outdoors.org – tons of general info

Restaurants:
As you return, drive west 3.0 miles on MA 16 and reach a small mall on the left that includes: • Apollo Pizza, Webster, MA (508) 943–1215 • Honey Farms Mini Market, Webster, MA (508) 949–0793 • Honeydew Donuts, Webster, MA (508) 943–1429 Another quarter-mile west is: • The Chowder Bowl Restaurant, Webster, MA (508) 949–7227 • Colonial Restaurant, Webster, MA (508) 943–4040 or http://colonialrestaurant.com

Organizations:
The Midstate Trail homepage: www.midstatetrail.org/index.htm – The Midstate Trail begins in Douglas State Forest, and runs 92 miles northward, connecting with New Hampshire's Wapack Trail on the northern border of Massachusetts.

Maps:
USGS maps: Webster, MA

Western
MASSACHUSETTS

Farther from the ocean, Massachusetts' western mountains stand tall. The state's tallest mountain—Mt. Greylock—and the surrounding Berkshire hills boast tracts of deep forest filled with the state's major wildlife, and through it all runs the long-distance Appalachian Trail, on its way from Georgia to Maine.

In fact, these mountains are much older than the Taconics, sitting just to their west. They are part of the ancient Appalachian mountain chain, which stretches south from Vermont's Green Mountains and New Hampshire's White Mountains. And even this far west, there was once an inland sea depositing limestone, which, in some places, later changed to marble.

Sounds peaceful, but the beginning of this mighty mountain chain was a car-wreck. Geologists tell us that plate tectonics have rammed North America into Africa three times, beginning with the Taconic orogeny 450 million years ago. That enormous impact forced the Berkshire and Taconic Mountains far into the air, with later collisions sparking volcanic activity, and leaving parts of African land stuck on our coast.

So Massachusetts is dominated by Wachusett in its center, and Greylock to the west. This is no coincidence—both peaks are monadnocks, super-tough chunks of mountain that stand alone, since their brothers have long since eroded away. The layout was the same when those early European settlers arrived; they found the Berkshires mighty inconvenient, standing as a major block to their western expansion. Building a train tunnel through the mountain range was one solution, but the engineers nearly got more than they bargained for—see the hike in Savoy Mountain State Forest for more tales of this struggle.

Even today, our modern autos must zig-zag painstakingly along MA 2 as the road winds slowly over Whitcomb Summit. Other hikes that visit these steep peaks include Chester-Blandford State Forest, Mohawk Trail State Forest, Monroe State Forest, October Mountain State Forest, and Pittsfield State Forest.

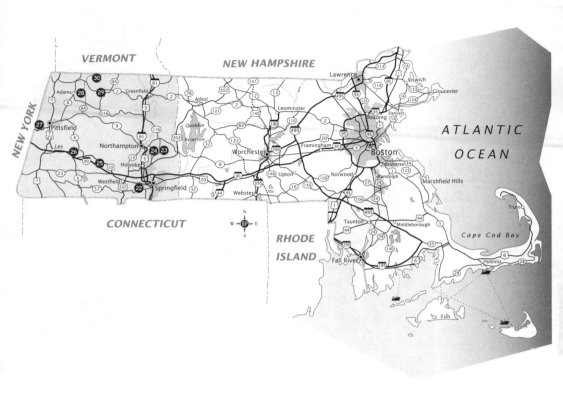

The Hikes

Section Overview

Robinson State Park

This out-and-back hike skirts the steep bluffs above the Westfield River, providing a surprising amount of solitude for a park just seven miles from downtown Springfield. But it's bigger than it looks—Robinson has over 800 acres, including more than five miles of river frontage. (*See page 118*)

Rattlesnake Knob

This modest loop climbs through forested trails to the saddle between Mt. Norwottuck (the highest peak of the Holyoke Range) and Long Mountain, reaching two stirring outlooks at Rattlesnake Knob. While you won't see many rattlers here, the region is rich with cultural and natural history, including a museum of locally found dinosaur footprints. (*See page 122*)

Skinner State Park

The Holyoke Range, including Skinner State Park and the adjacent Holyoke Range State Park, is one of the only east-west mountain ranges in the country—all others run north-south. This hike traverses two of the peaks in the range on a steep, rocky trail, then drops down to the valley floor to loop back on a flat dirt path that circles a small reservoir. (*See page 128*)

Chester-Blandford State Forest

The Westfield River begins as three streams draining the eastern slope of the Berkshire Hills, and then flows into the Connecticut River at Agawam. State highways and railroads run parallel along its length, including MA 20, which led you here. This loop begins with a steep climb to the cliffs above, with their soaring views up and down the river valley. The hike then traverses around these cliffs, called Observation Hill, before descending to the foot of a waterfall where Sanderson Brook flows into the Westfield River. (*See page 132*)

October Mountain State Forest

This hike follows the long-distance Appalachian Trail over Becket (2,200 feet) and Walling (2,220 feet) mountains, then drops down to the shore of Finerty Pond, illustrating the variety of this enormous forest. It then tracks the Cordonier Trail southward through low-lying forest lands, looping back to the Appalachian Trail for a short backtrack to your car. (*See page 136*)

Pittsfield State Forest

This loop traces a section of the historic Shaker Trail over Holy Mount, the religious group's consecrated peak, then returns on the Taconic Crest Trail, a quiet, long distance hiking trail that stretches back and forth across the New York border for 35 miles. Nearby sections of the Shaker Trail pass by dozens of historic foundations, mills, carriage roads, and holy sites. (*See page 140*)

Savoy Mountain State Forest

This loop follows a two-track multi-use trail through northern hardwood forests, then climbs past Lewis Hill to the fire tower on Borden Mountain. The return path passes Balance Rock, then parallels Ross Brook as it flows toward Tannery Falls on its way to the Deerfield River. You can swim here at either North Pond or South Pond, though there is only a lifeguard at the former. (*See page 146*)

Mohawk Trail State Forest

This out-and-back hike traces a traverse along the shoulder of Hawks Mountain (1,880 feet), to an exposed cliff that offers gorgeous views of the Deerfield River Valley. And if you want to do some extra exploring after this short hike, pick up a map at the park headquarters (on the north side of MA 2, 0.7 miles east of here) and walk along the gorgeous Thumper Mountain Trail and Nature Trail on the banks of the Deerfield River. (*See page 152*)

Monroe State Forest

From stone-age natives to a 4.8-mile train tunnel to a nuclear power plant, this region has been home to all stages of humanity. This varied loop climbs to the wooded peak of Spruce Mountain, with some beautiful views to the south along power line cuts. It then descends to Hunt Hill for a breathtaking view over the Deerfield River Valley and the Bear Swamp Upper Reservoir, which is drained daily to provide electric power through an underground "pumped storage

facility." Complete the loop with a flat hike along the dirt Raycroft Road. (*See page 156*)

Robinson State Park

Hike Specs

Start: From the grassy parking lot off River Road, 0.3 miles from the North Street entrance
Length: 3-mile out-and-back
Approximate Hiking Time: 1.5 hours
Difficulty Rating: Easy
Trail Surface: Hard packed dirt trails
Lay of the Land: Steep, wooded bluffs along a river bank
Land Status: MA Department of Environmental Management
Nearest Town: Agawam, MA
Other Trail Users: Mountain bikers
Canine Compatibility: Dogs permitted

Getting There

From Holyoke: Take I-91 south to exit 3. Follow MA 57 west for 2.1 miles, then turn right at the Main Street/West Springfield exit. Follow Main Street, and at the second traffic light (3.9 miles), bear right onto North Street. At 6.9 miles, turn right at a sign for the park entrance. Follow River Road, and, at 7.2 miles, park in a grassy lot on the right at the bottom of a hill. *DeLorme: Massachusetts Atlas & Gazetteer:* Page 46 J16

The Westfield River drains the creeks and brooks of the Berkshires into the Connecticut River at Springfield. This hike traces the southern bank of the river along some of its last five miles, touring through a mixed hemlock, maple, beech, and birch woodland punctuated by rhododendrons and fiddlehead ferns, and by several timber stands of white pine.

Agawam is perhaps best known as the home of Six Flags New England amusement park, and crowds at Robinson can be thick, especially when they're seeking a place to swim on a hot, summer day. It gets much quieter once you get out on the trails, but you still have to keep an eye out for speeding mountain bikes. The steep bluffs are dissected by power lines and shadowed by the active railroad track on the opposite bank. The park also includes a 17-acre island west of the falls at the Mittineague-Rexam dam, but this hike does not visit it. (Mittineague, which is Indian for "the place of falling waters," is a neighborhood in the adjacent town of West Springfield.) Overall, this urban park offers unexpected solitude and sweeping river views, without the elevation change or long drive of more remote spots.

The Westfield was Massachusetts's first river to gain federal protection under the 1968 Wild and Scenic Rivers Act, and is today watched over by the Westfield River Watershed Association. Founded in 1952, the group offers ecology education and speakers, as well as publishing a canoe guide and monitoring the salmon restoration program in these waters. The river drains an area of 517 square miles, including 78 lakes and ponds within the Westfield River basin, 48 of which have an area of 10 acres or more. The river is also a major source of drinking water for the Springfield region.

An effort to restore Atlantic salmon to the Connecticut River basin is underway, in a joint project between the states of Vermont, New Hampshire, Connecticut, and Massachusetts, together with the U.S. Fish and Wildlife Service. After declining throughout the 19th century, native Atlantic salmon disappeared from the river and its tributaries (including the Westfield River). Since 1983, this group has reintroduced the fish into the watershed. These anadromous fish are born in fresh water, mature in the open ocean, and return to their freshwater home rivers to spawn.

Superman, Batman, and Bugs Bunny are the attractions at Six Flags New England. The park is still expanding, launching three new roller coasters and a free-fall ride in 2000. And these coasters are not your average ride—the Superman Ride of Steel drags its passengers 20 stories into the air, drops them for 10 seconds of weightlessness, and flings them along the track at speeds up to 80 mph. The other rides have names like black diamond slopes on ski mountains—Scream, Time Warp, Cannonball Falls, Thunderbolt, Double Trouble, Cyclone, and Mind Eraser.

Also, the Agawam Cultural Council supports arts and humanities in the area, such as lectures and performances on the first Friday of each month, from October through May. Now in its fifth year, its Summer Series holds performances and concerts throughout July and August.

Hike Information

Trail Contacts:
Robinson State Park, Agawam, MA (413) 786–2877 or www.state.ma.us/dem/parks/robn.htm

Schedule:
10 A.M. to 6 P.M. daily

Fees/Permits:
No fees or permits required

Local Information:
Agawam, MA website: www.agawam.ma.us

Local Events/Attractions:
Sixflags New England, Springfield, MA (MA 159) (413) 786–9300 or www.sixflags.com/newengland – The city of Springfield is a seven-mile drive, just on the other side of the Connecticut River.

Other Resources:
Westfield River Watershed Association (413) 532–7290 or http://bondo.wsc.mass.edu/dept/garp/wrwa/wrwa.htm – offers educational programs, speakers, and newsletters, as well as a canoe guide to the river

Local Outdoor Retailers:
Backpacking Etc., Agawam, MA (413) 786–1023

Maps:
USGS maps: West Springfield, MA

MilesDirections

0.0 START in the grassy lot. Walk toward the river and bear right, following the dirt Yellow Trail northward as you follow the river downstream (this trail is not blazed).

0.1 Turn left at a fork, staying close to the river.

0.2 Bear left at an intersection with a broader dirt trail, following blue and yellow blazes into a thick birch grove.

0.3 Carry on as an unmarked trail enters from the right.

0.4 Cross a stream in a shallow ravine, and immediately turn left at an intersection, following the trail as it traces the edge of the steep bluff, 50 yards above the river to your left.

0.5 Bear left and leave the blue and yellow blazes behind as you enter a grove of tall maples.

0.7 Reach a spot where power lines cross the river, and carry on, following the pole line. Continue to walk northeast along the poles as several trails enter from the right.

1.1 Pass an intersection at a thick stand of white pine.

1.2 Continue to follow the pole line past a left fork. *[**FYI.** This low land can be very muddy, with lots of skunk cabbage.]*

1.4 Just two poles short of reaching another power line atop a steep ridge, turn sharp left at an intersection onto a two-track dirt path.

1.5 Reach the waterfront, where the river flows over a tall dam. Turn left here to begin your walk home.

Keeping the river close on your right hand side, soon bear right to follow a trail closer to the shore.

1.7 Go left at a T-intersection with a larger path, bearing away from the water.

1.8 Cross a small stream and bear right, following a broad dirt path parallel to the river, on your right.

1.9 Bear left at a fork, soon reaching the familiar pole line at the thick pine grove. *[**FYI.** The open, grassy meadow on the other side of the wires is a great spot to stop for lunch and enjoy the silence.]* But to get home, you bear right here, retracing your steps back to your car.

2.2 Pass the spot where the power lines cross the river.

2.4 Bear right at a T-intersection, picking up the blue and yellow blazes again.

2.5 Follow the blazes as the trail curves left away from the water, then curves quickly right, crossing the stream in the ravine.

2.8 Turn right onto a dirt trail just before you reach the paved River Road, and walk along the steep cliff above the river, passing by an unmarked trail that enters from the left.

3.0 Reach your car.

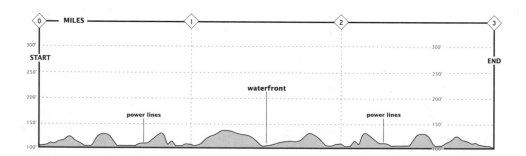

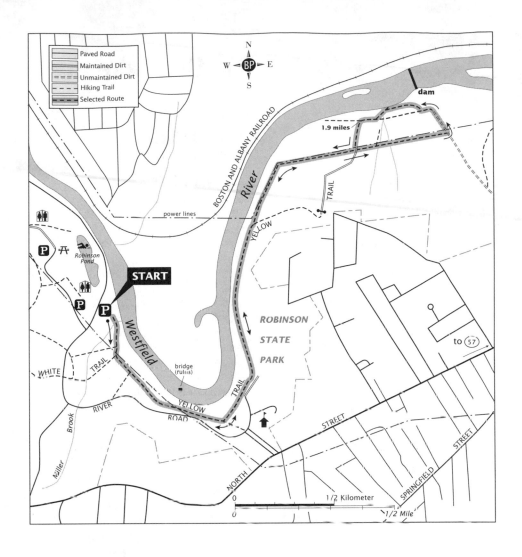

Legend:
- Paved Road
- Maintained Dirt
- Unmaintained Dirt
- Hiking Trail
- Selected Route

N
W — BP — E
S

BOSTON AND ALBANY RAILROAD

River

dam

1.9 miles

TRAIL

power lines

YELLOW

Robinson Pond

P

P

P

START

Westfield

ROBINSON STATE PARK

to 57

WHITE

TRAIL

RIVER

Miller Brook

bridge (ruins)

YELLOW

TRAIL

ROAD

STREET

NORTH

SPRINGFIELD

STREET

0   1/2 Kilometer
0   1/2 Mile

Rattlesnake Knob

Hike Specs

Start: From trailhead off Bachelor Street, south of Notch Visitors Center
Length: 3.9-mile loop
Approximate Hiking Time: 2 hours
Difficulty Rating: Medium, due to climbing
Trail Surface: Broad, dirt trails
Lay of the Land: Loop to the ridgeline and back for a combination of outlook and forested trails
Land Status: MA Department of Environmental Management
Nearest Town: Amherst, MA
Other Trail Users: Mountain bikers
Canine Compatibility: Dogs permitted

Getting There

From Springfield: Take I-91 north to exit 19. From the exit, follow MA 9 east, soon crossing the Connecticut River. At 0.5 miles, turn right onto Bay Road, following signs for MA 47 south. At 2.3 miles, turn left to remain on Bay Road and leave MA 47. At 5.2 miles, reach Atkins Farms Country Market, and turn right onto MA 116 southbound. At 6.4 miles, turn left into the Notch Visitor Center for restrooms, free maps, and a great natural history center. To reach the trailhead continue south on MA 116, and turn left onto Amherst Street at 7.5 miles, following a sign for MA 202 and Granby. At 7.9 miles, turn left onto Bachelor Street. Finally, at 8.6 miles, park on either shoulder of the road when you reach a brown metal gate on your left. *DeLorme: Massachusetts Atlas & Gazetteer:* Page 35 M24

T he short drive from I-91 to the trailhead provides stunning views of the Holyoke Range as you go up Bay Road. Pass pastures full of cows and fields full of pumpkins, corn, apples, and Christmas trees. From Rattlesnake Knob, you can hear the cattle mooing when the wind is right.

This hike is entirely in the town of Granby, except for the knob itself, just across the town line into Amherst. The colored shapes on trees are not trail blazes, but refer to the difficulty of cross-country ski slopes: green is easy, blue intermediate, and black expert. Together, Holyoke Range State Park and Skinner State Park include 2,936 acres along the mountain ridge.

Ever since it was settled in 1727, and incorporated in 1768, the town of Granby has struggled to establish agriculture on the shoulders of the Holyoke range, and to establish industry with its scarce water supply. The earliest residents overcame these hurdles by the early 19th century by growing grains, hops, pumpkins, and turnips, even opening several distilleries to use any surplus grain. They added to their income through dairy farming and by producing buttons and hats. Despite their determined efforts, dairy farming was all that remained by 1875. Today, an enormous milk bottle housing a dairy bar acts as a town landmark.

Nearby Hadley claims to have the most farmland acreage of any town in the Pioneer Valley (Connecticut River Valley). And these folks take their "pioneer" title seriously, claiming to be one of the oldest settlements in the state (founded in 1659).

Amherst, another local town, has moved on completely from its agricultural beginnings, to embrace its current main industry—education. As the home of UMass-Amherst and Amherst and Hampshire Colleges, this town sees its population whiplash between 35,000 in the academic year to less than 25,000 in the summer. If you're hungry for culture after your walk in

the woods, this is the place to be for museums and learning (see contact info below). Amherst College alone offers a Center for Russian Culture, poet Emily Dickinson's homestead, the Folger Shakespeare Library, Mead Art Museum, and the Pratt Museum of Natural History, featuring fossils, minerals, and dinosaur tracks.

Yes, dinosaurs once stomped around the Connecticut River Valley, leaving footprints in the then-soft sedimentary and sandstone rocks. The museum's ichnology department (the study of tracks) holds more than 1,100 slabs of stone dating to the Jurassic age (about 200 million years ago). A dinosaur called Anomocpus once passed through Turner's Falls, MA, and a famous series of tracks called "Noah's Raven" were discovered in 1802 in South Hadley, MA, the first dinosaur evidence in North America. There is also an extensive archeology collection of local Native American relics.

And if your tastes run more to the literary, stop by Emily Dickinson's home, found at 280 Main Street in Amherst (contact info below). It's open for tours from March through mid-

MilesDirections

0.0 START at a brown metal gate off Bachelor Street, walking up the two-track sandy path past a trailhead marked "Main Access."

0.2 Bear right at a fork, following a sign for the Upper Access Trail, and immediately crossing a stream.

0.9 Pass by a rusted car hulk on your left, and then pass an unmarked, wide path on your right.

1.0 Pass by a sign for the Technical Trail (a mountain bike path) on your left.

1.1 Pass by an unmarked footpath to your right.

1.3 Pass by the Southside Trail (blazed blue), joining from your left. Soon cross another stream, then pass by a blue-blazed path on your right.

1.6 Fork right toward the Cliffside Trail (blazed red), then immediately fork left to join the combined Robert Frost (blazed orange) and Metacomet-Monadnock trails (blazed white).

1.7 Fork left, still following the orange and white blazes, and immediately start to climb a steep, rocky hillside.

1.8 Bear right at the top of the ascent, following a sign for "Viewpoint, 100 feet" and passing by a sign for the Cuddebank Trail (blazed blue). *[FYI. The viewpoint is Rattlesnake Knob, with Long Mountain visible to the east (on your right), and the University of Massachusetts' famous brick library tower in Amherst visible to the north (on your left).]* Leave the knob and fork to your right, still following orange and white blazes. At a bend in the trail, pass by a metal post marked "A/G" for the town line.

2.0 Bear left at a fork as you continue to follow orange and white.

2.1 Turn left at the bottom of a short, steep descent, following a sign for "M&M Trail to Horse Caves, Mt. Norwottock." Then immediately merge

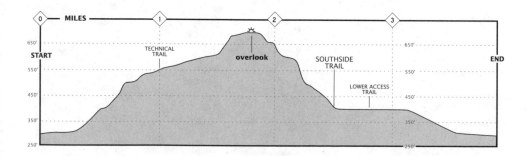

left again, at a sign for "Swamp Trail to Southside, 0.3 miles," now following blue blazes.

2.3 Turn right in a grassy junction to continue following the Swamp Trail, and continue a gentle descent.

2.5 Turn right onto the Southside Trail.

2.7 Pass by an unmarked trail joining from the right.

2.8 Merge left at a fork as you leave the Southside Trail, following a sign marked "Lower Access Trail to B. Street gate."

2.9 Pass by the unmarked Technical Trail on your left.

3.2 Reach a marshy beaver pond which has flooded the original trail, and swing right around its western edge, soon crossing two small wooden bridges just below the pond's south end.

3.7 Bear right, downhill, at the fork where you first turned to climb the Upper Access Trail.

3.9 Cross through the brown metal gate and reach your car.

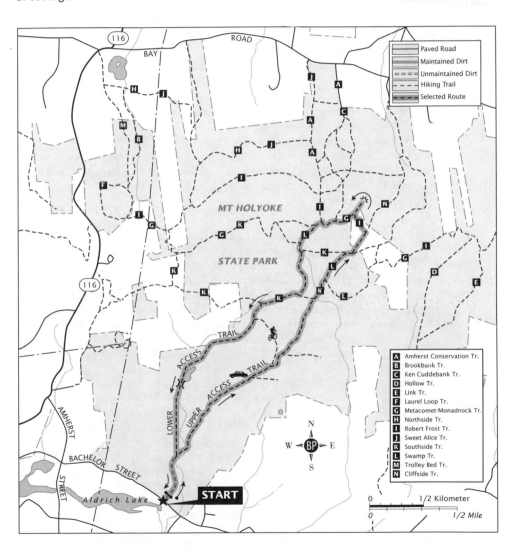

December. There's even an annual walk through town on the anniversary of her death, May 15, 1886, and a birthday party every December 8th.

So, will you find many rattlesnakes in the woods as the name of the hike implies? Probably not. Although they were widespread in colonial times, Massachusetts's rattlesnakes are so rare today they are scarcely ever seen by people. In fact, the Timber Rattler is an endangered species in the state, and there are none at all in Maine, Rhode Island, central New Hampshire, most of Vermont, or Long Island.

Massachusetts' Farms

There are 6,200 farms in Massachusetts, which cover 570,000 acres of open space in the form of scenic and productive farmland. More than 80 percent of these farms are family-owned. And together, all the farms totaled $459 million of agricultural cash receipts in 1998.

Check www.massdfa.org/farms_products for a list of pick-your-own (PYO) farms for apples, blueberries, raspberries, flowers, pumpkins, strawberries, and vegetables. The list is published online at www.massgrown.org/farms_products/pyo2000.pdf, as an alphabetical list of farms with address, hours, and directions.

Also, the Massachusetts Department of Food and Agriculture publishes a guide called The Green Book: A Directory of Wholesale Growers of Massachusetts Grown and Fresher Products, which can lead you to places through the state to buy locally grown produce. County by county, it lists producers of organic produce. The fruits list alone can make your mouth water: apple cider, blackberries, blueberries, cranberries, nectarines, grapes, melons, peaches, pears, plums, raspberries, rhubarb, and strawberries. And each listing includes the farm name, contact name, and fax and phone numbers, with an index for addresses, too. There is a version online at www.massdfa.org/farms_products/gbook.pdf.

For further information, there's plenty of information on the web. Try www.massgrown.org or www.centralmassfresh.com or www.berkshiregrown.com.

Hike Information

Trail Contacts:
Skinner State Park, Hadley, MA (413) 586–0350 or *www.state.ma.us/dem/parks/ skin.htm* • **Holyoke Range State Park-Notch Visitors Center**, Amherst, MA (413) 253–2883 or *www.state.ma.us/dem/parks/ hksp.htm*

Schedule:
Open year round

Fees/Permits:
No fees or permits required

Local Information:
Trail maps online: *www.state.ma.us/dem/ parks/trails/skin.pdf*

Local Events/Attractions:
Museums of Amherst College: *www.amherst. edu/about_amh/museums.html* • **Emily Dickinson Homestead**, Amherst, MA (413) 542–8161 or *www.dickinsonhomestead.org* • **Blizniak Christmas Tree Farm**, Hadley, MA (413) 586–0723

Restaurants:
Atkins Farm Country Market, Amherst, MA (413) 253–9528 — *serves breakfast and lunch, but can be very crowded on weekends*

Other Resources:
Amherst, MA website: *www.town.amherst. ma.us* – *loaded with links and information* • **Amherst Online:** *www.amherstonline.com* – *great for cultural and culinary listings* • **Amherst History Museum**, Amherst, MA: *www.amhersthistory.org www.amherstcommon. com* – *has tons more info, including a useful hiking page:* *www.amherstcommon.com/ recreation/hiking.html* • **Hitchcock Center for the Environment**, Amherst, MA (413) 256–6006 or *www.hitchcockcenter.org.*

Maps:
USGS maps: Mount Holyoke, MA

24

Skinner State Park

Hike Specs

Start: From Notch Visitors Center

Length: 4.6-mile loop

Approximate Hiking Time: 3 hours

Difficulty Rating: Difficult, due to steep, rocky sections

Trail Surface: First half is steep and rocky, second half is a flat dirt trail

Lay of the Land: This hike traverses two peaks in the Holyoke Range, then loops back in the valley below

Land Status: MA Department of Environmental Management

Nearest Town: Northampton, MA

Other Trail Users: Mountain bikers, cross-country skiers, and equestrians

Canine Compatibility: Dogs permitted

Getting There

From Springfield: Take I-91 north to exit 19 (MA 9, Northampton, Amherst). Drive east on MA 9 for 7.0 miles, and then turn right onto MA 116 south. At 11.9 miles, turn left at the sign for the Notch Visitors Center. *DeLorme: Massachusetts Atlas & Gazetteer:* Page 35 L24

The loop begins with a steep climb to Bare Mountain, and provides splendid views along the ridgeline to Mt. Hitchcock. The trail then drops quickly to the cool valley floor and soon reaches a small reservoir, created by the military to support a nearby, now-defunct, underground command center. Today the reservoir is filled with enormous bullfrogs and bright orange koy fish. The trail soon reaches the fenced-in former military compound, now converted into a library for Amherst College. This post-cold war renovation stands in stark contrast to the millennia of occupation by Native Americans, from the Nonotuck to the Algonquin, who first arrived more than 6,000 years ago and were known locally as the Norwottuck.

In 1821, the hotel atop Mount Holyoke was America's first summit house, and in 1854 the train to reach it was the state's first mountain tram. Original proprietors John and Fannie French offered accommodations including a bowling alley. Throughout its heyday from 1861 to 1894, details like this placed the Summit House among the region's premier attractions, alongside Mount Greylock's Bascom Lodge. A silk manufacturer named Joseph Allen Skinner donated this land to the state in 1940, and today the park is larger than 3,000 acres. The visitors center is packed with information on the human and natural history, as well as providing restrooms and maps. And you can still tour the Summit House.

For hundreds of years, the Pioneer Valley has been a farming community, and much of that heritage is intact in the layout of the towns here. Hadley boasts that its square-mile town common is the largest in New England, and says it has the most farmland acreage of any town in the valley. It offers the Porter-Phelps Huntington House (built in 1752) and Hadley Farm Museum to illustrate this history. But perhaps Hadley's best claim to fame is as "the birthplace of broom-making," ever since they first mechanized the process in 1797 and became one of the leading growers of broomcorn. Of course, the famous five-college area (Smith, Amherst,

Mount Holyoke, Hampshire, and UMass-Amherst) offers countless attractions, so check with those institutions for further opportunities.

In the fall, the peaks are favorite spots to watch the annual bird migrations, such as broad wing and red tail hawks and kestrels. But in the moist spring months, the air can be thick with annoying midges and black flies. The mountains have two basic habitats: oak-hickory forests on south-facing slopes, and a mix of hemlock, white pine, birch, beech, and maple on the northern slopes. The south-side habitat usually occurs much further south, and the north-side trees are usually found further north in New England. But the range's odd orientation (it was formed glacially, not tectonically) provides the unique exposure to support them.

Together, Holyoke Range State Park and Skinner State Park contain 2,936 acres along the spine of the mountain range, which rises nearly 1,000 feet above the surrounding valley floor.

Hike Information

📞 Trail Contacts:
Skinner State Park, Hadley, MA (413) 586–0350 or www.state.ma.us/dem/parks/skin.htm

🕐 Schedule:
Open year round – visitors center is open 9 A.M. to 5 P.M. daily.

💲 Fees/Permits:
No fees or permits required

❓ Local Information:
Hadley Guide: www.hadleyonline.com • **Town of Hadley website**: www.magnet.state.ma.us/cc/hadley.html • **Northampton's homepage**: www.ci.northampton.ma.us

💡 Local Events/Attractions:
Atkins Farm Country Market and Apple Orchard, South Amherst, MA (413) 253–9528 or 1–800–594–9537 or www.atkinsfarms.com – as you leave the visitors center, follow MA 116 north for 1.0 mile to reach the market.

🚶 Hike Tours:
Available at the visitors center

🏃 Organizations:
Friends of the Mount Holyoke Range, South Hadley, MA: http://fomhr.tripod.com • **Save the Mountain (STM):** www.savemtholyokerange.com – a group that fights private development of this land

⏱ Other Resources:
Notch Visitors Center: (413) 253–2883 • **Summit House (atop Mt. Holyoke):** (413) 586–0350

🏬 Local Outdoor Retailers:
There are several along Russell Street, which is MA 9, just west of its intersection with MA 116: **Adventure Outfitters**, Hadley, MA 1–800–835–2925 or www.adventureoutfitter.com • **Competitive Edge Ski and Bike**, Hadley, MA (413) 585–8833 or www.compedgeskibike.com • **Eastern Mountain Sports (EMS)**, Hadley, MA (413) 584–3554 or www.emsonline.com • **Amherst Drop Zone**, Hadley, MA (413) 585–5800

Ⓝ Maps:
USGS maps: Mount Holyoke, MA

Friends of the Mount Holyoke Range is a group that organizes hikes and supports wilderness preservation in the area. Subscribe to their newsletter for dates and contacts. There is even an annual 5k (3.1-mile) footrace to the summit of Mount Holyoke each September.

MilesDirections

0.0 START at the Notch Visitors Center. Cross MA 116 to a sign for Bare Mountain, Mt. Hitchcock, and the Summit House, and begin a steep climb up the white-blazed Metacomet-Monadnock Trail. The trail includes several switchbacks across slopes of loose, rocky scree.

0.4 Reach the top of Bare Mountain, with views of a sprawling gravel quarry at the base of Mount Norwottock, the campuses of Amherst and Hampshire colleges, and the parking lot where your car sits.

0.5 Continue along the white-blazed ridgeline, soon reaching a fenced-in shack and a pipeline. Follow the blazes along a pipeline. You'll soon drop into a cool, shaded saddle between the two peaks.

1.2 Keep your eyes open as you come over a rise, and soon follow the white blazes in a right turn down the side of the ridge.

1.7 Reach the top of Mount Hitchcock with its fallen fire tower (knocked down by the state for insurance reasons) and super views of the Connecticut River. Continue to follow your white blazes as you begin a descent through rocky, rolling terrain.

2.3 Pass by a left turn for the blue-blazed Low Place Trail. Then immediately bear right onto the blue-blazed Parker Trail.

2.5 Turn right onto the yellow-blazed Northside Trail.

2.7 Bear right at a fork. *[**FYI.** The red-blazed College Trail leads left here.]*

3.0 Bear left at a fork, continuing to follow the yellow blazes.

3.3 Pass by several unmarked trails entering from the right.

3.4 Bear right at an intersection in an open clearing, soon crossing straight through another intersection.

3.5 Go left at a fork to reach the small reservoir. Bear right around the far edge of the small reservoir, picking up the trail where it heads back into the trees.

3.7 Bear left at a fork.

4.2 Reach the fenced Amherst College library property, and bear left, following the fence line toward the compound's entrance.

4.3 Bear left onto the paved Military Road.

4.5 Turn right onto MA 116.

4.6 Reach the Notch Visitors Center, and your car.

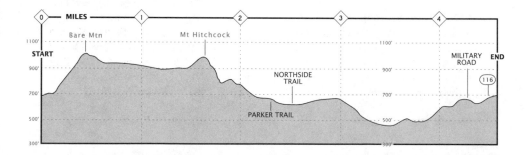

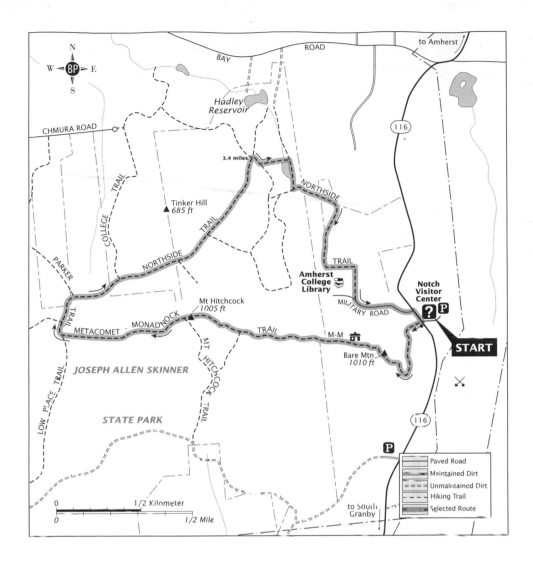

N

W ⊕ BP E
S

to Amherst

BAY ROAD

Hadley
Reservoir

116

CHMURA ROAD

3.4 miles

NORTHSIDE

COLLEGE TRAIL

Tinker Hill
▲ 685 ft

NORTHSIDE TRAIL

TRAIL

Amherst
College
Library

Notch
Visitor
Center

? P

PARKER TRAIL

MILITARY ROAD

METACOMET   MONADNOCK TRAIL

Mt Hitchcock
1005 ft

TRAIL

M-M

START

JOSEPH ALLEN SKINNER

MT HITCHCOCK TRAIL

LOW PLACE TRAIL

Bare Mtn
1010 ft

STATE PARK

116

P

to South
Granby

0   1/2 Kilometer
0   1/2 Mile

Paved Road
Maintained Dirt
Unmaintained Dirt
Hiking Trail
Selected Route

25

Chester-Blandford State Forest

Hike Specs

Start: From Sanderson Brook Road, off MA 20
Length: 3.8-mile loop
Approximate Hiking Time: 2 hours
Difficulty Rating: Medium, due to some very steep sections of trail
Trail Surface: Short steep section is a narrow dirt trail; majority of the hike is on broad gravel roads
Lay of the Land: Steep hills above the Westfield River valley, with sweeping views of the valley and a trip to a waterfall in the bottom
Land Status: MA Department of Environmental Management
Nearest Town: Chester, MA
Other Trail Users: Mountain bikers, ATV riders (although land is posted for no motorized vehicles)
Canine Compatibility: Dogs permitted

Getting There

From Westfield: Take U.S. 20 west, passing its junction with MA 23 west at 5.8 miles, and its junction with MA 112 north at 12.1 miles. Pass the headquarters of Chester-Blandford State Forest on your left at 14.7 miles. Turn left at 16.4 miles onto Sanderson Brook Road, immediately opposite the Bannish Lumber Yard. Park in the small dirt lot on your right. *DeLorme: Massachusetts Atlas & Gazetteer:* Page 45 28A

T he hike begins on the H. Newman Marsh Memorial Trail, named for the man (1924–96) who helped develop the Jacob's Ladder Trail Scenic Byway. The byway is known today as MA 20, but it has been used since the days when Mahican and Woronoake Native American tribes used it to travel between the Connecticut and Hudson river valleys. Jacob's Ladder itself is a 2,100-foot-high mountain ridge about a half-hour's drive west.

A Civilian Conservation Corps crew working in this forest first cleared the Newman Marsh Trail as a firebreak in the 1930s. About 100 men lived in a camp nearby, where they built two bridges and the Sanderson Brook Road, cut timber, planted trees, and exterminated the gypsy moths that were killing those trees. Today, the Newman Marsh Trail features numbered posts marking points of interest. At Post #7, huge boulders of quartz, surrounded by rhododendron, poke up into a forest of pine and maple. And Post #8 marks a stunning overlook with views up and down the valley.

This land contains so much quartz and mica that it often seems there must be shards of glass in the soil at your feet. Indeed, mining used to be the local business—removing mica, emery, and corundum (a mineral found in rubies and sapphires but more commonly used as an abrasive) from these hills. And in the wet summer months, there are enormous mushrooms splashing color—orange, red, silver, white, black, and scarlet—throughout the forest floor.

The nearby town of Chester enjoyed busy industry from the 1930s to 60s with its emery mill, granite quarrying, and stone carving. Yet today, only the small emery mill remains, so the town must search for a new economic engine. One candidate is the Bannish Lumber Company, located just across the street from the trailhead. Other businesses include tourism, blueberry and produce farms, and maple sugaring. But one of the most promising developments is the Miniature Theatre of Chester, founded in 1990 and located in the town hall. This

summer-stock theater plays works by such famed playwrights as South African Athol Fugard. There are matinee performances at 2 P.M. on Thursdays and Sundays in season.

Did I mention blueberries? Well, this is no average roadside, pick-your-own, type of place. The Chester Hill Winery makes blueberry wine. The area's 1,370-foot elevation is too high for most wine grapes, but blueberries grow very well here. And the berry is flexible: "The wine can be made sweet or dry, still or effervescent, light or strong, and all of it is good," say owners Joe and Mary Ann Sullivan on their website. For their "nouveau" style wines, the berries are picked in July, fermented with red wine yeast, and sold in November. Port or reserve styles take longer to mature; choices are New Blue, Best Blue, or Bay Blue. The vineyard also produces some white wine from hardy, indigenous grapes. They can even personalize bottle labels with any (legal) text.

Hike Information

Trail Contacts:
Chester–Blandford State Forest headquarters, Chester, MA (413) 354–6347 or *www.state.ma.us/dem/parks/chbl.htm*

Schedule:
Open year round

Fees/Permits:
No fees or permits required

Local Information:
Jacob's Ladder Trail Scenic Byway Inc., Huntington, MA: *www.berkshireweb.com/jacobsladdertrail* – *The 33-mile stretch of MA 20 between Westfield and Lee is nicknamed "The Jacob's Ladder Trail." The path was first blazed by the Mahican and Woronoake native American tribes, then expanded in 1910 as one of the first highways built for automobiles.*

Local Events/Attractions:
Chester Hill Winery, Chester, MA (413) 354–2340 or *www.blueberrywine.com*

Accommodations:
Lee Lodging Association, Lee, MA: *www.leelodging.org* • **Lee Chamber of Commerce**, Lee, MA (413) 243–0852 or *www.leechamber.org*

Organizations:
The Miniature Theatre of Chester, Chester, MA (413) 354–7770, box office (413) 354–7771 or *www.miniaturetheatre.org* – *the Theater is located at the Chester Town Hall, on Middlefield Street, just off of MA 20.*

Other Resources:
The Berkshire Web: *www.berkshireweb.com* – *a great Internet resource for weather, maps, shopping, restaurants and hotels* • **Hidden Hills** *(western MA) website: www.hidden-hills.com – includes a general map of Chester at www.hidden-hills.com/map/chestermap. html*

Local Outdoor Retailers:
Backpacking Etc., Agawam, MA (413) 786–1023

Maps:
USGS maps: Chester, MA; Blandford, MA

MilesDirections

0.0 START at your car, and walk southward up the gravel Sanderson Brook Road, following signs for Sanderson Brook Falls.

0.1 Cross a gated bridge over Sanderson Brook.

0.2 Turn left onto the Newman Marsh Trail, a blue-blazed, narrow dirt path that leads steeply uphill.

0.4 The trail climbs a steep ravine and crosses a small stream to your left.

0.5 Bear left at a fork, following a sign toward "Overlook Trail and Vistas." Shortly after this turn, the trail flattens out from its steep climb.

0.6 Pass Post # 7, with its quartz boulders.

0.8 Reach a breathtaking overlook of the Westfield River Valley (Post # 8), with the river sandwiched between U.S. 20 and the Conrail train tracks.

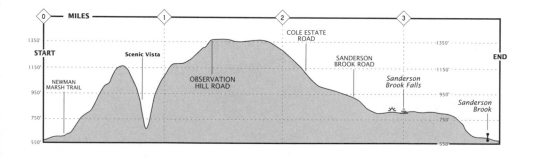

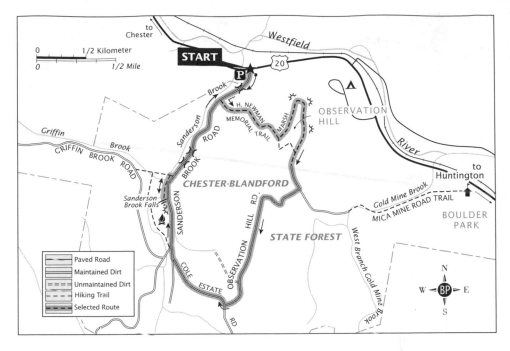

0.9 Reach another overlook, at Post # 9.

1.2 Bear left at a fork, away from a sign for Sanderson Brook Road. *[**Note**. The blue blazes continue in both directions.]*

1.3 The Newman Marsh Trail ends, and you continue southward along a gravel road.

1.4 Go right at a fork, onto Observation Hill Road.

2.1 Pass by an old dirt road that enters from the right.

2.2 Go right at a T-intersection onto the Cole Estate Road, heading north on this broad, gravel road.

2.5 Pass by a dirt road that enters from your left, as you descend from the hill and begin to hear the roar of Sanderson Brook.

2.6 Pass straight through a large clearing. *[**FYI**. There are several riverside fire circles and campsites on the trails to your left.]* You are now on Sanderson Brook Road.

2.9 Walk between a line of boulders set in the gravel road to prevent motorized vehicles from entering. Then immediately reach an overlook of Sanderson Brook Falls to your left.

3.0 Take a hairpin left turn onto a blue-blazed path that drops into the ravine and leads to the base of the falls, a swimming hole in summer. When you are done exploring the falls, backtrack to the road.

3.2 Rejoin Sanderson Brook Road, continuing your descent.

3.3 Cross two metal bridges over Sanderson Brook.

3.6 Pass by the original turn you took to climb the Newman Marsh Trail.

3.7 Cross the gated bridge.

3.8 Reach your car.

October Mountain
State Forest

Hike Specs

Start: From the trailhead on U.S. 20, near Greenwater Pond

Length: 6.1-mile loop

Approximate Hiking Time: 3.5 hours

Difficulty Rating: Difficult, due to distance and steep climbs

Trail Surface: Steep dirt trails, and broad two-track carriage roads

Lay of the Land: Roll over two peaks then trace a lakefront to return on this loop

Land Status: MA Department of Environmental Management

Nearest Town: Lee, MA

Other Trail Users: Mountain bikers, dirt bikers, ATVs, snowmobilers

Canine Compatibility: Dogs permitted

Getting There

From Lee: Follow U.S. 20 east. About four miles past its junction with I-90 (exit 2), cross from Lee County into Becket County, then pass a large white house called the Belden Restaurant and Tavern. Take your next right off U.S. 20, onto a small jug handle road. This rest area is 4.4 miles east of the I-90/U.S. 20 junction, and bears an historic marker sign for the town of Lee and Jacob's Ladder Trail (today called MA 20). Be sure to park on the grass island adjacent to the highway, and not on the private lawns. *DeLorme: Massachusetts Atlas & Gazetteer:* Page 33 L17

N amed for George Washington's top aide, General Charles Lee, the town of Lee was settled as an agriculture and lumber village in 1760, adding textile and paper mills along the Housatonic River by 1806. The demand for its textiles soon declined, but Lee claimed 25 paper mills by 1857. And at one point, the local Smith Paper Company was the largest in the world, fueled by the region's seemingly endless forests. But of course, the lumber supply was soon exhausted, and the mills were destroyed by a series of floods, with the largest in 1886. Still, the region rebounded, prospering through its marble quarries. Discovered by builders in 1852, premium Lee Marble was reputed to be the hardest in the world.

Today's Berkshires specialize in tourism, and boast of Tanglewood, the summer home of the Boston Symphony Orchestra, as well as outdoor theater and outlet malls.

The deep woods of October Mountain State Forest remain far away from all of this. It is the largest state forest in Massachusetts, containing over 16,000 acres and nearly 10 miles of the 2,100-mile Appalachian Trail, on which this loop begins.

October Mountain stands between the Taconic Range and the Green Mountains, and this altitude and distance inland combine to present a very different ecosystem from coastal Massachusetts. One sign of this is the Mountain Maple, which covers the slopes of Becket Mountain. The familiar five-lobed maple leaf appears to have just three lobes on this small tree, although the remaining pieces are visible if you look closely. Hop Hornbeam also grows here on the mountain slopes, with hemlock dominating in the low lands. In the lower, swampy land, puddles on the trail are filled with frogs in the spring, and toads can be found traveling between water sources.

But the balance of animals was once much different. The forest began as the estate of William C. Whitney, Grover Cleveland's Secretary of the Navy. Whitney used it for hunting,

and kept it stocked with buffalo, elk, black tailed and Virginia deer, moose, pheasants, grouse, quail, Belgian hare, and angora sheep. Local lore says that Herman Melville was the first to dub it "October Mountain," during the time he lived at Arrowhead, in Pittsfield.

Today, the forest is so large that, in addition to Lee, it spreads into three towns: Becket, Lenox, and Washington. These towns were so tough to settle that the largest industry in 18th-century Washington was charcoal making; the residents' only way to make a living was to burn the trees around them. And in 1798, times were so hard in Becket that the townspeople repealed their compulsory church tax, making all religious contributions voluntary—a practice that soon spread across the entire country.

Modern Becket and Lenox are well-known artistic centers, fly-fishing meccas, and popular spots for vacationers with second homes. In fact, Lenox was called "the inland Newport" in the 19th century, with its mansions called "Berkshire cottages." If you're sleeping here, there is a 50-site campground in the section in Lee. But be careful not to pollute; the forest is the watershed for drinking water in Pittsfield and Lee, and also drains into the Housatonic and Westfield Rivers.

Hike Information

● Trail Contacts:
October Mountain State Forest Headquarters, Lee, MA (413) 243-1778 or *www.state.ma.us/dem/parks/octm.htm* • **Appalachian Trail website:** *www.state.ma.us/dem/parks/appl.htm* – for information on the Appalachian Trail in Massachusetts

● Schedule:
Open year round

● Fees/Permits:
No fees or permits required

● Local Events/Attractions:
Lee, MA website: *www.berkshireweb.com/themap/lee/lee.html* • **Herman Melville Homestead**, Pittsfield, MA (413) 442-1793 or *www.mobydick.org*

● Accommodations:
Bucksteep Manor, Washington, MA (413) 623-5535 or *www.bucksteepmanor.com*

● Restaurants:
Juice n' Java, Lee, MA (413) 243-3131 – has sandwiches, bagels and good coffee. To get there, follow MA 20 west 5.2 miles to the center of Lee. • **Cactus Café**, Lee, MA (413) 243-4300 – for those who like Mexican food • **Angelinas's Sub Shop**, Lee, MA (413) 243-4752

● Other Resources:
Lee Chamber of Commerce, Lee, MA: *www.leechamber.org* – lists restaurants, lodging, special events, etc.
Berkshire website: *www.newberkshire.com*

● Local Outdoor Retailers:
Appalachian Mountain Gear, Great Barrington, MA (413) 528-8811 or *www.amggear.com*

● Maps:
USGS maps: East Lee, MA

MilesDirections

0.0 START at the rest area, and cross to the north side of U.S. 20, then walk east along the road (continuing away from Lee).

0.2 Turn left at a sign for the Appalachian Trail, and follow the AT's white blazes steeply uphill.

0.4 Cross an intersection with a blue-blazed vehicle trail marked S.A.M. (Snowmobile Association of Massachusetts). Soon bear left at a fork near a stream crossing, continuing to follow the white blazes along a boardwalk as you pass under a power line.

0.8 Reach the paved Becket Road (may be called Yokum Pond Road or Tyne Road on maps) and cross it, picking up the AT on the other side.

1.2 Reach the top of Becket Mountain, a wooded plateau marked by an AT log book in a wooden box, and four concrete foundations that once anchored a tower. There is also a USGS survey marker in the bedrock, and no shortage of mosquitoes. Continue

to follow the AT along this ridge, soon dropping steeply downhill.

2.2 Turn right at an intersection onto the Finerty Trail, leaving the Appalachian Trail. Then soon turn left, following a spur trail marked S.A.M. 50 yards to the shore of Finerty Pond. After enjoying the waters, backtrack on the spur trail, and turn left, heading east with the pond on your left.

2.6 Cross a wooden footbridge over a stream.

2.8 Turn right at a large intersection onto the Finerty Pond Trail (marked "95" on the S.A.M. blazes). This is a muddy, rutted two-track trail. It is unblazed, but the intersections are clearly marked with trail names and distances.

2.9 Cross a wooden footbridge.

3.0 Turn right at a T-intersection onto the Buckley Dutton Trail.

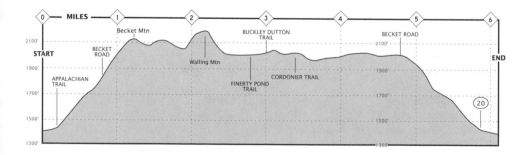

138

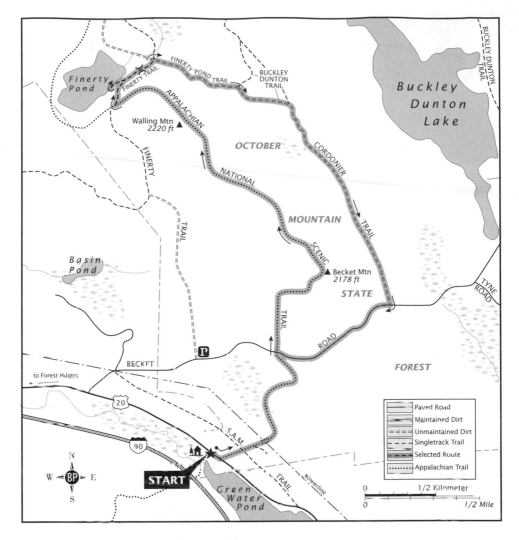

3.4 Turn right onto the Cordonier Trail. This broad-vehicle trail is deeply rutted in places, and unfortunately people have dumped trash along the way, including couches, TV sets, and hub caps.

4.8 Reach the paved Becket Road (a.k.a. Yokum Pond Road), and turn right, heading downhill.

5.3 Turn left onto the Appalachian Trail, retracing your steps from the beginning of the hike.

5.6 Cross under the power line and along the boardwalk.

5.7 Pass by an unmarked trail entering from the

left, then soon bear right at an intersection, following the white blazes steeply downhill.

5.9 Reach the paved road and turn right onto MA 20, heading west.

6.1 Reach your car.

Pittsfield State Forest

Hike Specs

Start: From the trailhead in the rest stop parking area on U.S. 20 about a mile east of the New York state line

Length: 4.2-mile loop

Approximate Hiking Time: 3 hours

Difficulty Rating: Medium, since the dirt trail can be deeply rutted in places, and demands a lot of scrambling

Trail Surface: Half of the hike is on dirt two-track trails, and half is on narrow dirt hiking paths

Lay of the Land: This loop climbs some gentle peaks before returning by a long traverse along a heavily wooded hiking trail

Land Status: MA Department of Environmental Management

Nearest Town: Pittsfield, MA

Other Trail Users: ATV riders, mountain bikers, cross-country skiers

Canine Compatibility: Dogs permitted

Getting There

From Pittsfield: Drive west on U.S. 20 (a.k.a. Housatonic Street) from its intersection with U.S. 7. Pass a sign for Pittsfield State Forest and Hungerford Street at 2.6 miles, and pass an intersection with MA 41 south at 4.3 miles. Pass the Hancock Shaker Village at 4.9 miles, then turn right at 6.8 miles into a small rest stop off of U.S. 20. Park on the side of the paved crescent road. *DeLorme: Massachusetts Atlas & Gazetteer:* Page 32 D4

S tarting at the nearby museum-village, the Hancock Shaker Trail loops through Pittsfield State Forest, marking significant spots with numbered posts. As you come over the low peak called Holy Mount, you'll reach one that reads "Sacred Lot. You are on consecrated ground. Please show respect."

This hike begins on the Griffin Trail, a broad, multi-use path marked with a sign at the start, but unblazed along its length. Like its neighbor, the Taconic Skyline Trail, it is heavily rutted with the tracks of ATV and dirt bike riders. These ruts have filled with mud, and subsequent riders have steered around them, widening the trail at several points to greater than 30 feet. The only redeeming point is that all the ruts are teeming with frogs in the spring and summer months (though they may live only long enough to see the next knobby tire roll through).

These woods also hold garter snakes and Eastern Redbacked Salamanders. But the brightest coloring surely belongs to the red eft, a neon orange salamander that lives under rotting logs. The eft is an immature form of the Eastern Newt, which begins life as a larva in a stream, spends 2–3 years as an eft, and then returns to the water as a mature aquatic newt.

From the Griffin Trail, you'll turn onto the Shaker Trail for your climb to Holy Mount—the center of the Shakers' philosophy of hard work and pure thoughts. With only the most primitive tools, they began working a marble quarry in this park in 1785, and inhabited the nearby village from as early as 1790. They used the quarried stone to help build a carding and fulling mill (for wool), a grist mill, and saw mill, all located along the banks of Shaker Brook.

In more recent years, this park housed a very different group of hard-working people. A camp of President Franklin D. Roosevelt's Civilian Conservation Corps (CCC) lived here

from 1933–41. At their peak in the state, Massachusetts had 51 camps employing 10,000 men. They set up campsites, practiced forest management, and did fire hazard reduction, pest control, wildlife enhancement, and recreational development.

After a few intersections, you'll soon pick up the Taconic Crest Trail, a quiet, idyllic path that seems far from the whines and ruts of motorbikes and four-wheelers. In contrast to those multi-use trails (a friend calls them "multi-abuse trails"), it is very faint at times, though always clearly blazed.

Pittsfield also has a proud literary history, beginning with Herman Melville's residence, Arrowhead. Now a museum and National Historic Landmark, this building where the writer

lived from 1850 to 1862 is open for tours. Melville's wealthy father bought land here in 1816, but later went bankrupt and died shortly thereafter, leaving him to search for work. The young man drifted through jobs as a bank teller, fur store clerk, and Pittsfield schoolteacher, before heading west for a surveying job and then to sea with the merchant marine. Finally, he sailed on a whaling ship out of Cape Cod. This was the beginning of his adventures, island-hopping through the South Pacific. He worked as a bowling pin setter in Hawaii and then joined the U.S. Navy until finally coming home to New England. Bursting with stories, sights, and sounds, he visited the family farm in 1850 and fell in love with the region. In the company of other literary Berkshire residents like Nathaniel Hawthorne and Oliver Wendell Holmes, he wrote Moby Dick at Arrowhead.

MilesDirections

0.0 START Walk toward the eastern end of the rest stop, and turn left through the chain link fence, immediately bearing right onto the Griffin Trail, a wide multi-use trail.

0.5 Pass by a small trail entering from your left; this is just a detour around the deep ruts and mud puddles caused by ATV traffic.

0.8 Cross North Branch Brook.

0.9 Continue uphill on Griffin as you cross an intersection with the Brook Trail. Soon the trail passes over exposed bedrock—a welcome change from the muddy ruts.

1.3 Cross Shaker Brook. A detour path has a wooden walkway here.

1.4 Turn left uphill onto a smaller, unmarked trail, the Shaker Trail. This trail is not labeled, but it's marked clearly with green triangles around white circles. For the purposes of this loop we're walking it backwards, so the markers are only visible over your shoulder.

This is a narrow path, with almost no ATV ruts.

1.6 Cross a small brook and stone wall, marked with Post #11 of the Hancock Shaker Trail.

1.8 Reach Holy Mount, covered in ferns and ancient stone works. Post #10 and #9 mark significant sites. Soon descend from Holy Mount, walking parallel to a stone wall on your left.

2.0 Bear left at an intersection in a large clearing, leaving the Shaker Trail, and joining a wide dirt path that runs parallel to another stone wall.

2.3 Pass by a wide, rutted trail that enters from your right, the Doll Mountain Trail. Then immediately turn left at a T-intersection, heading downhill. (A sign here for "Pittsfield State Forest" points in the other direction, presumably toward the park headquarters, on the northern end of the property.)

2.4 Merge right, continuing downhill and crossing a brook. Immediately after the brook, turn left

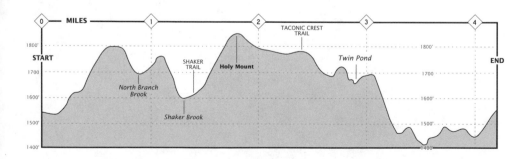

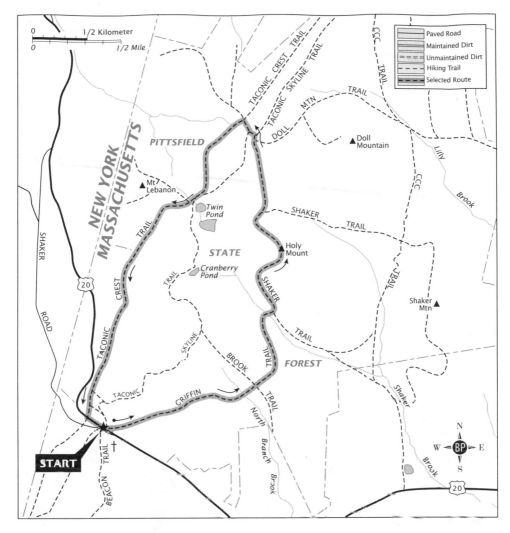

onto the white-blazed Taconic Crest Trail. This intersection is about halfway down a short slope, and is very easy to miss! *[Note. If you reach an intersection marked with a stack of rusting furniture and boards, you've gone about 50 yards too far.]*

2.8 Cross a small stream.

2.9 Reach Twin Pond and turn right, following your white blazes as the Taconic Skyline and Taconic Crest trails briefly overlap.

3.0 Turn right onto the narrow Taconic Crest Trail, heading uphill and southward. (Pass by a wider, unblazed trail here that also branches right, and heads into New York state).

3.3 Cross a small stream. Cross similar streams at 3.6 and 4.0 miles.

4.1 Bear right at a fork, still following white blazes. You can hear the traffic now from U.S. 20. Pass by several trails joining from the left, as the parking area comes into view.

4.2 Reach your car.

City of Peace

You pass Hancock Shaker Village on your way to the trailhead from the east. The Shakers called this commune their "City of Peace," and lived here from 1790 to 1960.

The Shakers, whose full name is the United Society of Believers in Christ's Second Appearing, emigrated from England to America in 1774 and established their first community in nearby Albany, NY. Their leader Ann Lee attracted so many followers that there were 19 Shaker communities by 1830, located in Connecticut, Indiana, Kentucky, Maine, Massachusetts, New Hampshire, New York, and Ohio. Today only one Shaker community remains, at Sabbathday Lake, Maine.

Shakers held all property in common and practiced pacifism, celibacy, and equality and separation of the sexes. The City of Peace is now a 1,200-acre "living history museum," with activities at any time of year, including hikes through the nearby woods, with visits to Holy Mount and Shaker Mountain, sleigh rides, archeology, crafts and livestock shows, antique shows, barn dances, auctions, harvest dinners, and a Christmas celebration.

For more information, phone (413) 443–0188 or (800) 817–1137, or check www. hancockshakervillage.org. Open daily except holidays.

Hike Information

📞 Trail Contacts:
Pittsfield State Forest, Pittsfield, MA (413) 442–8992 or *www.state.ma.us/dem/parks/pitt.htm*

🕐 Schedule:
Open year round

💲 Fees/Permits:
No fees or permits required

💡 Local Events/Attractions:
Herman Melville Homestead, MA (413) 442–1793 or *www.mobydick.org*

🏢 Organizations:
The New England Mountain Biking Association: *http://nemba.org/ma/p_Pittsfield_State_Forest.html* – sometimes has useful information on the region such as weather reports and trail conditions.

🔄 Other Resources:
Columbia Regional net: *www.regionnet.com/colberk* – offers information and resources for the greater region covering Berkshire County, Massachusetts and Columbia County, New York.

🚴 Local Outdoor Retailers:
Plaine's Bike, Ski, and Snowboard, Pittsfield, MA (413) 499–0294 or *www.plaines.com* • **Arcadian Shop Outdoor Specialty Store**, Lenox, MA 1–800–239–3391 or *www.arcadian.com* • **Berkshire Outfitters**, Adams, MA (413) 743–5900 or *www.berkshireoutfitters.com* – on MA 8 along the town line between Adams and Chesire

Ⓝ Maps:
USGS maps: Pittsfield West, MA

Savoy Mountain
State Forest

Hike Specs

Start: From Tannery Falls parking lot, off Tannery Road
Length: 7-mile loop
Approximate Hiking Time: 3.5 hours
Difficulty Rating: Difficult, due to length and steepness
Trail Surface: Wide, packed dirt, all-use trails
Lay of the Land: Climb thickly forested slopes to the wooded summit of Borden Mountain, then wind alongside Ross Brook to close the loop
Land Status: MA Department of Environmental Management
Nearest Town: North Adams, MA
Other Trail Users: Mountain bikes, ATV and dirt bike riders, snowmobilers, cross-country skiers
Canine Compatibility: Dogs permitted

Getting There

From Greenfield: At the intersection of I-91 and MA 2, follow MA 2 west to its intersection with MA 8A south, just west of Charlemont. Continue along MA 2, passing the entrance to Mohawk State Forest in 3.6 miles. Cross a bridge that veers left, and at 6.3 miles take a sharp left onto Black Brook Road, immediately before a sign that reads "Entering Town of Florida." *[Note. This turn is easy to miss, since it comes immediately before MA 2 climbs a mountain pass, and there's no road sign.]* Follow Black Brook Road as it crosses a small bridge at 6.5 miles and forks right at 7.8 miles. Turn right at 8.8 miles onto Tannery Road, crossing from pavement onto dirt. In 9.5 miles, turn right into the Tannery Falls parking lot.

If you're coming along MA 2 from the west, Black Brook Road is 2.0 miles downhill from Brown's Garage, which is opposite the giant "Caution – Steep Hill" sign at the intersection with South County Road. *DeLorme: Massachusetts Atlas & Gazetteer:* Page 21 H25

The Hoosac Range is a watershed between the Connecticut and Deerfield Rivers to the east and the Hoosic River and Berkshire Range to the west. MA 2 goes through switchback contortions as it scales these heights, culminating in the hotel and observation tower at Whitcomb Summit (on MA 2 just west of this hike).

This range is the site of one of the great engineering feats of the 19th century, the Hoosac Tunnel, carved through the mountain by the Boston & Maine Railroad so trains could pass from the steep-walled Deerfield River gorge to North Adams. At 4.8 miles, it was the longest tunnel in North America when the first train passed through in 1875, pulling 22 carloads of grain. Though it is fully 26 feet wide by 22 feet tall, air is precious underground. So the workers relied on ventilation pumps driven by Deerfield River water wheels, and a series of vertical airshafts that were drilled through 1,000 feet of rock. In the end, its plans were so precise that when the workers tunneling from each end met in the center, they were less than an inch off-target.

But the achievement came at great cost. The construction depended on the first commercial use of the famously powerful and unstable explosive nitroglycerine, and 196 workers were killed over the 20 years it took to build, earning it the nickname "the bloody pit."

In addition to reaching the top of Borden Mountain, this loop through the 10,500-acre state forest passes two points of interest: Tannery Falls (near your parked car) and Balance Rock (along your return path). You begin by following the Tannery Trail through northern hardwood forests typical of the eastern slopes of the Hoosac Range. Then the Lewis Hill Trail provides a steady climb over Lewis Hill before steeply ascending Borden Mountain. This wooded peak doesn't offer much of a view, but on a summer day the wildflower meadow around the fire tower is worth the climb on its own. You return downhill along the Balance Rock Trail, and then along the Ross Brook Trail.

As a consequence of being open to vehicles, the Tannery Trail and Balance Rock Trail are deeply rutted, with wide mud puddles that create even wider trails as hikers and bikers swerve around them. Try to be sensitive to this trend, and skirt the puddles closely to avoid making the trails even worse. There is some silver lining to the erosion, since in spring and summer these ruts are vernal pools, filled with mating frogs and salamanders. Another consequence of all this standing water is to create a tremendous population of hungry mosquitoes, so be sure to bring your favorite bug dope.

If you're staying here overnight, there are 45 campsites at South Pond, available from May to October. And at the forest's Interpretive Center, there are guided hikes, natural and cultural history walks, slide shows, games, and exhibits.

MilesDirections

0.0 START at Tannery Falls parking lot. Return to Tannery Road and turn right, heading west across a small bridge over Ross Brook, then immediately turning right onto the Tannery Trail. *[FYI. White pines and striped and mountain maples dominate this forest, along with beech and birch. Gulf Brook gurgles in the valley below.]*

1.8 Emerge from the woods at the intersection of Tannery and New State Roads, turning left to head east on Tannery Road.

1.9 Pass by an unmarked trail entering from the right.

2.1 Turn right on Lewis Hill Trail, a broad uphill path marked with several signs (though none for the trail name itself).

2.2 Reach an early 19th-century cemetery on your left, bounded with stone walls.

3.2 Cross a wide wooden boardwalk.

3.8 Turn right on the dirt Adams Road, heading west. Immediately pass by the unmarked Kamick Trail heading uphill to your left.

4.0 Turn left at a power line, passing through a metal gate and climbing steeply uphill on the paved Fire Tower Trail.

4.3 At the top of the pavement and power line, reach Borden Mountain, with its grassy meadow and fire tower. *[FYI. This clearing is a great place to stop for lunch. And you can catch a limited view southward if you walk just beyond the fire tower to the*

microwave/radio relay station.] Then retrace your steps down the paved Fire Tower Trail.

4.6 Go right on Adams Road, heading east.

4.9 Pass by the Lewis Hill Trail on your left.

5.1 Turn left, heading downhill on the Balance Rock Trail, again well-marked but not with the trail name.

5.9 Turn left, steeply downhill, on a dirt road. *[Side-trip. If you'd like to see Balance Rock, turn right instead, and reach the boulder in a quarter mile. Then return to this junction.]*

6.0 Turn right onto the narrow, blue-blazed Ross Brook Trail.

6.4 Follow the trail as it crosses Ross Brook, then crosses back again.

6.8 Cross a wooden boardwalk.

6.9 Fork left over a wooden bridge.

7.0 Cross Tannery Road and reach your car.

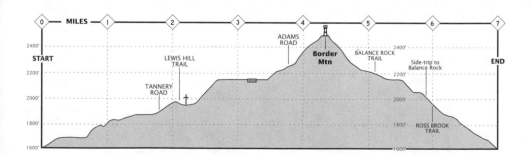

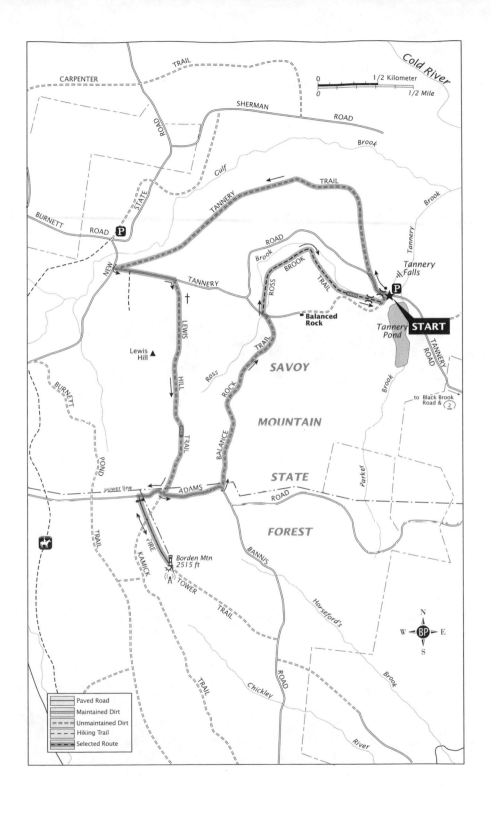

Cold River

CARPENTER

TRAIL

SHERMAN ROAD

0   1/2 Kilometer
0   1/2 Mile

Brook

BURNETT ROAD

STATE

Gulf

TANNERY

TRAIL

Brook

Brook

ROAD

BROOK

Tannery
Falls

NEW

TANNERY

ROSS

BROOK

TRAIL

P

Brook

Tannery

**Balanced
Rock**

Tannery
Pond

START

LEWIS

Lewis
Hill

Ross

ROCK

TRAIL

SAVOY

to Black Brook
Road & 2

HILL

TRAIL

BALANCE

MOUNTAIN

Brook

Parker

BURNETT

POND

power line

ADAMS

STATE

TRAIL

KAMICK

FIRE

ROAD

FOREST

Borden Mtn
2515 ft

BANNIS

Horseford's

TOWER

N
W   BP   E
S

TRAIL

Brook

TRAIL

ROAD

Chickley

River

Paved Road
Maintained Dirt
Unmaintained Dirt
Hiking Trail
Selected Route

Story of a Headstone

The cemetery along the Lewis Hill Trail tells the sad tale of 45 years in the Dunham family, early homesteaders who expressed their grief in poetry on the headstones here.

The oldest named grave belongs to James Cornell, who died Nov. 3, 1819, aged 64 years. The next is young Alfred J., son of Bradish and Candance Dunham, who died Feb. 1, 1843, aged 3 months. His headstone bears this couplet: "Short below has been thy stay/So fade the joys of earth away."

A young couple shares the next tombstone: Charles R. Dunham died Sept. 2, 1854, aged 29 years; and his wife Caroline M. died August 1, 1853, aged 26 years. The stone describes their passing thusly: "In hope they lived, in hope they died/They had no fear of death or grave/Their bodies mouldering side by side/Their spirits gone to God, who gains."

The patriarch himself, Bradish Dunham died March 18, 1862, aged 67 years. And his wife Candance died Sept. 5, 1864, also at 67.

Hike Information

☎ Trail Contacts:
Savoy Mountain State Forest Headquarters, Florida, MA (413) 663–8469 or *www.state. ma.us/dem/parks/svym.htm*

🕐 Schedule:
Open year round

💲 Fees/Permits:
No fees or permits required

❓ Local Information:
Mohawk Trail: Savoy Mountain State website: *www.berkshireweb.com/mohawktrail/ savoy.html* • **Mohawk Trail website**: *www. mohawktrail.com*

💡 Local Events/Attractions:
Mass MoCA (Museum of Contemporary Art), North Adams, MA (413) 664–4481 *www.massmoca.org* or *www.berkshireweb. com/mohawktrail/massmoca.html* – Open daily from 10 A.M. – 6 P.M., $8 admission for adults

🛏 Accommodations:
Whitcomb Summit Motel and Spa (413) 662–2625 (for information) or 1–800–547–0944 (for reservations) or *www. whitcombsummit.com – located "at the highest point on The Mohawk Trail, 2,240 feet" – there are also 45 campsites and three log cabins in the state forest.*

🍴 Restaurants:
Appalachian Bean Café, North Adams, MA (413) 663–7543 or *www.northadams.com – check out the website for more listings.*

👥 Organizations:
The Berkshire Web: *http://berkshireweb. com/mohawktrail/savoy.html – for information on everything from hikes and hotels to restaurants and realtors*

🏪 Local Outdoor Retailers:
The Mountain Goat, Williamstown, MA (413) 458–8445 or *www.northadams.com/store-front/mountaingoat* • **Berkshire Outfitters**, Adams, MA (413) 743–5900 or *www. berkshireoutfitters.com*

Ⓝ Maps:
USGS maps: Cheshire, MA

Mohawk Trail State Forest

Hike Specs

Start: From the gatehouse
Length: 2.4-mile out-and-back
Approximate Hiking Time: 1.5 hours
Difficulty Rating: Medium, due to steepness
Trail Surface: Narrow dirt trail
Lay of the Land: Traverse the shoulder of Hawks Mountain for an overview of the Deerfield River Valley
Land Status: Massachusetts Department of Environmental Management
Nearest Town: North Adams, MA
Other Trail Users: Hikers only
Canine Compatibility: Dogs permitted

Getting There

From Greenfield: Drive west on MA 2 from its intersection with I-91 (exit 26 off I-91) passing through Charlemont at 17 miles. Pass the intersection of MA 2 with MA 8A north at 17.1 miles, and with MA 8A south at 17.8 miles. Pass the main entrance to Mohawk Trail State Forest at 21.3 miles. Then at 22 miles turn right, into a state forest picnic area immediately after a sign on MA 2 reading "Leaving Pioneer Valley." This turn is easy to miss, but brown forest service buildings and a gatehouse, with scattered picnic tables, mark the picnic area. Park in the dirt lot just west of the front gate. *DeLorme: Massachusetts Atlas & Gazetteer:* Page 21 G29

Y ou know you're graduating from the Pioneer Valley to the Berkshire Hills when the road signs along MA 2 begin to read "Warning: Bear Crossing." And indeed, hikers picking up trail maps at the park headquarters here are also given pamphlets asking them to store food carefully and not to feed the bears. The literature also warns that bears are active in daylight hours, and "typically inhabit wooded wetlands, swamps, and mixed hardwood conifer forest with a dense understory adjacent to water sources." Never surprise a bear, and in an encounter, make loud noises until he goes away.

MA 2 is also known as the Mohawk Trail, since the famous Native American tribe first blazed this path. The paved automobile road was completed in 1914, constructed for a total cost of $368,000 in an effort to connect the state highway system from Boston to New York, and the west beyond. This short 12-mile section was the most challenging section to build, since it had to climb over Hoosac Mountain from Florida, near the Deerfield River, to North Adams. The task was made more difficult since the mountain was not a monolith, but had two ridges—Whitcomb Summit to the east, and Perry's Pass to the west—with an elevated valley in between. The railroad also needed to cross this range, but it did so 1,200 feet underground, through the Hoosac Tunnel.

On the north side of MA 2, there are restrooms and telephones at the picnic area where you parked, and a swimming hole in the Cold River, a tributary of the Deerfield River. Also, at forest headquarters there are five cabins and 56 tent sites. But this hike follows the Totem Trail for a quick tour of the forest's quiet, south side. The trail follows a gorgeous, fern-lined traverse along the slope, passing frequent animal scat and tracks. From your observation post on the hillside, it is easy to watch the lines of tiny cars below, carrying their canoes and kayaks to the Deerfield River. This is a popular spot for whitewater paddling, not only because of the beauty of the countryside, but because the nearby hydroelectric power station stages daily releases of flood water, creating predictable rapids.

Nearby outfitters like Zoar Outdoor rent all the gear and instruction you need to play in these waters from April through October. Zoar offers whitewater rafting, canoeing, and kayaking trips, as well as rock climbing expeditions. A favorite stretch for paddlers of all stripes is the unimpeded length of the Deerfield River that runs 17 miles from Fife Brook Dam in Florida, MA to the Number 4 dam in Buckland. Of course, the reason this water is so popular with boaters is the regular release schedule. According to Zoar, ten hydroelectric dams have operated on the river since 1974, all pumping out power for insatiable New England. Call (888) 356–3663 for a daily river level report from U.S. Generating Company, the utility that operates the hydro dams. You can even check the U.S. Geological Survey's site to see how high any Massachusetts river is running, with real-time reports. See http://water.usgs.gov/ma/nwis/rt for a state map with links to river-by-river listings.

Hike Information

● Trail Contacts:
Mohawk Trail State Forest, Charlemont, MA (413) 339–5504 or *www.state.ma.us/dem/parks/mhwk.htm*

● Schedule:
Open year round – no restricted hours for trails, but picnic area is posted 9:30 A.M. – 7:30 P.M., with a $2 parking fee.

● Fees/Permits:
No fees or permits required

● Local Information:
Williamstown, MA website: *www.williamstownchamber.com* • **Mohawk Trail website:** *www.berkshireweb.com/mohawktrail/index.html* or *www.berkshireweb.com/mohawktrail/mtsf.html*

● Accommodations:
The state forest has many **campgrounds** for rent from mid-April through mid-October, and cabins year round. Leashed pets are allowed. For rates and rules, visit the park headquarters.

● Restaurants:
Appalachian Bean Café, North Adams, MA (413) 663–7543 – *located near the Holiday Inn*

● Organizations:
Smola's Fly Fishing Guide Service, Enfield, CT (860) 763–1856 or *www.jacksmola.com* – *provides trout fishing guide service for the Deerfield, Farmington, Westfield and Swift Rivers* • **Zoar Outdoor**, Charlemont, MA 1 800 532 7483 or *www.zoaroutdoor.com*

● Local Outdoor Retailers:
Corner Sports, North Adams, MA (413) 664–8654 – *at the corner of Main and Holden streets in downtown North Adams, near the Holiday Inn*

● Maps:
USGS maps: Rowe, MA

Mass MoCA

The Massachusetts Museum of Contemporary Art—known everywhere as Mass MoCA—features displays like Tree Logic *(1999), by Australian artist Natalie Jeremijenko. The arrangement consists of six flame maple trees hung upside down from a latticework of cables strung between eight 35-foot telephone poles. Their root balls are encased in stainless steel planters and watered by a drip irrigation system.*

Open since May, 1999, the museum is an enormous renovation of a 13-acre, 27-building mill complex. The buildings were first purchased in 1872 for a dye and textile company, then sold in 1940 to an electrical component manufacturer, which went out of business in 1985. Today it's on the National Register of Historic Places. Mass MoCA, 87 Marshall Street, North Adams. Check its web site at www.massmoca.org. It's open daily from 10 A.M.–6 P.M., with admission of $8 for adults. Phone (413) 664-4481 for more information.

Two other local museums include the Sterling and Francine Clark Art Institute, 225 South St., Williamstown, (413) 458-9545, www.clark.williams.edu; and the Williams College Museum of Art, 15 Lawrence Hall Drive, Williamstown, (413) 597-2429, www.williams.edu/WCMA. Hours are Tuesday–Saturday, 10 A.M.–5 P.M., Sunday 1 P.M.–5 P.M.; free admission, wheelchair accessible.

MilesDirections

0.0 START at the gatehouse to the state forest picnic area, and carefully cross MA 2. Briefly walk east on the shoulder of the road.

0.1 At the road sign for the Pioneer Valley boundary, turn right at a trailhead marked by a stone monument with a plaque reading, "Mohawk Trail State Forest, established 1921."

0.2 Turn left as soon as you enter the woods, crossing a dry stream bed below a brown wooden pump house. Follow this trail gently uphill as it runs southeast, roughly parallel to MA 2. The path is sporadically marked with blue blazes, but is easy to follow.

0.9 Turn right at a T-intersection, heading uphill, then immediately bear left at a fork (this section of the trail splits and rejoins itself later anyway).

1.2 Emerge onto a rock outcropping that supplies a terrific view of the river below. The trail ends here, so turn around and retrace your steps downhill.

1.5 Turn left at the T-intersection.

2.3 Turn left, heading briefly west along MA 2.

2.4 Carefully cross the highway to reach your car.

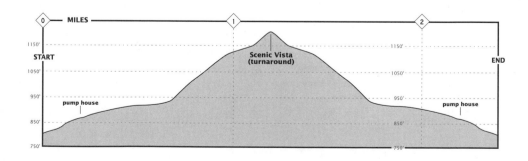

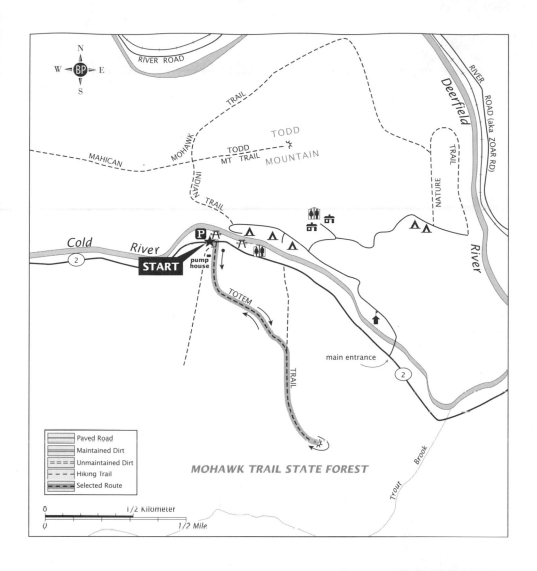

N
W—BP—E
S

RIVER ROAD

MOHAWK   TRAIL

MAHICAN

TODD
TODD   MOUNTAIN
MT   TRAIL

INDIAN   TRAIL

Deerfield

RIVER ROAD (aka ZOAR RD)

TRAIL

NATURE

River

Cold   River

2

START

P

pump
house

TOTEM

TRAIL

main entrance

2

Trout   Brook

MOHAWK TRAIL STATE FOREST

Paved Road
Maintained Dirt
Unmaintained Dirt
Hiking Trail
Selected Route

0   1/2 Kilometer
0   1/2 Mile

Monroe State Forest

Hike Specs

Start: From the trailhead at the junction of Main and North Roads

Length: 4.4-mile loop (or 5.4 miles, including the overlook spur)

Approximate Hiking Time: 3 hours

Difficulty Rating: Intermediate, with some scrambling uphill pitches

Trail Surface: Half scrambling uphill pitches and half flat, broad two-track

Lay of the Land: Northern hardwood forest on the steep slopes above the Deerfield River Valley

Land Status: MA Department of Environmental Management

Nearest Town: North Adams, MA

Other Trail Users: 4-wheel drive vehicles (on Raycroft Road), and mountain bikers on trail sections

Canine Compatibility: Dogs permitted

Getting There

From Greenfield: Find the intersection of I-91 and MA 2. Drive west on MA 2 for 18 miles to Charlemont. Continue on MA 2 for about 10 miles past the junction with MA 8A south, going up a steep mountain road. At the top, pass the Whitcomb Summit House, and in 0.9 miles, turn right on Tilda Hill Road, following signs for the town of Monroe. At 5.0 miles, turn right at a trailhead sign onto Raycroft Road (called South Road on some maps), just opposite North Road. Park on the shoulder of the dirt road there.

From North Adams: Drive east on MA 2 until you reach the Golden Eagle restaurant at the hairpin turn. Drive 2.5 miles past the restaurant and turn left onto Tilda Hill Road. At 6.6 miles, turn right at a trailhead sign onto Raycroft Road (called South Road on some maps), just opposite North Road. Park on the shoulder of the dirt road there. *DeLorme: Massachusetts Atlas & Gazetteer:* Page 21 B26

As you drive west on MA 2 from Charlemont, you'll leave the Pioneer Valley and climb a roller-coaster steep mountain pass through the Hoosac Range, with rocky cliffs so high your car radio loses reception. A series of hotels and souvenir shops boast 50-mile views from observation towers along the hairpin switchbacks, culminating at the 2,240-foot Whitcomb Summit.

Monroe State Forest is 4,321 acres of woodland that borders Vermont on its northern edge, and nestles in a bend of the Deerfield River on its southern end. The classic northern hardwood forest contains mostly birch, beech, and maple, with a smattering of hemlock, spruce, and fir. Moose prints and droppings are common, and grouse may leap up from the brush underfoot, sounding like helicopters as they frantically beat their wings. And keep an eye out for wild turkeys, which had disappeared from the region until the state released 37 birds in the Berkshires in 1972. By 1986 there were 5,000 birds, and it seems like there are many more today.

Trails were once well-marked with blue paint blazes, but these are fading and peeling off trees, so keep a close eye on your path. There are two lean-tos and many tent sites along Dunbar Brook in the park's lower, eastern half if you're looking for an overnight spot. But the park is known for its aggressive mosquito population, so be sure to bring plenty of bug dope. The falls in Dunbar Creek at the trailhead are a popular swimming hole, and may be just what you need to cool off after this loop.

Colonial settlement began here in 1750, but natives had been fishing and hunting here since 400 B.C. At a settlement where Fife Brook joins the river, they left behind flaked scraping knives and spear points made from quartzite, schist, and chert. There have been three major engineering marvels in the years since then: the Hoosac railroad tunnel in 1875, Yankee Nuclear Power Station in 1961, and the Bear Swamp "pumped storage" hydroelectric plant. The railroad tunnel is scarcely used anymore. The nuclear plant, called Yankee Rowe, shut down in 1992, and is nearly finished with a lengthy decommission process. The hydro plant is located underground in the hollowed-out mountain under the Bear Swamp Upper Reservoir, high above the river's eastern bank.

Despite its name, the town of Florida is actually one of the coldest in the state. It had a boom time in the second half of the 19th century while the railroad tunnel was constructed. This boom took its toll, as all but the most inaccessible sections of Monroe State Forest were cleared for agriculture in the 19th century, and have since been harvested at least once for timber. But the modern economy is based more on its natural splendors, specifically fly-fishing. The section of the Deerfield River that runs through here is famed for its brown, rainbow, and brook trout. Its neighbor Monroe, named for President James Monroe, was even slower to develop. Hindered by its mountainous terrain and lack of water, it relied on dairy farming. Likewise, the tunnel brought prosperity here. Modern hydroelectric plants in the Deerfield River continued the trend, and today the region is relying increasingly on the charms of its natural beauty. Canoes and kayaks on car-tops in the summer months reveal that whitewater junkies don't mind river dams, as long as they know when the water releases will create killer rapids.

MilesDirections

0.0 START at the map kiosk at the trailhead, and follow the dirt Raycroft Road, crossing a bridge over Dunbar Brook. On the other side, bear right along the road, following it into the forest.

0.2 Turn right onto the Spruce Hill Trail, a small, blue-blazed path leading steeply uphill. Be careful, as this turn is very easy to miss. After a short climb, the trail flattens out for a ridgeline walk.

1.0 Pass by an unmarked trail entering from the left. [**FYI**. This is a shortcut back to the Raycroft Road.]

1.4 Fork left at a T-intersection.

1.5 Reach Spruce Mountain, marked only by a small clearing and a fire circle. It's a wooded summit, but for a limited view, walk 20 yards to a granite outcropping to your right. Then return to your trail and follow it southeast, downhill.

1.8 [**Side-trip.** For another quick view, turn right off the trail to another outcropping about 20 yards away.]

2.7 Cross a power line, with great views to either side.

2.8 Reach an intersection with three dirt roads, and go sharp left, to head north on the dirt Raycroft Road. [**Option.** The middle road here leads in about 0.5 mile to Hunt Hill and the Raycroft Lookout, with its stone viewing platform on a cliff-side above the Deerfield River.]

2.9 Pass under the power line again.

3.2 Pass by the blue-blazed Smith Hollow Trail as it branches off to the right. Immediately pass by another trail branching off to the right.

3.3 Pass by the Raycroft Extension Road, a rough dirt two-track leading to your right.

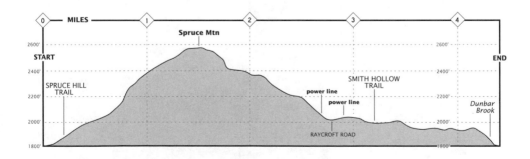

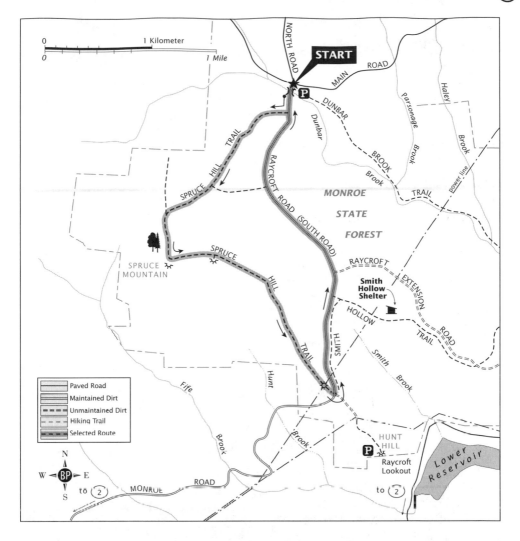

3.9 Pass by an unmarked trail entering from your left. This is the terminus of the shortcut you passed on your way up Spruce Mountain.

4.2 Pass by your original turn onto the Spruce Hill Trail, leading uphill to your left.

4.3 Cross Dunbar Brook across the wooden bridge.

4.4 Reach your car.

Local Power Supplies

This region is home to two major power plants—a hydroelectric dam and a decommissioned nuclear power plant.

The Bear Swamp Pumped Storage Facility produces 600 megawatts of power by switching water between the upper and lower reservoirs daily. Run by PG&E Generating Co., the plant fills the upper pond by night, when electricity is cheap, then releases it by day to fulfill demand. The water cascades 770 feet through tunnels within the mountain, driving two turbines. It then flows through a second plant, driving turbines at the Fife Brook dam, a comparatively small 10-megawatt station.

To reach the underground Bear Swamp Visitor Center from the trailhead, turn right onto Main Road and head west. At 1.6 miles, stay on Main Road by bearing right at an intersection with Davis Road. At 2.0 miles, turn right onto Kingsley Hill Road, bearing left at 2.4 miles. After a very steep descent, turn right at 3.3 miles onto River Road. Turn left at 5.8 miles at a sign for the visitor center. Check www.usgen.com/fact/bearswamp.html for more information.

The Yankee Nuclear Power Station was the third nuclear power plant built in the country, and the first built in New England. It operated from 1961–1992, and is now in the process of being dismantled, with various parts shipped to secure storage sites around the country. The plant is owned and operated by a consortium of 10 power companies in Maine, Massachusetts, New Hampshire, and Vermont.

There is a visitors center in Rowe, MA, with hours on Mondays and Tuesdays (or by appointment). Phone (413) 424–5498 for more information, or check http://yankee.com.

Hike Information

📞 Trail Contacts:
Monroe State Forest, Charlemont, MA (413) 339–5504 or *www.state.ma.us/dem/parks/mnro.htm*

🕐 Schedule:
Open year round

💲 Fees/Permits:
No fees or permits required

❓ Local Information:
The Mohawk Trail region website: *www.mohawktrail.com*

🍴 Accommodations:
Whitcomb Summit Motel and Spa (413) 662–2625 (for information) or 1–800–547–0944 (for reservations) or *www.whitcombsummit.com – located "at the highest point on The Mohawk Trail, 2,240 feet"; there are also 45 campsites and three log cabins in the state forest*

🍴 Restaurants:
Appalachian Bean Café, North Adams, MA (413) 663–7543 or *www.northadams.com – website has more listings*

🅡 Other Resources:
Great Outdoor Recreation Pages (GORP): *www.gorp.com/gorp/activity/byway/ma_mohaw.htm*

🏪 Local Outdoor Retailers:
The Mountain Goat, Williamstown, MA (413) 458–8445 or *www.northadams.com/storefront/mountaingoat* • **Berkshire Outfitters**, Adams, MA (on MA 8 along the town line between Adams and Chesire) (413) 743–5900 or *www.berkshireoutfitters.com*

Ⓝ Maps:
USGS maps: Rowe, MA

Midstate
TRAIL

H ow do you get from Rhode Island to New Hampshire?
If you're in Massachusetts' Worcester County, you can walk from state to state on the 92-mile Midstate Trail, completed in 1985. And there's no reason to stop once you get there—it connects on its northern end to the Wapack Trail, heading 21 miles to North Pack Mountain in Greenfield, NH; and it connects on its southern end to a planned 63-mile hiking trail to the Rhode Island seashore.

In between, the trail tours natural wonders like the autumnal hawk migration over Mount Wachusett, the path's highest point. And it passes manmade sights like the Barre Falls and Hodges Village dams, both flood control projects, not hydroelectric plants. There's plenty of peaceful walking, though of course a long-distance trail must follow some paved roads to cross an entire state. The Midstate Trail depends on a great variety of land holders, including federal land at the dams, Audubon and Boy Scout preserves, wildlife management areas and state forests, and dozens of generous private property owners. Please be respectful when passing near these homes. Leash your dog and keep your voice down, for the future of the trail depends on their largesse.

The Midstate Trail is well-blazed with yellow triangles nailed to trees at head height. Since it is a conglomeration of independently maintained sections, always remember that the trail is subject to change according to erosion, traffic, seasons, private property rights, etc. This guide gives the main landmarks and distances, but it is up to you to bring a map and compass, and to carefully follow the blazes. If you're camping overnight on the trail, there are five designated shelters: Douglas State Forest, Moose Hill, Buck Hill, Long Pond, and Muddy Pond.

There are two important guides to have if you're hiking the Midstate Trail: the Appalachian Mountain Club's Midstate Trail Guide, third edition (a 44-page pamphlet), and the AMC's Massachusetts and Rhode Island Trail Guide, seventh edition (a 370-page book, though just nine pages cover this trail). Both publications include maps. Note, however, that both these guides are written for the southbound hiker, so you may have to extrapolate some distances and directions. To buy either guide book, check with local outdoor stores, or contact the AMC at 5 Joy Street, Boston, MA, 02108. Phone (617) 523–0636. You could also phone the AMC's Worcester Chapter at (508) 797–9744. Always hike with a map; for the Midstate Trail, I rely on *DeLorme's Massachusetts Atlas and Gazetteer*.

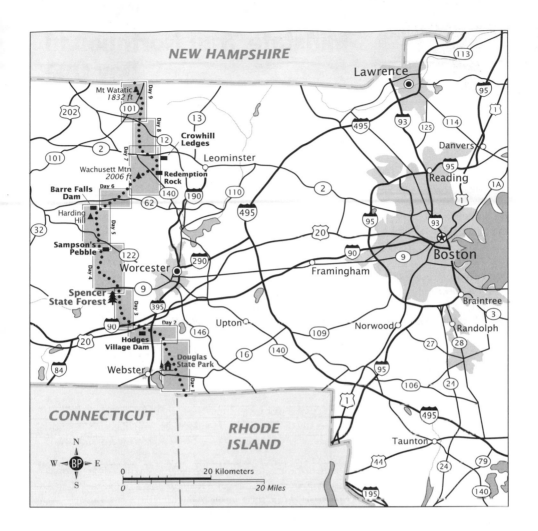

The Hikes

Midstate Trail Northbound
Day One

Hike Specs

Start: Southwest Main Street, in Douglas State Forest

Length: 8.0 miles one way

Approximate Hiking Time: 3.5 hours

Difficulty Rating: Easy and mostly flat

Trail Surface: Broad, sandy, two-track dirt paths

Lay of the Land: Cedars and hemlock fill this swampy, sandy land, which drains into ponds and reservoirs

Nearest Town: Webster, MA

Other Trail Users: Mountain bikers, cross-country skiers, and equestrians

Canine Compatibility: Dog friendly

Getting There

From Worcester: Take I-395 south to exit 2. Drive east on MA 16 (a.k.a. Webster Street) for about five miles, and turn right onto Cedar Street at signs for the forest entrance. In one mile, turn right onto Southwest Main Street, and follow this gravel road about two miles to a wooden Midstate Trail sign.

Alternatively, you could continue on Cedar Street until you reach the park's main entrance and nature center, located on Wallum Lake. There are picnic tables, map kiosks, park rangers, and a boat launching ramp here. *DeLorme: Massachusetts Atlas & Gazetteer:* Page 50 M8

The sandy flats of southern Massachusetts don't provide the climbs or views of the mountainous north, but Douglas State Forest offers more solitude than you'll find anywhere else on the trail.

Douglas State Forest is a 5,000-acre plot wedged into the corner of three state borders—Massachusetts, Connecticut, and Rhode Island. The 92-mile Midstate Trail begins its northward trek here, at a granite monument on the border between Massachusetts and Rhode Island.

But this hike begins just north of the line, since there is no parking area directly at the trail's southern terminus. If you'd like to start this long-distance trail with one foot in Rhode Island, you can hike the 3.5 miles southbound first, then double back.

For more details about the region, see this book's Whitin Reservoir hike (Hike 21), also in Douglas State Forest. That loop circles through the park's northern end, above MA 16.

Hike Information

Trail Contacts:
MA Dept. of Environmental Management, Douglas, MA, (508) 476–7872. *www.state. ma.us/dem/parks/doug.htm*

Schedule:
The picnic area at the main entrance is open 10 A.M. to 8 PM.

Fees/Permits:
No fees or permits required

Local Information:
Local town web sites are *www.douglas.ma.us* and *www.magnet.state.ma.us/cc/webster. html*

Organizations:
Midstate Trail Association, *www.midstate trail.org/index.htm*

Maps:
USGS maps: Webster, MA

MilesDirections

0.0 START on Southwest Main Street and head north, following the yellow triangles.

1.5 The trail merges with two broad paths from the east, as you continue following the yellow blazes.

1.9 Cross the paved MA 16 (a.k.a. Webster Street). This is the same trailhead as the Douglas State Forest loop (Hike 21) in this book, and is also a point you passed in your car, a mere 4.25 miles east of I-395.

4.0 Cross a wooden bridge, ignoring the blue blazes. Shortly thereafter, cross two junctions with logging roads.

4.7 Trace the shore of Whitin Reservoir, on your right, and soon continue eastward on a gravel road.

4.9 Pass through a metal gate as you leave the state forest.

5.4 Merge onto a rocky road and soon pass behind a private home.

6.0 Reach a junction with Northwest Main Street and follow it, heading northwest.

7.1 Bear right onto Douglas Road. [**Note**. Be careful, the left fork is also called Douglas Road.]

7.5 Pass by Waters Road on your right.

8.0 Reach Central Turnpike (a.k.a. Sutton Avenue) at West Sutton.

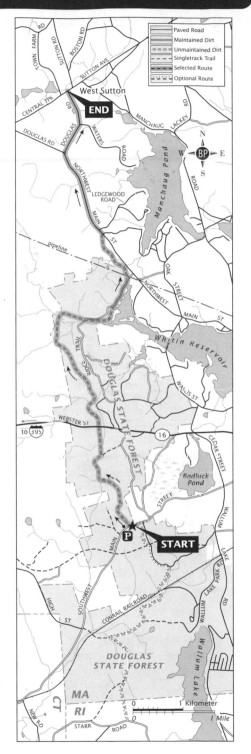

Midstate Trail Northbound
Day Two

Hike Specs

Start: Central Turnpike in West Sutton
Length: 11.6 miles one way
Approximate Hiking Time: 5 hours
Difficulty Rating: Easy, with minimal elevation change
Trail Surface: Mixture of dirt, gravel, and paved roads
Lay of the Land: Pass through the French River Basin on flat roads
Nearest Town: Webster, MA
Other Trail Users: Non-motorized use only: mountain bikers, cross country skiers, and equestrians
Canine Compatibility: Dog-friendly

Getting There

From Worcester: Take I-395 south to exit 4. Head east on Sutton Avenue (a.k.a. Central Turnpike), toward Sutton, not Oxford. In 3.2 miles reach West Sutton, where you'll park. The trail heads north on Town Farm Road, on your left.
DeLorme: Massachusetts Atlas & Gazetteer: Page 50 I8

T his stretch of the Midstate Trail is fairly urban, crossing I-395, coming through the town of Oxford, and passing along the spillway of the U.S. Army Corps of Engineers' Hodges Village Dam, which is on the French River.

The Army Corps of Engineers says Hodges Village Dam's 1,200 acres are filled with upland hardwoods, red oak, white oak, and hickory. The federal government manages the land for flood control, wildlife habitat, forest production, watershed protection, and outdoor recreation. In the autumn there is hunting on this land, but it is allowed only on the west side of the French River.

Hike Information

Trail Contacts:
Midstate Trail Association, *www.midstate trail.org/index.htm*

Schedule:
Open year round

Fees/Permits:
No fees or permits required

Local Information:
Buffumville Lake and Hodges Village Dam, P. O. Box 155, Oxford, MA 01540; phone (508) 248–5697 • **Nearest Army Corps of Engineers office:** New England District, 696 Virginia Road, Concord, MA 01742-2751

Accommodations:
The Webster KOA is open 4/15 to 10/15: (508) 943–1895 or try *www.koa.com/where/ma/21112.htm*

Local Outdoor Retailers:
Bolio Sporting Goods, 131 Main St., Webster, MA (508) 943–8007 • **Bert's Outdoor Store**, 9 E Main St., Webster, MA (508) 943–3335 • **Home Court Athletic Supply**, 2 Millbury Blvd., Oxford, MA (508) 987–3870

Maps:
USGS maps: Webster, MA

The nearby Buffumville Lake Project is a double reservoir resulting from the flood control dams. Bisected by Putnam Road, the north pond is 265 acres, and the south 186 acres. Both are shallow, averaging about six feet deep.

MilesDirections

0.0 START on Central Turnpike (a.k.a. Sutton Ave.) in West Sutton. Head north on the paved Town Farm Road.

0.9 Turn left on a dirt road, heading west.

1.5 Continue following blazes along a badly eroded, rocky road.

1.8 Cross a stone bridge over a stream, then two more.

2.2 Cross through a cable gate onto Lovett Road, with Sacarrappa Pond (a.k.a. Slaters Pond) on your left.

2.8 Pass the paved Sacarrappa Road on your left.

3.1 Turn right onto Brown Road, heading north.

4.4 Turn left onto Dana Road, heading west.

4.8 Cross under I-395, following Dana Road.

5.0 Cross over railroad tracks.

5.2 Turn right on MA 12 (a.k.a. Main Street), then immediately turn left onto Rocky Hill Road, heading west.

5.8 Cross onto wide dirt trail. This path alternates between dirt and gravel footing for the next three-quarters of a mile.

7.0 Cross a log boom, then cross the spillway base of the Hodges Village Dam and the French River.

8.2 The trail changes to the gravel-surfaced Trap Rock Road.

8.3 Back onto the trail.

8.6 Turn left onto Old Charlton Road, heading west.

9.5 Pass Conlin Road on your left (Old Charlton Road is also known as Buffum Road).

10.1 Turn left onto Turner Road, and pass over the Little River as it flows southward toward Buffumville Lake. Shortly thereafter come onto a dirt road.

10.6 Pass under a power line.

11.3 Come onto a gravel road, which soon becomes paved.

11.5 Trail becomes a dirt road.

11.6 Cross under MA 20 through a tunnel, between Charlton and Richardson Corners.

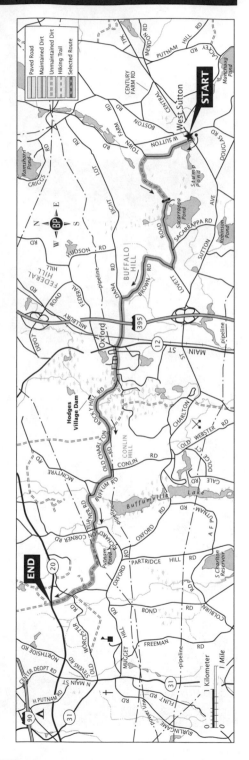

Midstate Trail Northbound Day Three

33

Hike Specs

Start: MA 20 near Charlton
Length: 11.0 miles one way
Approximate Hiking Time: 5 hours
Difficulty Rating: Moderate, alternating between swamp land and rolling hills
Trail Surface: Variable, including narrow hiking paths, broad logging roads, gravel and pavement
Lay of the Land: This region is full of swamps and small ponds, all draining toward Quabbin Rerservoir, just to the west
Nearest Town: Charlton, MA
Other Trail Users: Snowmobilers and cross-country skiers
Canine Compatibility: Dog friendly

Getting There

From Worcester: Take MA 20 west. Cross MA 56, and in three miles turn left onto Old Worcester Road. At mile 3.1, turn left and park on the shoulder. *DeLorme: Massachusetts Atlas & Gazetteer:* Page 49 G29

T his section of trail alternates between pavement and swamp land as it winds between ponds and crosses two major state highways.

Beginning on MA 20 between the rural neighborhoods of Charlton and Richardson Corners, it crosses the busy Mass Pike (I-90), then returns to more rural surroundings in the Four Chimneys Wildlife Management Area. Continuing northward, it crosses briefly through 965-acre Spencer State Forest, passing just west of Stiles Reservoir, and just north of Burncoat Pond. This section finally passes through Audubon land before reaching MA 9.

MilesDirections

0.0 START by passing under MA 20, walking north on paved Carroll Hill Road.

0.4 Follow the yellow blazes onto an old logging road, which soon runs by an abandoned factory, then a pipeline.

1.6 Merge onto paved Northside Road, which soon passes over the Mass Turnpike (I-90).

2.1 Turn left onto paved Leicester Turnpike (a.k.a. Stafford Street), then immediately turn right, heading north on paved Cemetery Road.

2.8 Bear right onto Gould Road and continue north, passing a campground on your right.

3.1 Cross a railroad bridge and follow Gould Road as it bends east.

3.3 Turn left, to begin following a pipeline.

4.0 Cross Borkum Road and climb Long Hill, entering Four Chimneys Wildlife Management Area.

4.6 Cross a pipeline on top of a hill.

4.9 Pass through a metal gate and turn left on the gravel Borkum Road, heading north and leaving Four Chimneys.

5.4 Turn left onto paved Clark Road, heading west.

5.5 Turn right onto paved East Charlton Road, heading north.

6.5 Pass by the junction with Marble Road, then turn right onto paved G.H. Wilson Road.

6.6 Turn left onto hiking trail, heading north and crossing several logging trails, passing briefly through Spencer State Forest.

7.9 Cross Jones Road, then carefully follow yellow blazes as you wind through Morgan Swamp.

9.1 Turn left on paved Greenville Street, then immediately right onto a woods path and climb a hill.

10.0 Enter Audubon land.

10.4 Descend the hill and cross a boardwalk as you skirt the northern edge of Burncoat Pond.

10.7 Leave Audubon land.

11.0 Reach MA 9, between its intersection with Bond and Watson streets in Spencer. This spot is just east of Tafts Corner.

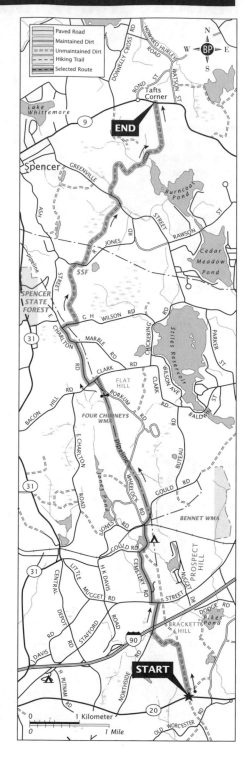

Hike Information

📞 **Trail Contacts:**
Spencer State Forest, Howe Pond Road, Spencer, MA. (508) 886–6333

🕐 **Schedule:**
Open year round

💲 **Fees/Permits:**
No fees or permits required

🎒 **Local Outdoor Retailers:**
Sports Store, 105 Masonic Home Road, Charlton, MA (508) 248–0800

Ⓝ **Maps:**
USGS maps: Worcester South, MA

Midstate Trail Northbound Day Four

Hike Specs

Start: From the courthouse on MA 9, just east of Tafts Corner

Length: 12.5 miles one way

Approximate Hiking Time: 5 hours

Difficulty Rating: Strenuous, with many rolling hills and stream crossings

Trail Surface: Alternating between marshy footpaths, steep hilltop scrambles, and gravel and paved roads

Lay of the Land: Marshy land full of glacial features like morrains and erratics

Nearest Town: Spencer, MA

Other Trail Users: Various

Canine Compatibility: Dog-friendly

Getting There

From Worcester: Go west on MA 9. About four miles after its intersection with MA 56 in Leicester, look for an abandoned courthouse across the street from the Spencer Country Inn (500 Main Street, Spencer). Park in the courthouse lot. *DeLorme: Massachusetts Atlas & Gazetteer:* Page 37 O28

Passing through a patchwork quilt of public land, you curve between ponds and reservoirs, cross the Midstate Trail's halfway point (about 46 miles to the state line, either north or south) near the end of this segment.

The section starts on MA 9 between its intersection with Bond and Watson Streets, just east of Tafts Corner. You first pass though 632-acre Moose Hill Wildlife Management Area and over Moose Hill itself, with great views of Sugdens (a.k.a. Moose Hill) Reservoir. Pass just east of Spencer Airport, and then cut through a corner of the 965-acre Spencer State Forest. This brings you to Buck Hill Reserve's four self-guided nature trails, including ecology and wildflower paths with views of Thompson Pond. Then pass along 89-acre Browning Pond (maximum depth 42 feet) before reaching Samson's Pebble, an enormous glacial erratic. Finally, enter the Boy Scout's Treasure Valley Scout Reservation, maintained by Troop 126 in Leicester, MA, before walking through a section of Oakham State Forest, where you pass the Midstate Trail's halfway sign, just half a mile shy of your end point.

Hike Information

Trail Contacts:
Spencer State Forest, Howe Pond Road, Spencer, MA (508) 886–6333

Schedule:
Open year round

Fees/Permits:
No fees or permits required

Accommodations:
Spencer Country Inn, 500 Main Street, Spencer, MA (508) 885–9036

Maps:
USGS maps: Worcester North, MA

MilesDirections

0.0 START at the courthouse lot and walk east on MA 9 about 100 yards, turning left at yellow blazes to head north along the footpath.

1.0 Cross gravel Bond Street and climb steeply.

1.7 Cross Howard Hurley Road.

2.2 Cross a dam, then cross Moose Hill Road. Shortly thereafter, turn right on Donnelly Cross Road, then immediately turn left onto the footpath, entering the Moose Hill Wildlife Management Area.

2.6 Cross over the top of Moose Hill.

3.8 Crossing several streams, pass just east of the Spencer Airport (1,040 feet elevation).

4.4 Cross paved Paxton Road, then shortly thereafter enter Spencer State Forest and begin climbing.

5.6 Cross Turkey Hill Brook on concrete bridge, then climb again.

6.1 Reach open shelter at Buck Hill, then walk along the Buck Hill Reserve's ecology and wildflower trails.

6.7 Cross paved McCormack Road.

7.8 Turn left on Thompson Pond Road and cross MA 31 (a.k.a. North Spencer Road) in North Spencer. Continue on this street, now called Browning Pond Road.

8.0 Turn right onto a hiking path.

8.5 Turn left onto gravel Browning Pond Lane.

8.6 Turn right onto Browning Pond Road.

8.8 Turn right onto a woods trail, and pass along the shore of Browning Pond.

10.0 Pass Sampson's Pebble, and soon enter Boy Scout land.

11.5 Cross a log bridge, then walk under a power line.

12.0 Reach the Midstate Trail's halfway sign.

12.5 Reach dirt East Hill Road, and leave Boy Scout land. This is the end of day four.

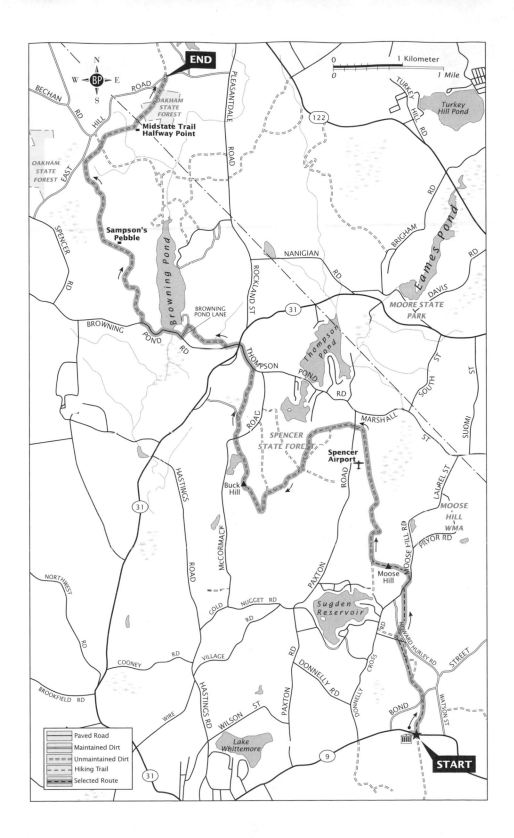

Midstate Trail Northbound
Day Five

Hike Specs

Start: East Hill Road, just south of Long Pond
Length: 7.8 miles one way
Approximate Hiking Time: 3 hours
Difficulty Rating: Easy and flat
Trail Surface: Wide dirt paths and roads
Lay of the Land: Winding through low-lying ponds and marsh lands
Nearest City: Worcester, MA
Other Trail Users: Various
Canine Compatibility: Dog-friendly

Getting There

From Worcester: Take MA 122 west to its intersection with MA 31 in Paxton. Continue on MA 122 about four miles, crossing the town line into Rutland, then turn left onto Pleasantdale Road. At 4.5 miles, turn right onto the dirt East Hill Road, which intersects the Midstate Trail at 5.5 miles. *DeLorme: Massachusetts Atlas & Gazetteer:* Page 37 J26

This hike begins near the Long Pond lean-to shelter then proceeds into 300-acre Rutland State Park, skirts the western edge of Blood Swamp, crosses busy MA 122, and finally reaches Barre Falls Dam.

Long Pond actually comprises three ponds—an 81-acre southern pond with a maximum depth of 25 feet, a much shallower middle pond (just a couple feet deep), and the 30-acre north pond, which is shallow and weedy like the middle one—bisected by MA 122. The Mass Department of Fish and Wildlife recently counted 13 species of fish in these ponds: largemouth and smallmouth bass, chain pickerel, yellow perch, white perch, black crappie, bluegill, pumpkinseed, rockbass, brown bullheads, white suckers, golden shiners, and rainbow trout (stocked).

MilesDirections

0.0 START on East Hill Road and head north on a hiking trail.

0.1 Cross a dirt road near the shore of Long Pond.

0.5 Reach a lean-to shelter, then climb steeply as you continue north on a wide path.

1.5 Cross paved Crawford Street and soon enter Rutland State Park.

2.1 Cross MA 122, carefully!

2.7 Cross Whitehall Road.

4.1 Pass through a metal gate, then under a power line.

4.5 Cross over Dike #3 and Stevens Brook.

6.5 Cross Blake Road.

7.8 Reach Barre Falls Dam, which makes a nice stopping point for day five.

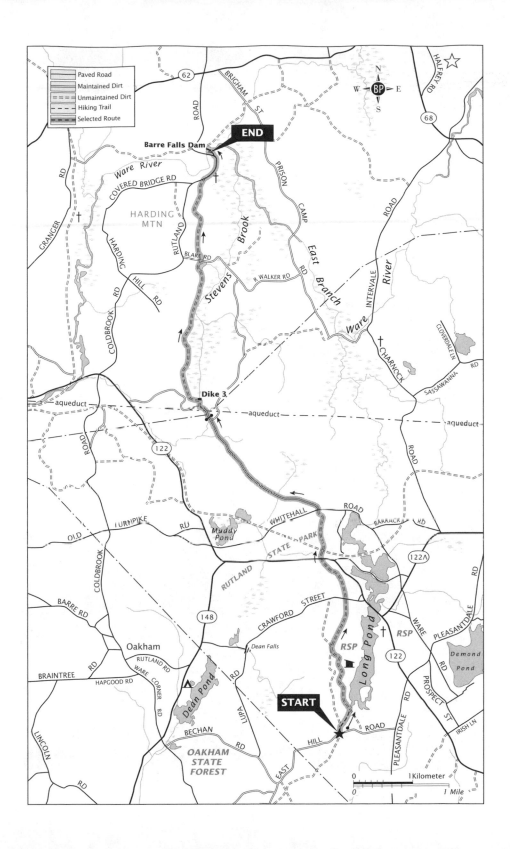

Paved Road
Maintained Dirt
Unmaintained Dirt
Hiking Trail
Selected Route

62
68
HALFREY RD

N
W — BP — E
S

Barre Falls Dam
END

Ware River
COVERED BRIDGE RD

GRANGER RD
HARDING MTN

COLDBROOK RD
HARDING HILL RD

RUTLAND RD
BLAKE RD
R. WALKER RD

Stevens Brook

PRISON CAMP RD

East Branch

Ware River
INTERVALE RD

CHARNOCK

CLOVERDALE LN

SASSAWANNA RD

aqueduct
Dike 3
aqueduct
aqueduct

122

ROAD

OLD TURNPIKE RD

Muddy Pond

WHITEHALL ROAD

BARRACK RD

STATE PARK

122A

COLDBROOK

RUTLAND

148

BARRE RD

CRAWFORD STREET

Long Pond

WARE RD

PLEASANTDALE RD

122A

RD

Oakham
Dean Falls
RSP

RSP
Demond Pond

BRAINTREE RD
RUTLAND RD
WARE CORNER RD
HAPGOOD RD

LUPA RD

122

PROSPECT ST

IRISH LN

Dean Pond

START

HILL ROAD

PLEASANTDALE RD

LINCOLN RD

BECHAN RD

EAST

OAKHAM STATE FOREST

0   1 Kilometer
0   1 Mile

Hike Information

☎ Trail Contacts:
Rutland State Park, MA 112A, Rutland, MA (508) 886–6333, *www.state.ma.us/dem/parks/rtld.htm*

🕐 Schedule:
Barre Falls Dam park hours are sunrise to sunset

💲 Fees/Permits:
No fees or permits required

🌐 Local Outdoor Retailers:
Eastern Mountain Sports, 7 Neponset Street, Worcester, MA (508) 856–9606

Ⓝ Maps:
USGS maps: Worcester North, MA

Midstate Trail Northbound Day Six

Hike Specs

Start: Barre Falls Dam

Length: 8.3 miles one way

Approximate Hiking Time: 3 hours

Difficulty Rating: Moderate, with narrow scrambly trails but without much elevation change

Trail Surface: Dirt footpaths

Lay of the Land: Thick forest in the Ware River valley drainage

Nearest Town: Hubbardston, MA

Other Trail Users: Mountain bikers and snowmobilers

Canine Compatibility: Dog friendly

Getting There

From Leominster: Follow MA 2 west to exit 22, for MA 68 south, Gardner, and Hubbardston. Circle a rotary to follow MA 68 south. At 0.5 miles, cross MA 2A. At 6.8 miles, pass a white church in the center of Hubbardston. At 9.4 miles, turn right at a flashing yellow light onto MA 62 west. At 11.7 miles turn left onto Barre Road, at signs for the Barre Falls Dam Picnic Area and U.S. Army Corps of Engineers. Pass a scenic overlook area at 12.3 miles, then cross the dam and park at 12.8 miles. *DeLorme: Massachusetts Atlas & Gazetteer:* Page 37 E24

This hike begins along the Ware River, then wanders through thick forest in somewhat higher ground. This is a tricky section of trail since it includes a large zig-zag, heading south for nearly a mile even as you continue to move north overall. At the point where it crosses Intervale Road, there is even a trail sign pointing north and south, but the sign is correct by the compass only — to continue toward the New Hampshire border, you head "south." The route continues on dirt roads to Audubon's Wachusett Meadow Wildlife Sanctuary in Princeton.

Barre Falls Dam is a flood control reservoir for the Ware River. With normal water levels, the river flows right through it, so there is no lake visible. The U.S. Army Corps of Engineers completed it in 1958 at a cost of about $2 million. Its 885-foot length and 62-foot height give it a capacity of 7.9 billion gallons.

Today there are many bluebird boxes in the floodplain below the dam. At the trailhead, the parking area at the dam has restrooms, roofed picnic tables, and a map kiosk. But be careful; there is hunting in these woods from the Saturday after Columbus Day to the Saturday after Thanksgiving. Also, a deep snow pack can linger in these woods long into March, making the trail impassable unless you have snowshoes or backcountry skis.

Just shy of reaching Davis Street, hikers must take care to follow the trail carefully, since hungry beavers here have recently felled some trees with the Midstate Trail's yellow triangle blazes. Soon afterwards, you'll cross the busy MA 68, then skirt the southern edge of the 875-acre Savage Hill Wildlife Management Area. The hike ends at Wachusett Meadow Wildlife Sanctuary, which means you cannot bring a dog. But you'll see plenty of animals, both those living naturally in the sanctuary, and also the herd of sheep that often graze around sanctuary headquarters. There are restrooms, trail maps, and a natural history center at Wachusett Meadows. And the Audubon Sanctuary organizes hawk watching during the annual fall migration.

MilesDirections

0.0 START from your car at Barre Falls Dam.

0.1 Cross the dam, passing a three-story concrete tower and the white park office building, and then a bridge over a dry, concrete-walled canal.

0.2 Turn right immediately after the bridge, leaving the pavement and picking up the yellow Midstate Trail blazes. Walk parallel to a waist-high chain link fence along the canal bank.

0.3 Cross a small stream in a thick white pine forest.

0.4 Turn right on a dirt road, with views of the Ware River at your feet and the dam towering above your head.

0.5 Fork left. Several trails branch off, but stay on the main road.

0.9 Turn right at a T-intersection onto another dirt road (Brigham Road), and cross a wooden automobile bridge over the river. Then immediately turn left, passing through a yellow, metal gate onto a two-track jeep road. Proceed uphill, through a clearing between parallel stone walls.

1.3 Crest a ridge and continue straight over it. After a gentle decent, veer right onto a narrow woods trail, following blazes and shortly thereafter beginning to climb.

1.4 Turn right at a T-intersection between more stone walls, passing through a thick growth of ferns.

1.6 Cross a wide trail, continuing on your blazed path and soon passing through a birch grove.

1.7 Pass a rock pile on your left with grapefruit-sized stones stacked as high as a small car. Follow the blazes carefully as the trail winds through thick woods.

2.3 Cross a stream as you pass through a hemlock grove and skirt a steep hillside on your left.

3.3 Cross the paved Intervale Road, with its deceptive trail sign. To continue toward New Hampshire, follow the "south" arrow.

3.6 Cross two more streams and a stone wall.

3.7 Turn left where the trail meets the East Branch of the Ware River, heading upstream. The trail runs parallel between the river and Intervale Road.

3.8 Pass a dirt road on your left, which leads to the nearby Intervale Road.

3.9 Turn right on MA 68 at its intersection with Intervale Road, crossing a bridge over the river. Turn right again immediately after the bridge, onto Davis Street. Head uphill on the paved Davis Street, away from MA 68.

4.3 Turn right off the pavement onto a wide woods trail, and immediately take a left fork.

4.5 Leave the woods and cross paved MA 56, onto Bushy Lane.

4.6 Cross paved MA 68, continuing on Bushy Lane, which is now dirt.

4.9 Cross paved Paddock Road on a diagonal, continuing on Bushy Lane.

5.6 Continue straight ahead onto a wide woods road.

6.1 Emerge onto the dirt Bigelow Road.

6.8 Bear right at a T-intersection onto paved Hubardston Road, passing a cemetery on your left.

7.1 Turn left at a T-intersection onto Ball Hill Road (Wheeler Road ends here), passing under a railroad bridge marked "Providence and Worcester RR."

7.2 Cross a brook.

7.5 Turn right onto MA 62, cross the street, and immediately turn left onto a dirt road, entering the Audubon Sanctuary. Immediately turn left onto a narrow hiking path.

7.6 Bear right at a fork, onto Fern Forest Trail.

7.9 Pass a pond and viewing bench on your left.

8.1 Pass the intersection with Beaver Bend Trail.

8.2 Turn right on the two-track Beaver Bend Trail. The Midstate Trail branches left here, but you'll continue through a metal gate for a brief spur to the sanctuary headquarters.

8.3 Reach Audubon parking lot and buildings, with restrooms, free maps, and natural history displays.

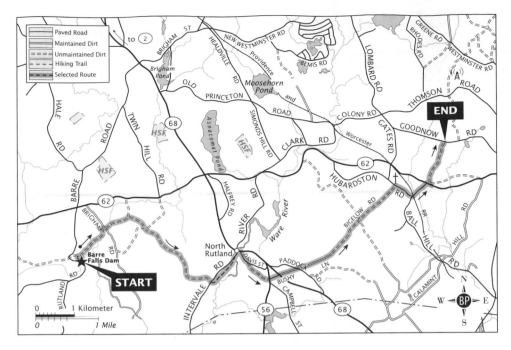

Hike Information

📞 Trail Contacts:
Barre Falls Dam, Project Office; phone (978) 928-4712

🕐 Schedule:
Barre Falls Dam park hours are sunrise to sunset

💲 Fees/Permits:
No fees or permits required

❓ Local Information:
Wachusett Meadow Wildlife Sanctuary, 113 Goodnow Road, Princeton, MA (978) 464-2712, *www.massaudubon.org/Nature_Connection/Sanctuaries/Wachusett_Meadow /index.html*

💡 Local Events/Attractions:
Apples, honey, and Christmas trees are for sale at private homes throughout this country

🎒 Local Outdoor Retailers:
Olympia Sports, Timpany Plaza Mall, on MA 68 0.6 miles south of MA 2.

📍 Maps:
USGS maps: Sterling, MA

Midstate Trail Northbound
Day Seven

Hike Specs

Start: From the Visitors Center at Wachusett Meadow Wildlife Sanctuary

Length: 8.5 miles one way

Approximate Hiking Time: 3 hours

Difficulty Rating: Intermediate, due to some steep sections on Mount Wachusett

Trail Surface: Dirt hiking trails, with some sections very rocky

Lay of the Land: Streams and stone walls cut through the flat, quiet sanctuary woods before the trail climbs steeply around the crowded shoulders of Mount Wachusett

Nearest Town: Princeton, MA

Other Trail Users: Only hikers are allowed on trails in Audubon sanctuaries, but you may find skiers and mountain bikers at Mount Wachusett State Reservation.

Canine Compatibility: There are no pets allowed in Audubon's sanctuaries, where this hike begins, but there are many dogs at Mount Wachusett State Reservation.

Getting There

From Leominster: Head west on MA 2 to exit 28 (Fitchburg and Princeton, MA 31). Head south on MA 31 through Leominster State Forest, and at 3.9 miles turn left at a blinking red light, continuing south on the combined MA 31 and MA 140. At 5.5 miles turn right on MA 31, a.k.a. Princeton Road, at a blinking yellow light, then right again at 8.1 miles onto the combined MA 31 and MA 62 west. At 8.4 miles, bear right through the blinking yellow light at Princeton Center, to continue on MA 62 west, a.k.a. Hubbardston Road. Pass the gazebo on the town green. At 9.0 miles turn right onto Goodnow Road. The Wildlife Sanctuary's parking lot is on the left in one mile.

DeLorme: Massachusetts Atlas & Gazetteer: Page 38 C1

Your reward at the middle of this hike is the sign in the parking lot at Mount Wachusett ski area: "Midstate Trail: New Hampshire 23 miles, Rhode Island 69 miles. Follow the yellow triangles." That sign sums up the Midstate Trail experience perfectly. Both ambitious and user-friendly, the trail leads hikers carefully through woods, between parks, across roads, and around ponds, all the while heading northward to Mount Watatic and the state border just beyond.

This section of the Midstate Trail climbs from the pristine Audubon Sanctuary up the steep shoulders of Mount Wachusett, with its crowds, cars, and frequent festivals at the ski area's base lodge. But the mountain also has great beauty, like the garter snakes that awaken in these woods each spring, and the dozens of tall, silent windmills on the mountain's flank.

After descending to the ski area parking lot, you head north, meandering through the city of Fitchburg's watershed land, to historic Redemption Rock, a quarter-acre historic site managed by the Trustees of Reservations. It marks the spot where an early Concord settler negotiated with Native Americans for the release of a kidnapped minister's wife during King Phillip's War in 1676, the bloody, last-gasp struggle by Native Americans against the pilgrims and settlers who were taking over their land.

Next, the trail climbs over the steep Crow Hill Ledges of Leominster State Forest. Rock climbers love the ledges for their steep exposed faces. And hikers love the ledges for their views of Crow Hill Pond and Crocker Pond just below, and glimpses of distant Boston far to the east. But it provides funny moments when the two meet, as hikers who stop to snack at cliff's edge can be suddenly joined by a helmeted head climbing up at their feet! This segment ends at Wyman Road, immediately off exit 26 of MA 2.

MilesDirections

0.0 START in the sanctuary parking lot and turn left to head west on the paved Goodnow Road.

0.1 Pass through a metal gate as the pavement changes to dirt, and immediately turn right, onto the Midstate Trail, blazed with yellow triangles (you can ignore the sanctuary's blazes, which are blue for trails leading away from the visitors center, yellow heading back, and white for connecting trails).

0.3 Turn left at a T-intersection, following a sign for "Chapman Trail, toward Glacial Boulder Trail."

0.4 Come through another stone wall and cross an intersection to continue on the Chapman Trail.

0.7 Bear right to continue northeast along the Chapman Trail, as the West Border Trail enters from your left.

0.8 Cross the paved Thompson Road, immediately passing Black Pond on the other side, and crossing a wooden footbridge over the stream that drains from it.

1.1 Pass the sanctuary boundary at a stone wall, marked by a small post marked #28 and a sign for the Midstate and Dickens trails.

1.4 Come through a metal gate, crossing the paved Westminster Road, and pick up the Harrington Trail/Midstate Trail on the other side, soon climbing through an open clearing.

1.5 Cross a stone wall and turn left at the top of the clearing, to continue following the yellow triangles along a broad, two-track trail. [*FYI. A trail on your right marked "To Windmills" is a spur that leads in 0.25-mile to a field of whining, spinning windmills with white, propeller-like blades.*]

1.6 Follow the blazes as the trail bears right.

1.7 Continue along the Harrington Trail as the Stage Coach Trail leads off to the right.

1.9 Cross a small wooden footbridge over West Wachusett Brook, then cross the dirt West Road and continue along Harrington.

2.1 Cross the paved Administration Road and continue on Harrington, soon crossing two wooden footbridges and a passing by a junction with the Lower Link Trail.

2.3 At the top of a steep climb, turn left onto Semuhenna Trail.

2.7 Cross the paved Summit Road and bear left onto Semuhenna/Westside Trail, then immediately right onto Semuhenna.

2.9 Cross Summit Road again.

3.2 Merge left at a T-intersection onto Old Indian Trail.

3.4 Cross the dirt Balance Rock Road, then cross an intersection and pick up Balance Rock Trail. Soon pass by the Balance Rock itself, and follow the yellow blazes as you veer left downhill.

3.8 At the bottom of the hill, pass by a left turn for the Pine Loop Trail, then take a left into the ski area's dirt parking lot.

4.0 Walk across the lot and reach the three flag-poles near a small pond at the paved entrance road. Turn right on Mile Hill Road, and walk uphill on the shoulder, following the Midstate Trail's yellow triangle blazes.

4.1 Turn left off the pavement onto a hiking path marked with a "Midstate Trail" sign, just before a road sign marking the Westminster/Princeton town line.

4.2 Cross an abandoned two-track dirt road and a stone wall, passing a sign posted by the Midstate Trail Committee: "This land is city of Fitchburg watershed. Landowner requests that you stay on the trail."

4.3 Cross a wooden footbridge over a small stream. You'll soon pass several more stream beds flowing downhill to your left as you traverse the slope.

4.6 Pass by an unmarked trail on your right and bear left, following the yellow blazes.

4.7 Turn right at a Y-intersection, following blazes.

4.8 Cross a stream on a stone causeway and turn right at a T-intersection. You immediately enter a small dirt parking lot at Redemption Rock. To follow the yellow blazes, turn left before

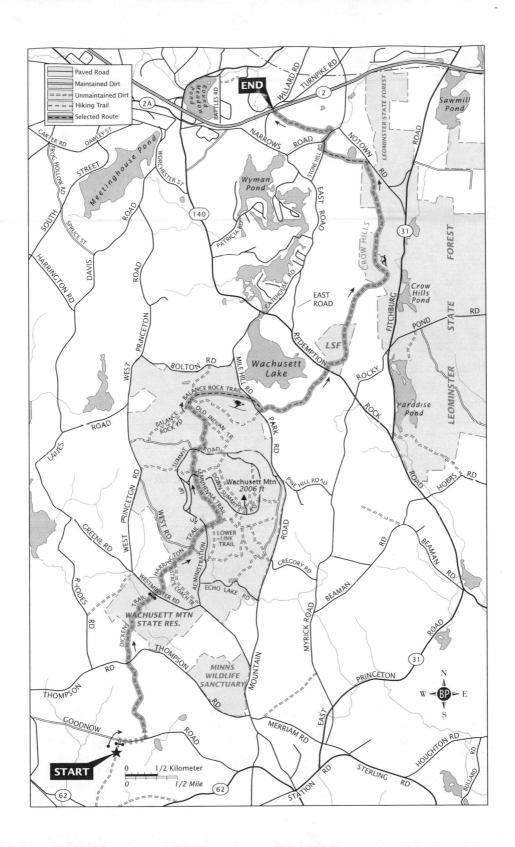

Paved Road
Maintained Dirt
Unmaintained Dirt
Hiking Trail
Selected Route

END

START

0   1/2 Kilometer
0   1/2 Mile

Fall Foliage

The visitors center at Wachusett Meadows explains that New England's famous foliage changes color in the autumn because leaves lose the green chlorophyll that has masked their true colors all year. As a rule of thumb, it offers the following guide to identifying trees by the color of their foliage.

Red: *blueberry, sumac, red maple*
Orange: *sugar maple, shadbush, white oak*
Yellow: *quaking aspen, alder*
Violet: *viburnum maple, white ash (may also be yellow)*

Mount Wachusett also has an excellent visitors center, accessible by trail or by car, on Mountain Road, near the ski area's base lodge.

reaching the rock, descend slightly, and soon cross the paved road, MA 140.

4.9 Pass by a large glacial boulder on your left and continue climbing uphill, soon scaling a steep cliff and reaching an overlook with great views of Mount Wachusett.

6.0 Pass several stone campfire circles, and turn sharp left, using your hands and feet to follow the yellow blazes up a series of rock cliffs—Crow Hill Ledges. Turn right at the top of the cliffs and soon reach an overlook with views of Crow Hills Pond and MA 31 to the southeast, and rock climbers under your feet.

6.1 Take a sharp left, following blazes as you circle counterclockwise around Crow Hill.

6.5 Descend from the ledges on a series of steep stone steps (built by the CCC), and turn left when you reach a large boulder at the base of the hill. [**FYI**. *A blue-blazed trail leads to the right here, toward park headquarters.*]

7.4 Cross a stone wall and proceed left, following the yellow blazes. You are quite near some private homes here, so keep your dog leashed and your voice down.

7.6 Cross a stone wall and turn right.

7.7 Emerge from the woods and turn right on the paved Stone Hill Road.

7.8 Cross Narrows Road and walk over a wooden car bridge, turning left onto a hiking path on the other side. Follow the yellow blazes very carefully here, as you walk parallel to Narrows Road on your left.

7.9 Fork left, following the blazes and staying very close to the stream.

8.2 Bear right, leaving the stream as you climb a series of switchbacks.

8.3 Continue to climb as you cross two wide dirt paths, and turn right onto a third two-track path.

8.4 Cross several more dirt roads, and emerge into a paved parking lot. Stay to your left and walk the perimeter of the lot until you reach yellow blazes on the other side, and turn left into the woods.

8.5 Emerge from the woods, cross the paved Wyman Road, cross a grassy triangle, then cross the paved Village Inn Road, reaching a bridge over MA 2 called Waterman Lane. On a road map, this is the exit 26 interchange off MA 2.

Hike Information

Trail Contacts:
Mass. Audubon Society, 113 Goodnow Road, Princeton, MA (978) 464–2712. *www.massaudubon.org* • **Wachusett Mountain State Reservation**, Princeton, MA, (978) 464–2987; *www.state.ma.us/dem/ parks/ wach.htm* • **Redemption Rock**, Trustees of Reservations, Leominster, MA (508) 840–4446; *www.thetrustees.org* • **Leominster State Forest**; Westminster, MA, (978) 874–2303; *www.state.ma.us/dem/ parks/ lmsf.htm*

Schedule:
Audubon Sanctuary trail hours are dawn to dusk, Tuesday through Sunday. Closed Monday except holidays.

Fees/Permits:
Audubon charges $3 per adult visitor (free for Audubon Society members)

Local Information:
The Holden Landmark is a small, weekly newspaper, full of local links and information; *www.thelandmark.com*

Local Events/Attractions:
The Sanctuary organizes events including a bird seed sale, fall harvest festival, bird-a-thon bird watching, and a book sale.

Accommodations:
Wachusett Village Inn; also offers sleigh rides in the winter; reservations required

Organizations:
Wachusett Mountain Ski Area hosts events and fairs year-round. Check their website for scheduling; *www.wachusett.com*

Maps:
USGS maps: Sterling, MA

Midstate Trail Northbound
Day Eight

Hike Specs

Start: Waterman Bridge overpass, which crosses MA 2 at exit 26

Length: 6.7 miles one way

Approximate Hiking Time: 2.5 hours

Difficulty Rating: Easy, with dirt paths and no major climbing

Trail Surface: Dirt footpaths winding through woods

Lay of the Land: Trail tracks a slight but steady rise from MA 2 through wooded slopes

Land Status: Westminster Conservation Commission

Nearest Town: Fitchburg, MA

Other Trail Users: None

Canine Compatibility: Trail passes close to private homes, so be careful of other dogs

Getting There

From Leominster: Take MA 2 west to exit 27, for Narrows Road and Depot Road. Follow Village Inn Road westbound, past the Wachusett Village Inn. At 0.8 miles, turn left onto Wyman Road, then immediately left again, as Wyman Road doubles back in a short jug handle that encircles a grassy triangle. Park on the shoulder. *DeLorme: Massachusetts Atlas & Gazetteer:* Page 26 M3

T his stretch of the Midstate Trail begins and ends on busy roads, but passes through quiet woods in between. Its reward is a visit to the beautiful Muddy Pond shelter at the hike's midpoint, before it finishes on MA 12 between Ashburnham and Blackburn Village.

The Midstate Trail follows a slow and steady climb from Round Meadow Pond through wooded agricultural land, passing tractors and caged turkeys and rabbits in rural backyards. It crosses under an MBTA rail line and over the Whitman River, emerging at the main intersection in Whitmanville, which is not really a town, but the intersection of four streets: Bragg Hill Road, South Ashburnham Road, Old Whitmanville Road, and Oakmont Avenue.

Climb gently from the Whitman River up Bragg Hill, reaching Muddy Pond in another 1.6 miles. With a lean-to shelter (maintained by the Westminster Conservation Commission), fire pit, and gorgeous lakeside views, this is a great spot for lunch. Muddy Pond drains into

Whitman Reservoir, which flows into the Whitman River and feeds Crocker Pond. The hike continues through tall trees and stone walls, ending when you cross Phillips Brook near Ashburnham.

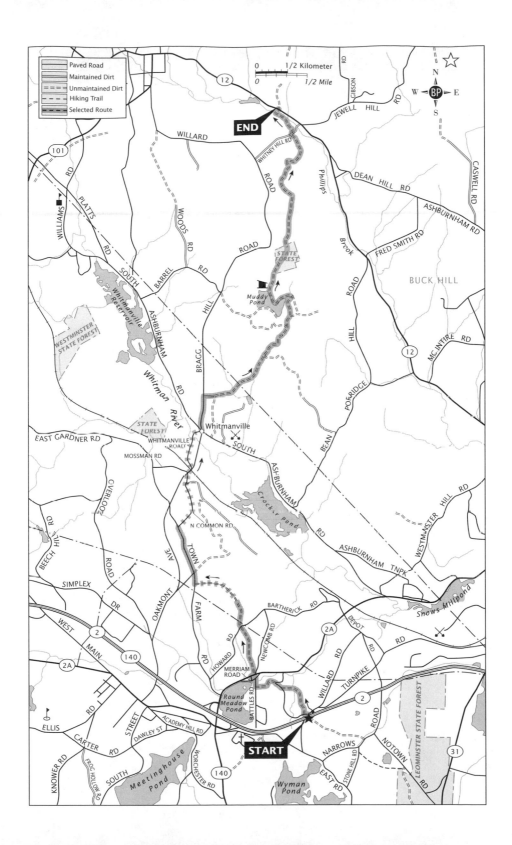

Paved Road
Maintained Dirt
Unmaintained Dirt
Hiking Trail
Selected Route

0   1/2 Kilometer
0   1/2 Mile

12

END

101

WILLARD

WHITNEY HILL RD

Phillips

JEWELL HILL

GIBSON RD

CASWELL RD

DEAN HILL RD

ASHBURNHAM RD

N
W   BP   E
S

WILLIAMS

PLATTS RD

WOODS RD

ROAD

STATE FOREST

Brook

FRED SMITH RD

BUCK HILL

SOUTH

BARREL

WESTMINSTER STATE FOREST

Whitmanville Reservoir

ASHBURNHAM

HILL

BRAGG

RD

Muddy Pond

ROAD

HILL

12

MC INTIRE RD

Whitman River

STATE FOREST

Whitmanville

SOUTH

PORRIDGE

EAST GARDNER RD

WHITMANVILLE ROAD

MOSSMAN RD

ASH-BURNHAM

BEAN

RD

Crocker Pond

N COMMON RD

ASHBURNHAM TNPK

WESTMINSTER HILL RD

BEECH HILL RD

OVERLOOK

ROAD

SIMPLEX DR

OAKMONT

AVE

TOWN FARM

Snows Millpond

WEST

2

140

MAIN

BARTHERICK RD

2A

DEPOT RD

RD

2A

HOWARD RD

NEWCOMB RD

WILLARD

TURNPIKE

2

RD

LEOMINSTER STATE FOREST

ELLIS RD

KNOWER RD

CARTER RD

STREET

DAWLEY ST

ACADEMY HILL RD

BATTLES RD

MERRIAM ROAD

Round Meadow Pond

ROAD

NARROWS RD

STONE HILL RD

EAST RD

NOTOWN RD

31

SOUTH

WORCHESTER RD

Meetinghouse Pond

140

Wyman Pond

START

FROG HOLLOW RD

MilesDirections

0.0 START at the Waterman Bridge overpass, at the intersection of Wyman and Village Inn Roads at exit 26 off MA 2. Follow Waterman Bridge as it crosses MA 2, immediately turning left on the north side, on a paved road through a metal gate.

0.2 Just before the pavement ends, turn left onto a yellow-blazed foot path. Soon cross a dirt road and gradually climb a small hill.

0.6 Come out of the woods and turn left onto a two-track dirt road.

0.7 Turn right onto paved Battles Road. You're very close to private homes here, so be sure to keep your dog leashed.

0.8 Turn left onto paved Merriam Road, then immediately right to cross a grassy wedge between a small bog and the D&D Farms flower and garden store. Then cross the paved MA 2A and bear right along its shoulder, heading northbound, away from Round Meadow Pond.

0.9 Turn left into the woods off of MA 2A. Be sure to follow the triangular yellow blazes very carefully for the next mile, since the trail takes many turns.

1.0 Fork right.

1.3 Cross Howard Road (a.k.a. Bartherick Road).

1.4 Cross under a power line.

1.5 Come down a short slope and bear right, soon crossing an intersection with another trail.

1.6 Turn left at a T-intersection, then right at a Y-intersection.

1.7 Bear right at a T-intersection.

1.9 Cross a two-track dirt path.

2.0 Come to a stone wall, and proceed left at a T-intersection. Then turn right onto paved Town Farm Road.

2.1 Turn right onto paved Syd Smith Road, which is at the corner of North Common and Town Farm Roads.

2.3 Syd Smith Road quickly turns to dirt, then you bear left onto a wide, two-track path that drops into the woods.

2.5 Turn left onto a smaller dirt path that heads uphill, parallel to a stone wall.

2.7 Traverse the top of the ridge, and pass through a waist-high gap in a beautiful stone wall.

2.8 Keep following the yellow blazes as they swing right.

3.1 Cross intersections with four abandoned dirt roads, then walk along a series of wooden boardwalks through a boggy area.

3.2 Turn right onto paved Oakmont Avenue, immediately crossing under a masonry railroad overpass that's covered with graffiti. On the other side turn left, climbing over a dirt pile onto the paved Old Whitmanville Road.

3.4 Follow this street, passing the Old Gardner Road on your left, then crossing the Whitman River.

3.6 Cross another bridge over the river, and reach Whitmanville. Cross South Ashburnham Road and head uphill on the paved Bragg Hill Road.

3.8 At the top of a rise, turn right onto a dirt road. Pass through a large clearing, and soon enter the woods on a two-track path.

4.1 Cross a small stream.

4.2 Pass under a power line.

4.3 Cross a stream, and bear left at a fork, following the yellow blazes.

4.5 Continue straight as you pass a fork to the right.

4.8 Cross a stone wall as you enter Westminster Conservation Land. Within a quarter mile, you'll catch glimpses of Muddy Pond through trees to your left.

5.2 Reach the wooden shelter with its fire circle and gorgeous views of the lake.

5.4 Follow the yellow blazes carefully as you pass through a clearing of timbered trees, cross an intersection with a blue-blazed trail, and turn right onto a narrow hiking trail.

5.7 Turn right at a T-intersection onto a broad trail, then fork left onto a narrow path. The trail is sometimes faint here, so be sure to follow the yellow blazes carefully.

5.9 Cross three stone walls in the next quarter mile.

6.5 Cross an intersection with the dirt Whitney Hill Road, and begin to hear traffic in the valley to your right.

6.7 Cross a wooden footbridge over Phillips Brook, climb a short dirt bank, and reach MA 12.

Hike Information

🕯 Trail Contacts:
AMC, Worcester Chapter, www.amcworcester. org. Also try Midstate Trail sites at *www. mtwatatic.com and http://midstatetrail. org*

🕐 Schedule:
Open year round

Ⓢ Fees/Permits:
No fees or permits required

🛏 Accommodations:
Wachusett Village Inn, 9 Village Inn Road, Westminster, MA 1–800–342–1905 or (978) 874–2000; *www.wachusettvillageinn. com*

🍴 Restaurants:
Mill No. 3 Farmstand is on MA 31, 0.9 miles north of its intersection with MA 2A south, and 0.2 miles south of its intersection with MA 12 north. It offers fresh produce, coffee, bakery, deli sandwiches, and even Christmas trees in season.

🏃 Hike Tours:
Outdoor Adventure Center, at the Wachusett Village Inn, 1–800–307–0426 • **Mountain Lynx Outdoor Adventures**, 180 Central Street, Leominster (978) 840–6464; *www. mountainlynx.com*

🜨 Other Resources:
Montachusett Regional Vo-Tech, at 1050 Westminster St., Fitchburg; *www.mtech. mec.edu. Website lists regional events, appearances, and performances.*

Ⓝ Maps:
USGS maps: Fitchburg, MA

Midstate Trail Northbound
Day Nine

Hike Specs

Start: MA 12 between Ashburnham and Blackburn Village

Length: 7.3 miles one way

Approximate Hiking Time: 2.5 hours

Difficulty Rating: Difficult, due to steep climbs and twisting trails

Trail Surface: Mostly dirt, with some rocky scrambling

Lay of the Land: Climb over an exposed rocky ridge between two valleys

Nearest Town: Ashburnham, MA

Other Trail Users: None

Canine Compatibility: Dog friendly

Getting There

From Leominster: Follow MA 2 west to exit 28, for MA 31, Fitchburg and Princeton. Follow MA 31 north toward Fitchburg, passing under a railroad bridge at 0.5 miles. Turn right at 1.0 miles to continue north on MA 31, as it merges with MA 2A at Waites Corner. At 2.1 miles, take a hairpin left turn at a stop sign, onto MA 12 north. At 7.3 miles, park in a grassy lot on the left, where a dam in Phillips Brook has created a large pond. (This lot is located at mile marker 52 on MA 12, and is 1.1 miles south of the junction of MA 101 north and MA 12.) *DeLorme: Massachusetts Atlas & Gazetteer:* Page 26 H2

After crossing Russell Hill Road, the trail climbs steeply and follows a rolling ridgeline between Brown Hill and Mount Hunger, with awesome views of Stodge Meadow Pond and surrounding hilltops to the north. These outlooks are a popular destination for hikers, so expect some company. Descending from the ridge, the trail threads between the 118-acre Winnekeag Lake and Stodge Meadow Pond, briefly tracing MA 101.

This is the last northbound leg of the 92-mile Midstate Trail, depositing the hiker on the New Hampshire line, just past the summit of Mount Watatic. At 1,832 feet in elevation, it is the second largest mountain in Massachusetts east of the Connecticut River (Mount Wachusett is 2,006 feet). Also, Watatic is a major viewing point for the annual hawk migration every fall, so keep your eyes on the skies if you're here in season. In truth, the summit is the emotional end of the line, unless you really want to walk the extra 1.2 miles to a nondescript stone wall in the woods, where a granite marker perches on the state line.

As you climb north from Russell Hill Road, you'll trace stone walls for nearly a mile along the rolling ridgeline of Mount Hunger. This series of gorgeous, 360-degree views culminates at 2.0 miles, as you come around a corner and suddenly reach a lookout point with views of surrounding lakes and ridges. The trail drops quickly, and emerges from the woods at Camp Winnekeag, a summer camp operated by the Southern New England Conference of Seventh Day Adventists.

Continue by, passing through rhododendron, white pine, and hemlock around Winnekeag, and then through thicker hemlock and pine stands in Ashburnham State Forest. Continuing north, you'll trace Old Pierce Road, which runs between Ashburnham State Forest on the right, and the Fitchburg Sportsmen's Club on left. Soon cross MA 119, where you reach the Mount Watatic trailhead with its sign: "Blueberry Lake Trail 0.25, Wapack Cutoff 0.74, New Hampshire 1.15." And a sign here for the Wapack Trail says: "Mount Watatic 1.1, shelter 1.0, Nutting Hill 1.9, New Ipswich Mtn. 5.8, NH Route 124 8.9."

Take care, a warning posted here says the most intensive hunting takes place during deer season, from Nov. 27 to Dec. 16. But don't fear; with Watatic's popularity, you won't be alone

in these woods—the trail is usually crowded with dogs and people, and the peak is scattered with concrete foundations of former fire towers, and steel poles from a former ski lift. At press time, a legal battle was raging over a telecommunication company's efforts to erect a new cell phone tower on this peak.

The Friends of the Wapack Trail, another long-distance path, have posted topo maps at major intersections through these woods. The Wapack Trail heads north from Mount Watatic to North Pack Monadnock, in Greenfield, NH, passing over the peaks of Pratt, New Ipswich, Barrett, and Temple mountains along the way. For a history of the ski area that formerly existed on the slopes of Mount Watatic, check the New England Lost Ski Areas Project at www.nelsap.org/ma/watatic.html.

Hike Information

Trail Contacts:
Friends of the Wapack Trail, *www.wapack. org*, or *www.mtwatatic.com*

Schedule:
Open year round

Fees/Permits:
No fees or permits required

Local Information:
Camp Winnekeag is a Christian youth camp and convention center operated by the Southern New England Conference of Seventh Day Adventists. See *www.tagnet. org/campwinnekeag* for more information.

Restaurants:
Cumberland Farms convenience store and Ashburnham Pizza are on MA 12, just north of its intersection with MA 101, and 1.3 miles north of the parking lot for this hike.

Organizations:
Friends of the Wapack, P. O. Box 115, West Peterborough, NH, 03468; *www.wapack.org*

Other Resources:
The Johnny Appleseed Visitors Information Center is a rest stop on MA 2 westbound, between exits 34 and 35. It offers food, restrooms, maps, and books on natural history and Native Americans.

Local Outdoor Retailers:
Outdoor Endeavors, Route 140 North, Winchendon, (978) 297–3114

Maps:
USGS maps: Ashburnham, MA

MilesDirections

0.0 START at the dam, and walk south on the shoulder of MA 12.

0.2 Pick up the yellow blazes, and turn left up a paved driveway marked with a mailbox for #139. Soon pass two private homes on your right, and enter the woods on a dirt road.

0.3 Pass a third home and fork right.

1.0 Come through a stone wall and follow the blazes as the trail swings left over a small ridge.

1.2 Emerge into a large mowed field between two private homes, and cross it, tracing the right edge of the field.

1.3 On the other side, cross the paved Russell Hill Road and bear left. Immediately enter the woods again, climbing steeply. At the top, a rolling ridgeline offers peeks of views through the trees for the next mile.

2.0 After dropping into a shallow saddle, you reach Mount Hunger. Come around a corner and suddenly see a gorgeous view of Stodge Meadow Pond and Mount Watatic to the north. Continue along the trail as it passes through a thick hemlock forest in a steep descent.

2.5 Turn right at a fork, onto a two-track lumber road. Then immediately bear right, back onto a narrow hiking path.

2.7 Briefly overlap with another logging road as you continue to follow yellow blazes.

2.8 Reach a telephone wire and follow the phone poles, heading downhill until you turn left on the paved Holt Road.

2.9 Turn right on MA 101, skirting the shore of Lake Winnekeag.

3.1 Turn left into a gravel parking lot at Camp Winnekeag, and walk west, keeping the lake on your left and MA 101 at your back. Follow the yellow blazes as you pass several other foot trails that wind around the camp.

3.4 Cross over three wooden boardwalks.

3.6 Begin to climb steeply.

3.8 Pass by a two-track path joining from the right. Then fork left at the top of a rise; this is Blueberry Hill.

3.9 Fork right, following blazes.

4.1 Pass a fire circle at the top of another rise; this is Fisher Hill.

4.2 Cross a stone wall and pass a sign for Ashburnham State Forest, passing through a thick forest of hemlock and white pine.

4.7 Go right on the paved Old Pierce Road

5.1 Cross MA 119 to a dirt parking lot with a kiosk bulletin board. Pass through the brown metal gate and up the two-track State Line Trail.

5.4 Turn right at a sign for the Midstate Trail, reading: "Mount Watatic 0.95, Midstate Trail Connector 2.15, NH Route 123/124 6.6." *[**Note**. Be careful, since the Wapack Trail is blazed identically to the Midstate Trail—with yellow triangles.]*

5.5 Cross a stream.

5.8 Reach a fabulous overlook to the south and west.

6.0 Pass a wooden lean-to shelter, built in 1981 by the Young Adult Conservation Corps.

6.1 Reach a stone cairn at the summit of Mount Watatic, with its 360-degree views and whipping winds. The Midstate Trail takes a hairpin left turn just BEFORE reaching the summit, so you must retreat slightly to carry on. Head northwest, parallel and to the left of a newly laid grinded rock road, keeping Mount Watatic's peak on your right as you head gently downhill.

6.7 Reach a series of stone cairns on Nutting Hill.

6.9 Bear left at a fork, as the Wapack Trail veers off to the right. And then turn right onto a hiking path. A sign here says "NH 0.41 (to right), Rt. 119 0.79 (to left)."

7.3 Reach the New Hampshire state line, marked by a granite monument set into a stone wall in the woods: "Midstate Trail, NH-RI, 1985."

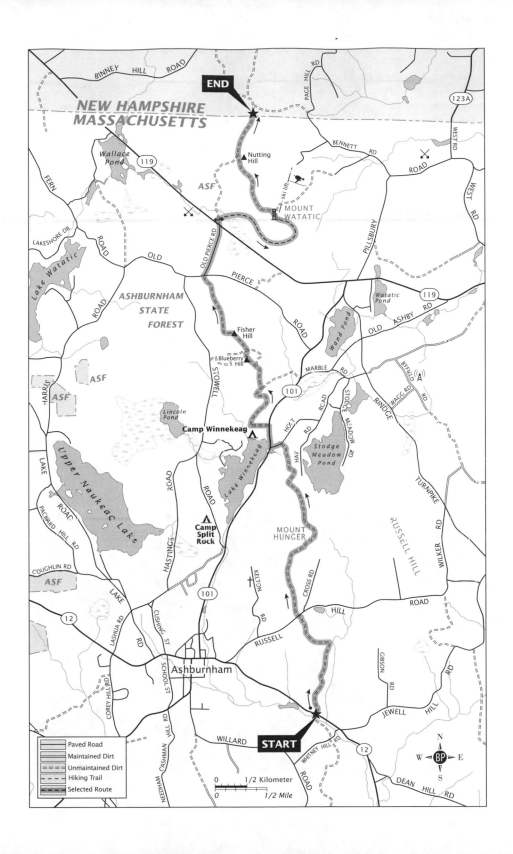

BINNEY HILL ROAD

END

NEW HAMPSHIRE
MASSACHUSETTS

PAGE HILL RD

123A

Wallace
Pond

119

FERN

Nutting
Hill

ASF

BENNETT RD

WEST RD

ROAD

WEST RD

LAKESHORE DR.

ROAD

OLD PIERCE RD

Ski lift

MOUNT
WATATIC

OLD

PIERCE

ROAD

PILLSBURY

ROAD

Lake Watatic

ASHBURNHAM
STATE
FOREST

ROAD

Watatic
Pond

119

OLD ASHBY RD

HARRIS

ASF

ASF

STOWELL

Fisher
Hill

Blueberry
Hill

Lincoln
Pond

Camp Winnekeag

ROAD

101

MARBLE

RD

BYFIELD RD

WACG RD

A

RD

RCAD

RINDGE

Wand Pond

STODGE

HAY RD

Stodge
Meadow
Pond

MEADOW RD

TURNPIKE

Upper Naukeag Lake

LAKE

ROAD

PACKARD HILL RD

Camp
Split
Rock

Lake Winnekeag

HASTINGS

MOUNT
HUNGER

RUSSELL HILL

WILKER RD

COUGHLIN RD

ASF

12

LASHUA RD

ROAD

CUSHING ST

101

KELTON RD

CROSS RD

HILL

ROAD

GIBSON RD

SCHOOL ST

CASHMAN HILL RD

Ashburnham

RUSSELL

JEWELL HILL RD

COREY HILL RD

NEEDHAM

WILLARD

START

ROAD

WHITNEY HILL RD

12

DEAN HILL RD

N
W   E
S
BP

Paved Road
Maintained Dirt
Unmaintained Dirt
Hiking Trail
Selected Route

0   1/2 Kilometer
0   1/2 Mile

Nursery Rhymes in Massachusetts

On Sept. 26, 1774, a boy named John Chapman was born in Leominster, MA. He traveled the country spreading seeds, eventually earning the name Johnny Appleseed. Today he is remembered by The Johnny Appleseed Trail, which is MA 2 from its junction with I-495 in the east to its junction with I-91 in the west.

Johnny is not the only nursery rhyme hero who hailed from Massachusetts. In the early 1800s, Mary Elizabeth Sawyer was born near Sterling, MA. Like most rural families of that era, the Sawyers kept sheep, and in 1816 Mary's father let her adopt a newborn lamb. She cared for it so well that it followed her as she walked to school that spring, so she snuck it into the classroom. The animal was quickly discovered, and someone wrote a poem about the pair—Mary had a little lamb. A replica of that original schoolhouse stands in Sudbury, MA, today.

For more information about the Johnny Appleseed Trail, phone (978) 534-2302 or check www.appleseed.org. If you're there in the fall, check the website for a list of more than 20 local orchards, and fill a sack with fresh fruits and vegetables after your hike.

The The
Art of
Hiking

The Art of Hiking

When standing nose to snout with a bear, you're probably not too concerned with the issue of ethical behavior in the wild. No doubt you're just wetting yourself. But let's be honest. How often are you nose to snout with a bear? For most of us, a hike into the "wild" means loading up the 4-Runner with everything North Face and driving to a toileted trailhead. Sure, you can mourn how civilized we've become—how GPS units have replaced natural instinct and GORE-TEX, true-grit—but the silly gadgets of civilization aside, we have plenty of reason to take pride in how we've matured. With survival now on the back-burner, we've begun to reason—and it's about time—that we have a responsibility to protect, no longer just conquer, our wild places; that they, not we, are at risk. So please, do what you can. A walk in the woods is a nice opportunity to marvel at the natural world and renew your energy to preserve it. Now, in keeping with our chronic tendency to reduce everything to a list, here are some rules to remember.

Zero impact. Always leave an area just like you found it—if not better than you found it. Avoid camping in fragile areas and along the banks of streams and lakes. Use a camp stove versus building a wood fire. Pack out all of your trash and extra food. Bury human waste at least 200 feet from water sources under six to eight inches of topsoil. Don't bathe with soap in a lake or stream—bathe in the water without soap. Leave what you find. As a general rule, don't gather plants, animals, artifacts or rocks. Some places, including national parks, prohibit taking anything. Know and abide by the rules and regulations of the land on which you travel.

Stay on the trail. It's true, a path anywhere leads nowhere new, but purists will just have to get over it. Paths serve an important purpose; they limit our impact on natural areas. Straying from a designated trail may seem innocent, but it can cause damage to sensitive areas—damage that may take years to recover, if it can recover at all. Even simple shortcuts can be destructive. So, please, stay on the trail. Take a moment to appreciate the work that went into the creation and maintenance of a trail for your enjoyment.

Keep your dog under control. You can buy a flexi-lead that allows your dog to go exploring along the trail, while allowing you the ability to reel him in should another hiker approach or should he decide to chase a rabbit. Massachusetts state parks require a six-foot maximum leash. Always obey leash laws, and be sure to bury your dog's waste or pack it in plastic bags.

Yield to horses. When you approach these animals on the trail, always step quietly off the trail and let them pass. If you are wearing a large backpack, it's a good idea to sit down. From a horse's perspective, a hiker wearing a large backpack is a scary trail monster and these sensitive animals can be spooked easily.

GETTING INTO SHAPE

Unless you want to be sore or, worse, sustain an injury —and possibly have to shorten your trip or vacation—be sure to get in shape before a big hike. If you're terribly out of shape, start a walking program early, preferably eight weeks in advance. Start with a 15-minute walk during your lunch hour or after work and gradually increase your walking time to an hour. You should also increase your elevation gain. Walking briskly up hills strengthens your leg muscles and gets your heart rate up. If you work in a storied office building, take the stairs instead of the elevator. If you prefer going to a gym, walk the treadmill or use a Stair-master. You can further increase your strength and endurance by walking with a loaded backpack. Stationary exercises you might consider are squats, leg lifts, sit-ups, and push-ups. Other good ways to get in shape include biking, running, aerobics, and, of course, short hikes.

PREPAREDNESS

It's been said that failing to plan means planning to fail. So do take the necessary time to plan your trip. Whether going on a short day hike or an extended backpack trip, always prepare for the worst. Traveling with an awareness and attitude of safety consciousness is the best way to prevent problems from arising in the first place. In order to remain comfortable, you need to concern yourself with the basics: water, food, and shelter. Don't go on a hike without having these bases covered. And don't go on a hike expecting to find these items in the woods.

Water. Even in frigid conditions, you need at least two quarts of water a day to function efficiently. Add heat and taxing terrain and you can bump that figure up to one gallon. That's simply a base to work from—your metabolism and your level of conditioning can raise or lower that amount. Unless you know your level, assume that you need one gallon of water a day. Now, where do you plan on getting the water?

Preferably not from natural water sources. These sources can be loaded with intestinal disturbers, such as bacteria, viruses, and fertilizers. *Giardia lamblia*, the most common of these disturbers, is a protozoan parasite that lives part of its lifecycle as a cyst in water sources. The parasite spreads when mammals defecate in water sources. Once ingested, Giardia can induce cramping, diarrhea, vomiting, and fatigue within two days to two weeks after ingestion. Giardia and other parasites are treatable. If you get sick after drinking untreated water, you may have a parasite. See a doctor immediately.

Treating water. The best and easiest solution to avoid polluted water is to carry your water with you. Yet, depending on the nature of your hike and the duration, this may not be an option—seeing as one gallon of water weighs 8.5 pounds. In that case, you'll need to look into treating water. Regardless of which method you choose, you should always carry some water with you in case of an emergency. Save this reserve until you absolutely need it.

There are three methods of treating water: boiling, chemical treatment, and filtering. If you boil water, it's recommended that you do so for 10 to 15 minutes; 20 minutes kills all disease-causing organisms including hepatitis. This is often impractical because you're forced to exhaust a great deal of your fuel supply. Giardia dies at 170 degrees Fahrenheit. Since water boils at 210

Lisann Dunegan

degrees Fahrenheit, bringing water to a boil is an easy and effective way to ensure water has reached 170 degrees. You can opt for chemical treatment (e.g. Potable Aqua), which will kill Giardia but will not take care of other chemical pollutants. Another drawback to chemical treatments can be the unpleasant taste of the water after it's treated. You can remedy this by adding neutralizing tablets after the water has finished treatment. Another way to minimize the taste is to add powdered drink mix to the already treated water. Filters are the preferred method for treating water. Filters remove Giardia, organic and inorganic contaminants, and don't leave an aftertaste. Water filters are far from perfect as they can easily become clogged or leak if a gasket wears out. It's always a good idea to carry a backup supply of chemical treatment tablets in case your filter decides to quit on you.

Food. If we're talking about "survival," you can go days without food, as long as you have water. But we're talking about "comfort" here. Try to avoid foods that are high in sugar and fat like candy bars and potato chips. These food types are harder to digest and are low in nutritional value. Remember, "you are what you eat" rings true and if you eat junk foods, that is what you'll feel like at the end of the day. Instead, bring along foods that are easy to pack, nutritious, and high in energy (e.g. bagels, nutrition bars, dehydrated fruit, gorp, and jerky). If you are on an overnight trip, easy-to-fix dinners include rice mixes with dehydrated potatoes, corn, pasta with cheese sauce, and soup mixes. For a tasty breakfast, you can fix hot oatmeal with brown sugar and reconstituted milk powder topped off with banana chips. If you like a hot drink in the morning, bring along herbal tea bags or hot chocolate. If you are a coffee junkie, you can purchase coffee that is packaged like tea bags. You can pre-package all of your meals in heavy-duty resealable plastic bags to keep food from spilling in your pack. These bags can be reused to pack out trash.

Shelter. The type of shelter you choose depends less on the conditions than on your tolerance for discomfort. Shelter comes in many forms—tent, tarp, lean-to, bivy sack, cabin, cave, etc. If you're camping in the desert, a bivy sack may suffice, but if you're above the treeline and a storm is approaching, a better choice is a three or four season tent. Tents are the logical and most popular choice for most backpackers as they're lightweight and packable—and you can rest assured that you always have shelter from the elements. Before you leave on your trip, anticipate what the weather and terrain will be like, and plan for the type of shelter that will work best for your comfort level.

Finding a campsite. If there are established campsites, stick to those. If not, start looking for a campsite early—like around 3:30 or 4:00 P.M. Stop at the first appropriate site you see, remembering that good campsites are found and not made. Depending on the area, it could be a long

time before you find another suitable location. Pitch your camp in an area that's reasonably level and clear of underbrush (which can harbor insects and conceal approaching animals). Make sure the area is at least 200 feet from fragile areas like lakeshores, meadows, and stream banks. Woody stemmed plants like kinnikinnik, blueberry, and whortleberry are easily damaged, so avoid plopping your tent on top of them. Try to avoid camping above treeline, as the tundra is fragile,

Lizann Dunegan

and you're exposing yourself to possible high winds and lightning.

If you are camping in stormy, rainy weather, look for a rock outcrop or a shelter in the trees to keep the wind from blowing your tent all night. Be sure that you don't camp under trees with dead limbs that might break off on top of you. Also, try to find an area that has an absorbent surface, such as sandy soil or forest duff. This, in addition to camping on a surface with a slight angle, will provide better drainage. By all means, don't dig trenches to provide drainage around your tent—remember you're practicing zero-impact camping.

If you're in bear country, steer clear of creek beds or animal paths. If you see any signs of a bear's presence (i.e. scat, footprints), relocate. You'll need to find a campsite near a tall tree where you can hang your food and other items that may attract bears such as deodorant, toothpaste, or soap. Carry a lightweight nylon rope with which to hang your food. As a rule, you should hang your food at least 15 feet from the ground and four feet away from the tree trunk. Trees at higher elevations don't often have branches longer than five feet so you may need to string rope between two trees or find a leaning snag. You can put food and other items in a waterproof stuff sack or a dry bag and tie one end of the rope to the stuff sack. To get the other end of the rope over the tree branch, tie a good size rock to it and gently toss the rock over the tree branch. Pull the stuff sack up until it reaches the top of the branch and tie it off securely. Don't hang your food near your tent! If possible, hang your food at least 100 feet away from your campsite. Alternatives to hanging your food are bear-proof plastic tubes and metal bear boxes. Chipmunks, ground squirrels, and pine martens will also steal your food if you don't hang it.

Lastly, think of comfort. Lie down on the ground where you intend to sleep and see if it's a good fit. Bring along an insulating pad for warmth and extra comfort. The days of using pine boughs or digging a hip depression in the ground are long gone. And for the final touch, have your tent face east. You'll appreciate the warmth of the morning sun and have a nice view to wake up to.

FIRST AID

If you plan to spend a lot of time outdoors hiking, spend a few hours and bucks to take a good wilderness or mountain-oriented first aid class. You'll not only learn first aid basics, but how to be creative miles from nowhere. Specialized companies like Wilderness Medicine Institute (WMI) offer such courses. Check out WMI for course dates and locations at *http://wmi.nols.edu*.

Now, we know you're tough, but get 10 miles into the woods and develop a blister, and you'll wish you had carried a first-aid kit. Face it; it's just plain good sense. Many companies produce lightweight, compact first-aid kits, just make sure yours contains at least the following:

First Aid

- Band-Aids
- moleskin, duct tape or athletic tape, and/or Band-Aid's Blister Relief Compeed
- various sterile gauze and dressings
- white surgical tape
- an Ace bandage
- an antihistamine
- aspirin, ibuprofen, or acetaminophen
- Betadine solution
- first-aid book
- Tums
- tweezers
- scissors
- anti-bacterial wipes
- triple-antibiotic ointment
- plastic gloves
- sterile cotton tip applicators
- a thermometer

Here are a few tips for dealing with and hopefully preventing certain ailments.

Sunburn. In most parts of Massachusetts, summer sun can be an intense and constant companion on hikes. It is a good idea to take along sunscreen or sun block, protective clothing, and a wide-brimmed hat. If you do get sunburn, treat the area with aloe vera gel and protect the area from further sun exposure.

Blisters. Be prepared to take care of these hike-spoilers by carrying moleskin (a lightly padded adhesive), gauze and tape, or Band-Aids. An effective way to apply moleskin is to cut

201

out a circle of moleskin and remove the center—like a doughnut—and place it over the blistered area. Cutting the center out will reduce the pressure applied to the sensitive skin. Other products that can help you combat blisters are Bodyglide and Second Skin. Bodyglide (1–888–263–9454) is applied to suspicious hot spots before a blister forms to help decrease friction to that area. Second Skin (made by Spenco) is applied to the blister after it has popped and acts as a second skin to help prevent further irritation.

Insect bites and stings. Prevention is the best approach to insect management. Massachusetts has a variety of biting insects, including mosquitoes, black flies, ticks, deer flies and no-see-ums. Insects are at their peak in the early summer and after wet weather. The best repellant for insects is protective clothing. Wear loose-fitting, tightly woven, light colored clothing, as insects are attracted to darker colors. Wear long sleeves and pants tucked into socks. A hat and/ or head net protects the face and head. A bandanna with insect repellant can also be worn tied around your neck. In general, having those layers available to put on if insects are troublesome is a good idea. Another preventative measure is to avoid any soaps, lotions, perfumes, or deodorants. These are all products designed to attract, not repel. A diet high in sugars can also attract insects. Being prepared can keep insects from ruining a great hiking experience.

You can treat most insect bites and stings by applying calamine lotion or hydrocortisone 1% cream topically and, for bites with moderate swelling, taking a pain medication such as ibuprofen or acetaminophen to reduce swelling. If you forgot to pack these items, a cold compress or a paste of mud and ashes can sometimes assuage the itching and discomfort. Remove any stingers by using tweezers or scraping the area with your fingernail or a knife blade. Don't pinch the area, as you'll only spread the venom.

Some hikers are highly sensitive to bites and stings and may have a systemic allergic reaction, anaphylaxis, that can be life threatening. This type of reaction usually follows quickly after an exposure, minutes after a sting or bite. Signs of a systemic allergic reaction can include generalized itching, generalized skin redness, hives, swelling of the mouth, face and neck, low blood pressure, upper and lower airway obstruction with labored breathing, and shock. The treatment for this severe type of reaction is epinephrine (Adrenaline) along with Benadryl. Epinephrine reverses the systemic reaction but does not help the ongoing allergic problem. Administration of Benadryl may prevent continued reaction to the sting, but will not reverse the cardio-vascular or respiratory symptoms which can be life threatening. If you know you're sensitive to bites and stings, carry Benadryl and a pre-packaged kit of epinephrine (e.g., Anakit), which can be obtained only by prescription from your doctor.

Ticks. As you well know, ticks can carry disease, such as Rocky Mountain spotted fever and Lyme disease. The best defense is, of course, prevention. If you know you're going to be hiking through an area littered with ticks, wear long pants tucked into socks and a long-sleeved shirt. You can apply a permethrin repellent to your clothing and a DEET repellent to exposed skin. At the end of your hike, do a spot check for ticks (and insects in general). If you do find a tick, coat the insect with Vaseline or tree sap to cut off its air supply. The tick should release its hold, but if it doesn't, grab the head of the tick firmly—with a pair of tweezers if you have them—and gently pull it away from the skin with a twisting motion. Sometimes the mouthparts linger, embedded in your skin. If this happens, try to remove them with a disinfected needle. Clean the affected area with an anti-bacterial cleanser and then apply triple antibiotic ointment. Monitor the area for a few days. If irritation persists or a white spot develops, see a doctor for possible infection.

Poison ivy, oak, and sumac. These skin irritants can be found most anywhere in North America and come in the form of a bush or a vine, having leaflets in groups of three, five, seven, or nine. Learn how to spot the plants. The oil they secrete can cause an allergic reac-

poison ivy

tion in the form of blisters, usually about 12 hours after exposure. The itchy rash can last from 10 days to several weeks. The best defense against these irritants is to wear protective clothing and to apply a non-prescription product called IvyBlock to exposed skin. This lotion is meant to guard against the effects of poison ivy/oak/sumac and can be washed off with soap and water. Washing with water immediately after contact with the plant can remove any lingering oil from your skin, as the oil is water-soluble. Should you contract a rash from any of these plants, use Benadryl or a similar product to reduce the itching. If the rash is localized, create a light Clorox/water wash or use Calamine lotion to dry up the area. If the rash has spread, either tough it out or see your doctor about getting a dose of Cortisone (available both orally and by injection).

Snakebites. First off, snakebites are rare in North America. Unless startled or provoked, the majority of snakes will not bite. If you're wise to their habitats and keep a careful eye on the trail, you should be just fine. If you see a snake of any kind, give it wide berth.

Dehydration. Have you ever hiked in hot weather and had a roaring headache and felt fatigued after only a few miles? More than likely you were dehydrated. Symptoms of dehydration include fatigue, headache, and decreased coordination and judgment. When you're hiking, your body's rate of fluid loss depends on the outside temperature, humidity, altitude, and your activity level. On average, a hiker walking in warm weather will lose four liters of fluid a day. That fluid loss is easily replaced by normal consumption of liquids and food. However, if a hiker is walking briskly in hot, dry weather and hauling a heavy pack, he can lose one to three liters of water an hour. It's important to always carry plenty of water and to stop often and drink fluids regularly, even if you aren't thirsty.

Heat exhaustion is the result of a loss of large amounts of electrolytes and often occurs if a hiker is dehydrated and has been under heavy exertion. Common symptoms of heat exhaustion include cramping, exhaustion, fatigue, lightheadedness, and nausea. You can treat heat exhaustion by getting out of the sun and drinking an electrolyte solution made up of one teaspoon of salt and one tablespoon of sugar dissolved in a liter of water. Drink this solution slowly over a period of one hour. Drinking plenty of fluids, more than the amount you are losing, can prevent heat exhaustion. Avoid hiking during the hottest parts of the day, and wear breathable clothing, a wide brimmed hat, and sunglasses. Untreated, heat exhaustion can lead to heat stroke, a life threatening condition.

Hypothermia is one of the biggest dangers in the backcountry—especially for day hikers in the summertime. That may sound strange, but imagine starting out on a hike in mid-summer when it's sunny and 80 degrees. You're clad in nylon shorts and a cotton T-shirt. About halfway through your hike, the sky begins to cloud up, and in the next hour a light drizzle begins to fall and the wind starts to pick up. Before you know it, you're soaking wet and shivering—the perfect recipe for hypothermia. More advanced signs include decreased coordination, slurred speech, and blurred vision. When a victim's temperature falls below 92 degrees Fahrenheit, the blood pressure and pulse plummet, possibly leading to coma and death.

To avoid hypothermia, always bring a windproof/rainproof shell, a fleece jacket and a hat. Remember that Massachusetts temperatures can vary a lot in one day. In spring or fall, or during rainy and windy weather, packing along Capilene tights and gloves is a good idea. Learn to adjust your clothing layers based on the temperature. If you're climbing uphill at a moderate pace you will stay warm, but when you stop for a break, you'll become cold quickly, unless you add more layers of clothing.

If a hiker is showing advanced signs of hypothermia, dress him in dry clothes, and make sure he's wearing a hat and gloves. Place him in a sleeping bag in a tent or shelter that will protect him from the wind and other elements. Give him warm fluids to drink, and keep him awake.

Frostbite. When the mercury dips below 32°F, your extremities begin to chill. If a persistent chill attacks a localized area, say your hands or your toes, the circulatory system reacts by cutting off blood flow to the affected area—the idea being to protect and preserve the body's overall temperature. And so it's death by attrition for the affected area. Ice crystals start to form from the water in the cells of the neglected tissue. Deprived of heat, nourishment, and now water, the tissue literally starves. This is frostbite.

Prevention is your best defense against this situation. Most prone to frostbite are your face, hands, and feet—so protect these areas well. Wool is the material of choice because it provides ample air space for insulation and draws moisture away from the skin. However, synthetic fabrics have recently made great strides in the cold weather clothing market. Do your research. A pair of light silk or polypro liners under your regular gloves or mittens is a good trick to keeping warm. They afford some additional warmth, but more importantly they'll allow you to remove your mitts for tedious work without exposing the skin.

Now, if your feet or hands start to feel cold or numb due to the elements, warm them as quickly as possible. Place cold hands under your armpits or bury them in your crotch. Carry hand and foot warmers if you can. If your feet are cold, change your socks. If there's plenty of room in your boots, add another pair of socks. Do remember though that constricting your feet in tight boots can restrict blood flow and actually make your feet colder more quickly. Your socks need to have breathing room if they're going to be effective. Dead air provides insulation. If your face is cold, place your warm hands over your face or simply wear a head stocking (called a balaclava).

Should your skin go numb and start to appear white and waxy but is still cold and soft, chances are you've got superficial frostbite. Rewarm as quickly as possible with skin-to-skin contact. No damage should occur. Do NOT let the area get frostbitten again!

If your skin is white and waxy but *dents* when you press on it, you have partial thickness frostbite. Rewarm as you would for superficial frostbite, but expect swelling and blisters to form. Don't massage the affected area, but do take ibuprofen for pain and reduction of tissue damage. If blisters form, you need to leave the backcountry.

If your skin is frozen hard like an ice cube, you have full thickness frostbite. Don't try to thaw the area unless you can maintain the warmth. In other words, don't stop to warm up your frostbitten feet only to head back on the trail. You'll do more damage than good. Tests have shown that hikers who walked on thawed feet did more harm, and endured more pain, than hikers who left the affected areas alone. Do your best to get out of the cold entirely and seek medical attention—which usually consists of performing a rapid rewarming in warm water (104°F–108°F) for 20 to 30 minutes. Get to a doctor as soon as possible!

The overall objective in preventing both hypothermia and frostbite is to keep the body's core warm. Protect key areas where heat escapes, like the top of the head, and maintain the proper nutrition and hydration levels. Foods that are high in calories aid the body in producing heat. Never smoke or drink alcohol when you're in situations where the cold is threatening. By affecting blood flow, these activities ultimately cool the body's core temperature.

NAVIGATION

Whether you are going on a short hike in a familiar area or planning a weeklong backpack trip, you should always be equipped with the proper navigational equipment—at the very least a detailed map and a sturdy compass. These tools are only useful if you know how to use them. Courses and books are available, so make sure your skills are up to snuff.

Maps. There are many different types of maps available to help you find your way on the trail. Easiest to find are Forest Service maps and Bureau of Land Management (BLM) maps. These maps tend to cover large areas, so be sure they are detailed enough for your particular trip. You can also obtain national park maps as well as high quality maps from private companies and trail groups. These maps can be obtained from either outdoor stores or ranger stations. Being large, these maps are best used for trip planning and driving, but not to navigate in the backcountry.

U.S. Geological Survey (USGS) topographic maps (topos) are particularly popular with hikers—especially serious backcountry hikers. These maps contain the standard map symbols such as roads, lakes, and rivers, as well as contour lines that show the details of the trail terrain like ridges, valleys, passes, and mountain peaks. The 7.5-minute series (one inch on the map equals approximately two-fifths of a mile on the ground) provides the closest inspection available. USGS maps are available by mail (U.S. Geological Survey, Map Distribution Branch, P.O. Box 25286, Denver, CO 80225), or you can visit them online at *http://mapping.usgs.gov/esic/to_order.html*.

If you want to check out the high tech world of maps, you can purchase topographic maps on CD-ROM. These software-mapping programs let you select a route on your computer, print it out, and then take it with you on the trail. Some software mapping programs let you insert symbols and labels, download waypoints from a GPS unit, and export the maps to other software programs. Mapping software programs such as DeLorme's TopoUSA (*www.delorme.com*) and MAPTECH's Terrain Navigator (*www.maptech.com*) let you do all of these things and more. Check out topos on websites such as *www.topozone.com*, too.

The art of map reading is a skill that you can develop by first practicing in an area you are familiar with. To begin, orient the map so it's lined up in the correct direction (i.e. north on the map is lined up with true north). Next, familiarize yourself with the map symbols and try to match them up with terrain features around you such as a high ridge, mountain peak, river, or lake. If you are practicing with a USGS map notice the contour lines. On gentler terrain these contour lines are spaced farther apart, and on steeper terrain they are closer together. Pick a short loop trail and stop frequently to check your position on the map. As you practice map reading, you'll learn how to anticipate a steep section on the trail or a good place to take a rest break, etc.

Compasses. First off, the sun is not a substitute for a compass. So, what kind of compass should you have? Here are some characteristics you should look for: a rectangular base with detailed scales, a liquid-filled housing, protective housing, a sighting line on the mirror, luminous alignment and back-bearing arrows, a luminous north-seeking arrow, and a well-defined bezel ring.

You can learn compass basics by reading the detailed instructions included with your compass. If you want to fine-tune your compass skills, sign up for an orienteering class or purchase a book on compass reading. Once you've learned the basic skills on using a compass, remember to practice these skills before you head into the backcountry.

Because magnetic north keeps moving around the north pole and topo maps use true north, using a map and compass together requires making adjustments for declination (the difference between magnetic and true north). Topo maps show the declination, but if you are looking at a 1970 map, the declination has changed. To determine the declination as of

Courtesy Magellan Systems

Magellan GPS unit

today, you can download shareware for Windows from the USGS (sorry Mac users!). Check out their website *http://geomag.usgs.gov.*

Global Positioning Systems (GPS). If you are a klutz at using a compass, you may be interested in checking out the technical wizardry of the GPS device. The GPS was developed by the Pentagon and works off 24 NAVSTAR satellites, which were designed to guide missiles to their targets. A GPS device is a handheld unit that calculates your latitude and longitude with the easy press of a button. The Department of Defense used to scramble the satellite signals a bit to prevent civilians (and spies!) from getting extremely accurate readings, but that practice was discontinued in May of 2000, and GPS units now provide nearly pinpoint accuracy (within 30 to 60 feet).

There are many different types of GPS units available, and they range in price from $100 to $400. In general, all GPS units have a display screen and keypad where you input information. In addition to acting as a compass, the unit allows you to plot your route, retrace your path, track your travelling speed, find the mileage between waypoints (straight line distance), and calculate the total mileage of your route. Despite the advances in GPS technology, don't put all of your trust in your GPS. Per the USGS, "GPS units do not replace basic map and compass skills." Keep in mind that these devices don't pick up signals indoors, in heavily wooded areas, or in deep valleys. And most important to remember, they run on batteries.

Pedometers. A pedometer is a handy device that can track your mileage as you hike. This device is a small, clip-on unit with a digital display that calculates your hiking distance in miles or kilometers based on your walking stride. Some units also calculate the calories you burn and your total hiking time. Pedometers are available at most large outdoor stores and range in price from $20 to $40.

TRIP PLANNING

Planning your hiking adventure begins with letting a friend or relative know your trip itinerary so they can call for help if you don't return at your scheduled time. Your next task is to make sure you are outfitted to experience the risks and rewards of the trail. This section highlights gear and clothing you may want to take with you to get the most out of your hike.

EQUIPMENT

With the outdoor market currently flooded with products, many of which are pure gimmickry, it seems impossible to both differentiate and choose. Do I really need a tropical-fish-lined collapsible shower? (No, you don't.) The only defense against the maddening quantity of items thrust in your face is to think practically—and to do so before you go shopping. The worst buys are impulsive buys. Since most of your name brands will differ only slightly in quality, it's best to know what you're looking for in terms of function. Buy only what you need. You will, don't forget, be carrying what you've bought on your back. Here are some things to keep in mind before you go shopping. Your pack should weigh no more than 30 percent of your body weight.

Clothes. Clothing is your armor against Mother Nature's little surprises. Massachusetts's weather can range from blistering heat to brutal cold, and hikers should be prepared for any possibility, especially when hiking in mountainous areas. The sun may feel hot until a cloud comes

Day Hikes

- daypack
- water and water bottles/water hydration system
- food and high energy snacks
- first-aid kit
- headlamp/flashlight with extra batteries and bulbs
- maps and compass/GPS unit
- knife/multi-purpose tool
- sunscreen and sunglasses
- matches in waterproof container and fire starter
- insulating top and bottom layers (fleece, wool, etc.)
- raingear
- winter hat and gloves
- wide-brimmed sun hat
- insect repellant
- backpacker's trowel, toilet paper, and resealable plastic bags
- whistle and/or mirror
- space blanket/bag
- camera/film
- guidebook
- watch
- water treatment tablets
- wet ones or other wet wipes
- hand and foot warmers if hiking high
- duct tape for repairs
- extra socks
- gaiters depending on season

along, and instantly the air temperature feels very cool.

During the summer, your main consideration is protecting your skin from sunburn and having layers to adapt to changeable weather conditions. Wearing long pants and a long sleeve shirt made out of materials such as Supplex nylon will protect your skin from the damaging rays of the sun. Avoid wearing 100 percent cotton, as it doesn't dry easily and offers no warmth when wet.

Since the weather can change from warm to chilly quickly, if you wear a t-shirt and shorts, make sure you have top and bottom "insulating" layers (see below) in your pack. Aside from keeping you warm, this layer needs to "breathe" so you stay dry while hiking. A fabric that provides insulation and dries quickly is fleece. It's interesting to note that this one-of-a-kind fabric is made out of recycled plastic. Purchasing a zip-up jacket or pullover made of this material is highly recommended.

Another important layer is the "shell" layer. You'll need some type of waterproof, windproof, breathable jacket that'll fit over all of your other layers. It should have a large hood that fits over a hat. You'll also need a good pair of rain pants made from a similar waterproof, breathable fabric. A fabric that easily fits the bill is GORE-TEX. However, while a quality GORE-TEX jacket can range in price from $100 to $450, you should know that there are more affordable fabrics out there that work just as well.

Now that you've learned the basics of layering, you can't forget to protect your hands and face. In cold, windy, rainy, or snowy weather you'll need a hat made of wool or fleece and insulated, waterproof gloves that will keep your hands warm and toasty. Buying a pair of light silk or polypro liners to wear under your regular gloves or mittens is a good idea. They'll allow you to remove your outer-gloves for tedious work without exposing the skin. Even in summer, a light winter hat and gloves can really help, too. Remember over 50 percent of our body heat is lost through our head, so if your extremities are cold, put on that hat! Carry packages of hand and foot warmers if you plan to be above treeline in case it gets really cold or snowy.

A handy item for those hot canyon or plains hikes is the neck cooler. You have to soak it in water for about 20 minutes, but then it stays damp and helps cool your body through your

Overnight Trips (include what's listed for Day Hikes)

- backpack and waterproof rain cover
- bandanna
- biodegradable soap
- collapsible water container (2–3 gallon capacity)
- clothing-extra wool socks, shirt and shorts, long pants
- cook set/utensils and pot scrubber
- stuff sacks to store gear
- extra plastic resealable bags
- garbage bags
- journal/pen
- nylon rope to hang food
- long underwear
- permit (if required)
- repair kit (tent, stove, pack, etc.)
- sandals or running shoes to wear around camp and to ford streams
- sleeping bag
- waterproof stuff sacks (one for hanging food)
- insulating ground pad
- hand towel
- stove and fuel
- tent and ground cloth
- toiletry items
- water filter

neck. Even wrapping a wet bandanna around your neck helps cool your body.

For winter hiking or snowshoeing, you'll need yet a lower "wicking" layer of long underwear that keeps perspiration away from your skin. Wearing long underwear made from synthetic fibers such as Capilene, Coolmax, or Thermax is an excellent choice. These fabrics wick moisture away from the skin and draw it toward the next layer of clothing where it then evaporates. Avoid wearing long underwear made of cotton as it is slow to dry and keeps moisture next to your skin.

Footwear. If you have any extra money to spend on your trip, put that money into boots or trail shoes. Poor-fitting boots will bring a hike to a halt faster than anything else. To avoid this annoyance, buy boots that provide support and are lightweight and flexible. When you purchase footwear, go to an outdoor store that specializes in backpacking and camping equipment. Knowledgeable salespeople can really help you find the right boot and the right fit for the type of hiking/backpacking you want to do. A lightweight hiking boot that can be waterproofed is usually adequate for most day hikes and short backpacks. Trail running shoes provide a little extra cushion and are made in a high-top style that many people wear for hiking. These running shoes are lighter, more flexible, and more breathable than hiking boots. Sturdier boots may be your best bet for rugged trails and multi-day backpacks. If you know you'll be hiking in wet weather or crossing streams or muddy areas often, purchase boots or shoes with a GORE-TEX liner, which will help keep your feet dry. Especially during spring and early summer when trails are muddy or snowy, make sure you wear waterproofed boots for maximum dryness. Walking around mud holes and snow damages wet ground and makes a bigger muddy mess. Get muddy! It's easier to clean your boots than repair damaged vegetation.

When buying your boots, be sure to wear the same type of socks you'll be wearing on the trail. If the boots you're buying are for heavy-duty or cold weather hiking, try the boots on while wearing two pairs of socks. Speaking of socks, a good sock combination is to wear a thinner sock made of wool or polypro/nylon covered by a heavier outer sock made of wool or wool/acrylic blend. New style socks such as SmartWool or Thorlos are excellent choices. The inner sock protects the foot from the rubbing effects of the outer sock and prevents blisters. Many outdoor stores have some type of ramp to simulate hiking uphill and downhill. Be sure to take advantage of this test, as toe-jamming boot fronts can be very painful and debilitating on the downhill trek.

Once you've purchased your footwear, be sure to break them in before you hit the trail. New footwear is often stiff and needs to be stretched and molded to your foot. A little leather conditioner such as Lexol can help the break-in process without major destruction to your foot in the process.

Hiking poles. Hiking with poles brings interesting comments ranging from "There's no snow now" to "Wow! I wish I had a pair of those on this trail!" Hiking poles help with balance and more importantly take pressure off your knees. The ones with shock absorbers are easier on your elbows and your knees. Some poles even come with a camera attachment to be used as a monopod. And heaven forbid you meet a moose, bear, or unfriendly dog, those poles make you look a lot bigger.

Packs. No matter what type of hiking you do you'll need a pack of some sort to carry the basic trail essentials. There are a variety of backpacks on the market, but let's first discuss what you intend to use it for. Day hikes or overnight trips?

If you plan on doing a day hike, a daypack should have some of the following characteristics: a padded hip belt that's at least two inches in diameter (avoid packs with only a small nylon piece of webbing for a hip belt); a chest strap (the chest strap helps stabilize the pack against your body); external pockets to carry water and other items that you want easy access to; an internal pocket to hold keys, a knife, a wallet, and other miscellaneous items; an external lashing system to hold a jacket; and maybe a hydration pocket for carrying a hydration system (which consists of a water bladder with an attachable drinking hose).

For short hikes, some hikers like to use a fanny pack to store just a camera, food, a compass, a map, and other trail essentials. Most fanny packs have pockets for two water bottles and a padded hip belt.

If you intend to do an extended, overnight trip, there are multiple considerations. First off, you need to decide what kind of framed pack you want. There are two backpack types for backpacking: the internal frame and the external frame. An internal frame pack rests closer to your body, making it more stable and easier to balance when hiking over rough terrain. An external frame pack is just that, an aluminum frame attached to the exterior of the pack. An external frame pack is better for long backpack trips because it distributes the pack weight better, and you can carry heavier loads. It's easier to pack, and your gear is more accessible. It also offers better back ventilation in hot weather.

The most critical measurement for fitting a pack is torso length. The pack needs to rest evenly on your hips without sagging. A good pack will come in two or three sizes and have straps and hip belts that are adjustable according to your body size and characteristics.

When you purchase a backpack, go to an outdoor store with salespeople who are knowledgeable in how to properly fit a pack. Once the pack is fitted for you, load the pack with the amount of weight you plan on taking on the trail. The weight of the pack should be distributed evenly and you should be able to swing your arms and walk briskly without feeling out of balance. Another good technique for evaluating a pack is to walk up and down stairs and make quick turns to the right and to the left to be sure the pack doesn't feel out of balance.

Other features that are nice to have on a backpack include a removable day pack or fanny pack, external pockets for extra water, and extra lash points to attach a jacket or other items. Remember all these extra features add

Courtesy Johnson Coleman

weight to the basic pack, cutting down on the amount of other stuff you can carry.

Sleeping bags and pads. Sleeping bags are rated by temperature. You can purchase a bag made of synthetic fiber such as Polarguard HV or DuPont Hollofil II, or you can buy a goose down bag. Goose down bags are more expensive, but they have a higher insulating capacity by weight and will keep their loft longer. You'll want to purchase a bag with a temperature rating that fits the time of year and conditions you are most likely to camp in. One caveat: the techno-standard for temperature ratings is far from perfect. Ratings vary from manufacturer to manufacturer, so to protect yourself you should purchase a bag rated 10 to 15 degrees below the temperature you expect to be camping in. Synthetic bags are more resistant to water than down bags, but many down bags are now made with a GORE-TEX shell that helps to repel water. Down bags are also more compressible than synthetic bags and take up less room in your pack, which is an important consideration if you are planning a multi-day backpack trip. Make sure to buy a compression stuff sack for your sleeping bag to minimize the space it consumes in your backpack. Features to look for in a sleeping bag include: a mummy style bag, a hood you can cinch down around your head in cold weather, and draft tubes along the zippers that help keep heat in and drafts out. Some sleeping bags are designed especially for a woman's anatomy.

You'll also want a sleeping pad to provide insulation and padding from the cold ground. There are different types of sleeping pads available, from the more expensive self-inflating air mattresses like Therm-a-Rest to the less expensive closed-cell foam pads (e.g., Ridge Rest). Self-inflating air mattresses are usually heavier than closed-cell foam mattresses and are prone to punctures but can be repaired.

Tents. The tent is your home away from home while on the trail. It provides protection from wind, snow, rain, and insects. A three-season tent is a good choice for backpacking and can range in price from $100 to $500. These lightweight and versatile tents provide protection in all types of weather, except heavy snowstorms or high winds, and range in weight from four to eight pounds. Look for a tent that's easy to set up and will easily fit two people with gear. Dome

type tents usually offer more headroom and places to store gear. Other tent designs include a vestibule where you can store wet boots. Some nice-to-have items in a tent include interior pockets to store small items and lashing points to hang a clothesline. Most three-season tents also come with stakes so you can secure the tent in high winds. Before you purchase a tent, set it up and take it down a few times to be sure it is easy to handle. Also, sit inside the tent and make sure it has enough room for you and your gear.

Cell phones. Many hikers are carrying their cell phones into the backcountry these days in case of emergency. That's fine and good, but please know that cell phone coverage is often poor to non-existent in valleys, canyons, and thick forest. More importantly, people have started to call for help because they're tired or lost. Let's go back to being prepared. You are responsible for yourself in the backcountry. Use your brain to avoid problems, and if you do encounter one, first use your brain to try to correct the situation. Only use your cell phone, if it works, in cases of true emergencies.

HIKING WITH CHILDREN

Hiking with children isn't a matter of how many miles you can cover or how much elevation gain you make in a day, it's about seeing and experiencing nature through their eyes.

Kids like to explore and have fun. They like to stop and point out bugs and plants, look under rocks, jump in puddles, and throw sticks. If you're taking a toddler or young child on a hike, start with a trail that you're familiar with. Trails that have interesting things for kids, like piles of leaves to play in or a small stream to wade through during the summer, will make the hike much more enjoyable for them and will keep them from getting bored.

You can keep your child's attention if you have a strategy before starting on the trail. Using games is not only an effective way to keep a child's attention, it's also a great way to teach him or her about nature. Play hide and seek, where your child is the mouse and you are the hawk. Quiz children on the names of plants and animals. If your children are old enough, let them carry their own daypack filled with snacks and water. So that you are sure to go at their pace and not yours, let them lead the way. Playing follow the leader works particularly well when you have a group of children. Have each child take a turn at being the leader. *Sharing Nature with Children* by Joseph Cornell, Dawn Publications, describes excellent activities such as those above.

With children, a lot of clothing is key. You always want to bring extra clothing for your children no matter what the season. In the winter, have your children wear wool socks, and warm layers such as long underwear, a polar fleece jacket and hat, wool mittens, and good winter parka. It's not a bad idea to have these along in late fall and early spring as well. Good footwear is also important. A sturdy pair of high top tennis shoes or lightweight hiking boots are the best bet for little ones. If you're hiking in the summer near a lake or stream, bring along a pair of old sneakers that your child can put on when he wants to go exploring in the water. Remember when you're near any type of water, always watch your child at all times. Also, keep a close eye on teething toddlers who may decide a rock or a poison mushroom is an interesting item to put in their mouth.

From spring through fall, you'll want your kids to wear a wide brimmed hat to keep their face, head, and ears protected from the hot sun. Also, make sure your children wear sunscreen at all times. Choose a brand without Paba—children have sensitive skin and may have an allergic reaction to sunscreen that contains Paba. If you are hiking with a child younger than six months, don't use sunscreen or insect repellent. Instead, be sure that their head, face, neck, and ears are protected from the sun with a wide brimmed hat, and that all other skin exposed to the sun is protected with the appropriate clothing.

Remember that food is fun. Kids like snacks so it's important to bring a lot of munchies for the trail. Stopping often for snack breaks is a fun way to keep the trail interesting. Raisins, apples, granola bars, crackers and cheese, Cheerios, and trail mix all make great snacks. If your child is old enough to carry his/her own backpack, fill it with treats before you leave. If your kids don't like drinking water, you can bring boxes of fruit juice.

Courtesy Johnson Outdoors

Avoid poorly designed child-carrying packs—you don't want to break your back carrying your child. Most child-carrying backpacks designed to hold a 40-pound child will contain a large carrying pocket to hold diapers and other items. Some have an optional rain/sun hood. Tough Traveler (1–800–GO–TOUGH or *www.toughtraveler.com*) is a company that specializes in making backpacks for carrying children and other outdoor gear for children.

HIKING WITH YOUR DOG

Bringing your furry friend with you is always more fun than leaving him behind. Our canine pals make great trail buddies because they never complain and always make good company. Hiking with your dog can be a rewarding experience, especially if you plan ahead.

Getting your dog in shape. Before you plan outdoor adventures with your dog, make sure he's in shape for the trail. Getting your dog into shape takes the same discipline as getting yourself into shape, but luckily, your dog can get in shape with you. Take your dog with you on your daily runs or walks. If there is a park near your house, hit a tennis ball or play Frisbee with your dog.

Swimming is also an excellent way to get your dog into shape. If there is a lake or river near where you live and your dog likes the water, have him retrieve a tennis ball or stick. Gradually build your dog's stamina up over a two to three month period. A good rule of thumb is to assume that your dog will travel twice as far as you will on the trail. If you plan on doing a five-mile hike, be sure your dog is in shape for a ten-mile hike.

Training your dog for the trail. Before you go on your first hiking adventure with your dog, be sure he has a firm grasp on the basics of canine etiquette and behavior. Make sure he can sit, lay down, stay, and come. One of the most important commands you can teach your canine pal is to "come" under any situation. It's easy for your friend's nose to lead him astray or possibly get lost. Another helpful command is the "get behind" command. When you're on a hiking trail that's narrow, you can have your dog follow behind you when other trail users approach. Nothing is more bothersome than an enthusiastic dog that runs back and forth on the trail and disrupts the peace of the trail for others. When you see other trail users approaching you on the trail, give them the right of way by quietly stepping off the trail and making your dog lie down and stay until they pass. The best bet is to keep your dog on a leash to prevent injury to him and to avoid harassing other hikers, horses, and wildlife. Complaints about dogs in the backcountry are on the rise. Be a responsible dog owner to make sure you can keep taking your buddy in the backcountry with you.

Equipment. The most critical pieces of equipment you can invest in for your dog are proper identification and a sturdy leash. Flexi-leads work well for hiking because they give your dog more freedom to explore but still leave you in control. Make sure your dog has identification that includes your name and address and a number for your veterinarian. Other forms of identification for your dog include a tattoo or a microchip. You should consult your veterinarian for more information on these last two options.

The next piece of equipment you'll want to consider is a pack for your dog. By no means should you hold all of your dog's essentials in your pack—let him carry his own gear! Dogs that are in good shape and don't have physical problems can carry up to 25 percent of their own weight for multiple days.

Companies that make good quality packs include RuffWear (1–888–RUFF–WEAR; www.ruffwear.com), Granite Gear (1–218–834-6157; www.granitegear.com), and Wolf Packs (1–541–482–7669; www.wolfpacks.com). Most packs are fitted by a dog's weight and girth measurement. Companies that make dog packs generally include guidelines to help you pick out the size that's right for your dog. Some characteristics to look for when purchasing a pack for your dog include: a harness that contains two padded girth straps, a padded chest strap, leash attachments, removable saddle bags, internal water bladders, and external gear cords.

You can introduce your dog to the pack by first placing the empty pack on his back and letting him wear it around the yard. Keep an eye on him during this first introduction. He may decide to chew through the straps if you aren't watching him closely. Once he learns to treat the pack as an object of fun and not a foreign enemy, fill the pack evenly on both sides with a few ounces of dog food in resealable plastic bags. Have your dog wear his pack on your daily walks for a period of two to three weeks. Each week add a little more weight to the pack until your dog will accept carrying the maximum amount of weight he can carry.

You can also purchase collapsible water and dog food bowls for your dog. Plastic storage containers also work well and double to protect your dog's food from getting wet. Some dogs don't like the collapsible bowls, so see what works before heading into the backcountry. These bowls are lightweight and can easily be stashed into your pack or your dog's. If you are hiking on rocky terrain or in the snow, you can purchase footwear for your dog that will protect his feet from cuts and bruises. All of these products can be purchased from RuffWear (1–888–RUFF–WEAR; *www.ruffwear.com*).

The following is a checklist of items to bring when you take your dog hiking: water bowls, a comb, a collar and a leash, dog food, a dog pack, flea/tick powder, paw protection, water, resealable plastic bags, and a First Aid kit that contains eye ointment, tweezers, scissors, stretchy foot wrap, gauze, antibacterial wash, sterile cotton tip applicators, antibiotic ointment, and cotton wrap. You might consider carrying saline solution for contact lenses for flushing any doggie wounds. For backpacking, consider bringing a pad or mat to put in your tent for your dog. Never leave your dog tied up in camp unattended. He might become a meal for a predator.

Cleaning up after your dog. Although it sounds awful, use resealable plastic bags to pick up and carry out your dog's waste or bury them like human feces.

Barking dogs. Most people hike and backpack to escape the sounds of the city, including barking dogs. If your dog is a barker, best to leave him at home to avoid dogs getting any more bad raps in the backcountry.

Bears and moose. If a dog discovers and provokes a bear or a moose, and the bear starts chasing him, you'll probably be the destination of this mad chase. In bear and moose country, keep your dog on a leash for his own safety.

Lost dogs. It's not unusual for an unleashed dog to stray from its owner, only to spoil a trip while you hunt for the wayward pooch or never to be seen again. If your dog does not respond well to voice commands, keep it leashed for its own safety.

First aid for your dog. Your dog is just as prone—if not more prone—to getting in trouble on the trail as you are, so be prepared. Here's a run down of the more likely misfortunes that might befall your little friend.

Bees and wasps. If a bee or wasp stings your dog, remove the stinger with a pair of tweezers and place a mudpack or a cloth dipped in cold water over the affected area.

Porcupines. One good reason to keep your dog on leash is to prevent it from getting a nose full of porcupine quills. You may be able to remove the quills with a pair of pliers, but a vet is the best person to do this nasty job because most dogs need to be sedated.

Heat stroke. Avoid hiking with your dog in really hot weather. Dogs with heat stroke will pant excessively, lie down and refuse to get up, and become lethargic and disoriented. If your dog shows any of these signs on the trail, have him lie down in the shade. If you are near a stream, pour cool water over your dog's entire body to help bring his body temperature back to normal.

Dehydration. Dogs may dehydrate faster than we humans, so make sure your dog is drinking enough water.

Heartworm. Dogs get heartworms from mosquitoes which carry the disease in the prime mosquito months of July and August. Giving your dog a monthly pill prescribed by your veterinarian easily prevents this condition.

Plant pitfalls. Plant hazards include burrs, thorns, thistles, and poison ivy. If you find any burrs, foxtails, or thistles on your dog, remove them as soon as possible before they become an unmanageable mat. Thorns can pierce a dog's foot and cause a great deal of pain. If you see that your dog is lame, stop and check his feet for thorns. Dogs are immune to poison ivy but they can pick

Lizann Dunegan

up the sticky, oily substance from the plant and transfer it to you.

Protect those paws. Be sure to keep your dog's nails trimmed so he avoids getting soft tissue or joint injuries. If your dog slows and refuses to go on, check to see that his paws aren't torn or worn. You can protect your dog's paws from trail hazards such as sharp gravel, talus, ice, snowballs, and thorns by purchasing dog boots.

Ticks and fleas. Dogs can get Rocky Mountain spotted fever from ticks, as well as other diseases, like Lyme disease. Before you hit the trail, treat your dog with a flea and tick spray or powder. You can also ask your veterinarian about a once-a-month pour-on treatment that repels fleas and ticks.

Mosquitoes and deer flies. These little flying machines can do a job on your dog's snout and ears. Best bet is to spray your dog with fly repellant for horses to discourage both pests from bothering your dog.

Giardia. Dogs can get giardia, which results in diarrhea. It is usually not debilitating, but definitely messy.

Mushrooms. Make sure your dog doesn't sample mushrooms along the trail. They could be poisonous to him, but he doesn't know that.

Websites. A number of websites have excellent hints about hiking and backpacking with your dog. Suggested sites include: *www.outdoor-dog.com*; *http://backpacking.about.com/recreation/backpacking/library/weekly/aa093000a.htm*; and *www.landfield.com/ftp/faqs/dogs-faq/misc/part1*.

Dog regulations. When you and your dog are finally ready to hit the trail, keep in mind that national parks and monuments and some state parks do not allow dogs on trails. Your best bet is to hike in national forests, BLM lands, and canine-friendly state parks. Always call ahead to see what the regulations are as they may change from time to time.

Meet the Author

When he's not cranking out newspaper and magazine stories on deadline, Ben has been lucky to call New England his outdoor playground. (He even proposed to his wife, Shannon, while they were cross-country skiing through the Vermont woods one January day.) Maybe growing up in New York City boosted his appreciation of the outdoors.

Ben's indoor education includes an economics degree from Colby College (Waterville, Maine) and a master's in journalism from Columbia University (NYC). But perhaps more important was his outdoor education, including childhood summers at Camp Chewonki (Wiscasset, Maine), and semesters at The Mountain School (Vershire, Vermont) and Sea Education Association (Woods Hole, Massachusetts).

Before he started earning a living in journalism, he worked outdoor jobs like commercial fishing for halibut in Alaska, running the harbor launch at a Maine yacht club, and guiding visitors around a New Mexico ranch on horseback. Those jobs pale in comparison to writing about something he loves—the hiking trails of Massachusetts.

Author

WHAT'S SO SPECIAL ABOUT UNSPOILED, NATURAL PLACES?

Beauty   Solitude   Wildness   Freedom   Quiet   Adventure

Serenity   Inspiration   Wonder   Excitement

Relaxation   Challenge

There's a lot to love about our treasured public lands, and the reasons are different for each of us. Whatever your reasons are, the national **Leave No Trace** education program will help you discover special outdoor places, enjoy them, and preserve them—today and for those who follow. By practicing and passing along these simple principles, you can help protect the special places you love from being loved to death.

THE PRINCIPLES OF LEAVE NO TRACE

- Plan ahead and prepare
- Travel and camp on durable surfaces
- Dispose of waste properly
- Leave what you find
- Minimize campfire impacts
- Respect wildlife
- Be considerate of other visitors

Leave No Trace is a national nonprofit organization dedicated to teaching responsible outdoor recreation skills and ethics to everyone who enjoys spending time outdoors.

To learn more or to become a member, please visit us at www.LNT.org or call (800) 332–4100.

Leave No Trace, P.O. Box 997, Boulder, CO 80306